MW00902884

The World That Then Was

Unveiling what the world was like before recorded history and transforming your world through God's eternal Word

Bill Seng

xulon PRESS

The World That Then Was
Unveiling what the world was like before recorded history and transforming your world through God's eternal Word
by Bill Seng

Printed in the United States of America

ISBN 9781626977259

www.xulonpress.com

Introduction

"Creationism is not science. There is nothing scientific about creationism." One of the teachers I respected the most at Findlay High School in Findlay, Ohio said these words. When he said this, he was level-headed, thoughtful, and sincere about what he was saying. I respected him for his demeanor and his opinion and I believed him. After all, he was the teacher and I was the student. But what my teacher had unwittingly accomplished was to plant a seed inside of one of his students that would one day transform the course of his life.

One might say that my teacher's statement was the beginning of *The World That Then Was*. Had he never made that statement, I may never have been exposed to creationism. I may have stayed inside the box of mainstream science; who knows what would have happened to my faith? Would I have casually come to reject spirituality in favor of materialism or would I have bought into an ideology that waters down key doctrines of the Bible? I am glad that I will never know the answer to that question and grateful that my honors Biology teacher exposed me to the concept of creationism for the first time in my life.

The negative side of his statement was that I instantly believed that creationism had nothing to do with science and I dismissed it as one might dismiss any other cultic belief. Every time that I heard the term "creationist" mentioned, from my freshman year of high school to my freshman year of college, I imagined an undereducated peon that may have been well-versed in the Bible, but totally ignorant of science. When I would discuss creationists with my classmates, I would often say, "Well, they just haven't heard the other side of the debate." I felt bad for them, because I thought that they had the potential to be good people, but they were too blinded by narrow-minded Biblical interpretations to see the truth that was so obvious to me. My sophomore year of college at Cleveland State University would challenge my confidence in the worldview I was adopting.

The first day of my college Biology class did not kick-off the new semester with a mind-blowing introduction to biology. No, it started off with my professor warning us about "crack-pot creationists." My Biology professor, needless to say, did not believe in God. The first week was dedicated to crack-pot creationists. We talked about young earth creationism and the vast array of information that disproves the notion that the world is only six thousand years old. This challenged me to consider the different possibilities regarding whether the theory that the universe evolved over a long span of time was compatible with the words of the Bible. After doing a fair amount of research I concluded that the earth was billions of years old, but that God created everything in six literal days. I know now that these two propositions are ideologically a contradiction. Back then, it seemed like a reasonable compromise. As time went on, I continued with my old earth presuppositions until one of my good friends helped me to become acclimated with true young earth creationism.

My friend Eric Duenke, who I met in high school, took me to his church one night to watch part of a video series. The speaker was the one and only Dr. Kent Hovind. Before going any further, I know that not everybody cares for Dr. Hovind and he has been in trouble for the past couple of years. That does not take away from the fact that he is well educated, well prepared, and a powerful authority when it comes to the topic of young earth creationism. I do not remember specifically what his topic was that night, but I was skeptical.

My friend, Eric, asked me what I thought and I berated him with a bunch of questions. He was able to answer a lot of my questions and the ones he could not answer would get resolved in time as I watched more of Kent Hovind and became acquainted with another ministry called Answers in Genesis. I did not immediately take kindly to young earth creationism, but then I realized that I always said that creationists never looked at the other side of the argument. I had not considered the possibility that I was the one ignoring the other side of the debate.

I learned that the scientific aspect of creationism is rejected by mainstream scientists because its conclusions are opposed to a naturalistic ideology. It uses Scripture to interpret the physical evidence that is present in the world to understand what the world was like shortly after it was created. Theories with an evolutionary premise do the exact same thing. They use naturalistic materialism to interpret the evidence present in the world and make their conclusions based off of those assumptions. Because the Bible is a source of testimony and naturalistic materialism is merely a line of logic, it could be argued that creationism is more scientific than science accomplished through naturalistic assumptions. Creationism establishes its worldview upon the words of the Bible. The Bible merely tells a person how to view the world as it currently exists. In all reality, it does not contradict the observations made in the natural world, it just contradicts the conclusions made by evolutionary scientists. The evolutionary scientist does not have a book of historic testimonies to tell them how to view the world. They start with their assumption of naturalistic materialism and interpret everything from that perspective. If you are anything like me, it probably angers you some that a naturalistic philosophy is taught as science inside of public schools, while creationism (which is consistent with the observations of the natural world) is exiled.

Although I began to form my roots in young earth creationism, it was not easy maintaining my convictions on the age of the earth and the appropriate interpretation of the Bible. New opposition began to rise from a front that I did not expect. While I was at Cleveland State University, I was involved in a Campus Ministry called Campus Bible Fellowship. One year, our office was right next door to the CSU Pagans. While I was investigating the scientific argument against the Theory of Evolution, I decided that the best way to test my knowledge on the subject would be to explain it to an unbiased third party. This way I could see if I could help the person to understand the case being made or even persuade him or her to believe in the content I was teaching. When I attempted to explain my argument to one of the CSU Pagans I encountered an unexpected twist. Many pagans actually believe in the Theory of Evolution. She immediately opposed and rejected my argument and then attempted to convince me that there was a clear contradiction between Genesis chapter one and Genesis chapter two. Her conclusion on the issue of Genesis was that it composed of two unique creation accounts that contradicted one another, meaning that the Bible was not truly God's authoritative Word. I will address the matter of Genesis chapters one and two later on. I rejected her claims but decided to pursue her arguments and beliefs further by educating myself about them. Aside from thoroughly studying the first few chapters of Genesis, I enrolled in a mythologies class to help with my understanding of the pagan myths.

I will not claim that it was the most comprehensive class in mythologies, but it was a great introduction to the topic. We discussed Greek, Roman, Norse, and Mesopotamian myths. You will notice that I cite these mythologies in the pages of this book and in most cases from the very books I used in that class. One grievance that I carried with me throughout this class was my professor's distaste for the stories in the Bible. Even though she had commented on several occasions that the Bible should have been required reading before taking such a course, she was not particularly fond of the Bible's teachings. To her, creation, the flood, and the life of Jesus were nothing more than forgeries from other ancient myths. This particular class did not leave much room for a student to continue to believe in that which is supernatural because it consistently attempted to refute all of the supernatural claims in each myth, as well as the supernatural claims of the Bible. With all of the similarities between the myths and the Biblical stories, many scholars have been led to believe that the Biblical stories really did originate from the pagan myths. The pagan myths are full of scientific impossibilities and outright absurdities meaning that the Bible's sources of information were flawed meaning that the Scriptures themselves were also flawed and not credible. The thought never crossed my professor's mind, or the minds of the mentioned scholars, that maybe the similarities between the Bible and the ancient myths were not really a result of forgery, but were really traces of harmony. You might be wondering what I am implying.

First of all, the assumption that the Bible is the forgery is because many of the Mesopotamian texts supposedly predate the earliest known Biblical texts. It should never be assumed that the earliest known manuscripts that have been discovered thus far are the originals unless the evidence suggests otherwise. For instance, according to the Bible the Law of the Old Testament was originally written in stone and entrusted to Moses to present to the people of Israel. No one has found these stone tablets, nor has anyone claimed to have found writings of the Old Testament that date back to the time of Moses. Nobody even claims to have the first reproductions of the original Old Testament Law on the ancient paper they would have used at the time. If such documents still exist it would be miraculous because of the brittle nature of the material they would be written on. Today, it is difficult enough to preserve a document written on a modern piece of paper.

Preserving a text written on this ancient material for thousands of years would have been nearly impossible.

Second, much of ancient history was preserved for long spans of time through oral tradition. This means that people communicated history and events of their day by word of mouth. This might sound horribly unreliable, but that was why many ancient oral traditions were communicated through songs and poetry. Employing such methods would allow for the possibility that an oral tradition could exist a long time without being altered too drastically. In our case, it could mean that certain elements of Genesis were preserved for a long time through oral tradition. It contains poetic elements that could support such a theory. Also, Moses, its supposed author, was not born until after the events he detailed in Genesis. Unless the Holy Spirit implanted these stories into Moses' mind, an oral tradition of some sort could have been responsible for many parts of Genesis. Unfortunately, such a hypothesis would be impossible to prove. Unless a document would be uncovered that would detail the nature of the oral tradition leading to Genesis, the evidence would have died out with the tradition itself and remain as nothing more than a rumor.

Thirdly, why should one assume that the Bible stole stories from other cultures just because the details of the stories sound similar? Is it not equally likely that the other traditions stole their ideas from the Biblical tradition? Or, better yet, is it not just as likely that maybe the other traditions were attempting to document the same stories from a different perspective? Most, if not all of the New Testament was written to codify acceptable doctrine and refute false doctrine. It was compiled into one book, the

Bible, so that the Church would be able to understand the difference between the doctrines and stories being circulated throughout their cultures and those that were actually written about by the Apostles. Interestingly enough, the Gospels of the New Testament were not the first documents written by the New Testament church. They were recorded with the intention of providing a clear understanding of what the life and works of Jesus really were. All one has to do to verify this would be to read the first chapter of any of the Gospels, especially Luke. The letters of the New Testament were written with a similar purpose in mind and their first chapters typically established such a premise as well. The authors of the Bible were constantly refuting false doctrine, even in the Old Testament. Genesis itself would have been understood by the Near Eastern religions to be a refutation of their contending creation myths. It established that there is only one God, not many. It clearly states that the heavens, the earth, and the seas were creations of God and not the remains of some slain deity. The sun, moon, and stars are also spoken of as inanimate objects that were created by God, even though many surrounding cultures believed them to be gods and heavenly beings of sorts. If Genesis was specifically written with such a motif in mind, it would explain the similarities and differences between Genesis and its regions contending religious tales. In order to set the record straight, Genesis would have to detail the same events as these other stories, but do so more accurately. Having encountered these challenges at Cleveland State helped me to develop such a method of thinking. It also prepared me for the road that was ahead of me.

I graduated from Cleveland State University with my faith fully intact and stronger than it was before. I earned a bachelor's in health science, but instead of pursuing a doctorate in physical therapy I set my sights on pursuing a theological education. This brought me back to the town I grew up in, Findlay, Ohio. I enrolled at Winebrenner Theological Seminary with the intention of earning a Master's of Divinity with a focus on Biblical studies. My Old Testament professor, Dr. Gary Staats, presented an open-ended assignment at the beginning of one of his classes that was supposed to be completed at the end of that term. The class was on the Pentateuch which, of course, included the book of Genesis. Within that class we discussed the age of the earth, creation from a literary perspective, and alternative interpretations of the first few chapters of Genesis. The content fascinated me and ultimately became the book that you now hold in your hands. Outside of my academic pursuit, there is still one event that I would like to recognize for being responsible for this book.

When I was in elementary school my dad recognized that I really enjoyed learning about dinosaurs. Many of the things I learned back then contradicted what I believed about the Bible, but as a child it is easy to believe two contradictory ideas at the same time. I remember that there was a day when my dad told my brothers and I, "There is going to be a day when people are going to tell you that you came from an ape. Don't believe it because it is not true." Of all things I have learned throughout my studies, this one statement stands out above them all. My dad was essentially declaring, "Hey, you were created in the image of God. Don't let anyone tell you otherwise."

What you will notice throughout this book is mankind's expectations, being created in the image of God, and its failure to live up to that calling. Despite mankind's failure to live up to its divine image, God continually pursues his creation even after it fails him time and time again.

Perhaps the best image to help you understand the purpose of this book is that of Michelangelo's depiction of the creation of man in the Sistine Chapel. The first man, Adam, sits relaxed and careless; hardly noticing what is happening in the world around him. He is slowly drifting further and further away from God. God, however, is unwilling to allow his creation to drift away without his own drastic action. He reaches out from his heavenly dwelling, in pursuit of Adam. He beckons him to return and stretches out his hand as far as he can to invite Adam into salvation. Adam in return does not pursue God. He continues to sit lazily in his field. As God reaches out for Adam with his hand outstretched, a tiny space remains between his forefinger and his creation's. Although the creation has turned away, God has continued to pursue his creation by filling the gap between he and Adam by coming down to earth as the person Jesus Christ. Through Jesus, God's pursuit of man was completed and everyone now has the opportunity to cross the gap between heaven and earth. Secular humanism and false religions have attempted to restore that void and forever separate mankind from its Creator. They have failed to prevent God from seeking more children for his kingdom. God overcomes these obstacles today the same way he has done in the past. His methods are, namely, the Word of God and the people he selects to carry his message to the world.

I have been greatly blessed to have encountered opposition throughout the years and even more blessed to be presenting to you a perspective on the Holy Scriptures that will renew your faith in their authoritative words. You might be reading this book at just the right time in your life. Maybe you are off to college. Maybe you are a scientist in pursuit of God. Maybe you are a skeptic that simply wants a different perspective on the debate. My hope is that you will read about the evidence from science, from myths, and from the Bible and conclude that there is something more to this life than what you are presently able to see. Like me, you will learn much about who you are and who God is as you explore *The World That Then Was*.

Section 1
In the Beginning

Chapter 1
Mountains, Boxes, Canyons, and Gaps

A new religion has been born. The stories about God, gods, and angels have been discredited through the dishonesty of self-seeking clergymen who promote a supernatural agenda. Those who approach religion in civilized communities now do so with much skepticism and caution. Ironically, this skepticism has given birth to a new religion that is better suited to modern man. It has done away with the gods and replaced them with mankind. This new religion has announced that humans are the only supreme intelligence on earth. The teachers of this religion have preached with such passion that the masses follow its statutes without question. They are so effective that you may not even know that you conform to its teachings. The name of this religion is "humanism." The man, Charles Darwin, is recognized as their chief prophet because he articulated their cornerstone doctrine. This doctrine is better known as the "Theory of Evolution."

The Theory of Evolution is the thrust behind the rapidly expanding religion of humanism. Before Darwin popularized the notion that all living things have a common ancestor a secular explanation for the existence of life could not hold up against scrutiny. Those who denounced the existence of God were nothing more than grumpy, depressing, cynics with no philosophical grounding to stake their claims of a godless existence. Darwin's proposed doctrine furthered the advancement of secular humanism by establishing a foundational principle: all life gradually evolved and made progressive advancements as time elapsed. Such a principle has been used to not only explain the existence of life, but also the entire universe.

Throughout this book one will recognize references to the "Theory of Evolution," that are not really referencing Darwin's Theory of Evolution. Darwin's theory discussed the descent of species from a common ancestor. The Theory of Evolution referenced in this study is not just referring to the mere descent of one species from an ancestor species, but the descent of all things from the birth of the universe to the present. Secular scientists found so much value in Darwin's Theory of Evolution that they recognized the principle he applied to the descent of life might also be applicable to the existence of the cosmos. Because of Darwin's influence on modern scientists, his Theory of Evolution cannot be divorced from the more complete form of his doctrine. Some people might find the notion that all things exist through unguided natural processes to be frightening, but many people find such a doctrine to be entirely liberating.

The beauty of the Theory of Evolution is that death, suffering, and the other ills of life are not a result of anybody's decision, but are natural results of life's existence.

Those who are considered religious often attribute one's suffering to some sort of immoral choice he or she made that was followed up by negative consequences divvied out by some divine authority. On the other hand, evolution teaches that nature has made progressive, unguided, and amoral steps to bring all things into a balance that allows the universe to continue to exist. This creates a worldview where morals are flexible and relative to each individual. Pagan religions are not far removed from humanism's moral relativity. Pagan religions often endorse a practice where their followers create images of their gods out of natural materials. This allows individuals freedom to create gods that represent a lifestyle that is more suitable to one's preferences instead of having to submit to a supreme authority that has established a standard to distinguish good from evil. Where the pagans justify their lifestyles through the idols they choose to worship, humanists justify their lifestyles through the principles taught through the Theory of Evolution.

Comparing humanism and evolution to ancient religions sounds like a stretch of the imagination. Religions are typically developed through the testimonies of people. Humanism is supposedly built upon facts that are interpreted through the Theory of Evolution. This book will show that the facts used to formulate the doctrine of evolution can be interpreted in more than one way. It will also show how the advocates for this religious doctrine interpret evidence in a manner that is irrational and often misleading. Humanism and its doctrine of Evolution contain nothing more in substance than any other legend or myth. Although the Theory of Evolution is a key doctrine of the religion of humanism, its scientific element can actually be useful for verifying past events spoken about in religious texts, specifically the Bible. It is incorrect to conclude that the Theory of Evolution and the Bible are compatible. They are not.

However, evidence used to prove past evolutionary events can be used just as easily to verify key Biblical events. This suggests that belief in such events derive from some sort of biased presupposition. A belief that is established through nothing more than an ideological preference is no better at defining reality than religion. For the sake of this writing, the title of the "doctrine of evolution" is more fitting than the "Theory of Evolution" because a doctrine is formulated on presuppositions where theories are based on observable data. Ironically, from a historic perspective the Bible's account of creation could be considered more scientific than the evolutionary model of origins. This is because nobody has ever observed life evolve from inanimate material, but Biblical testimony claims to be based on eyewitness information.

If the witnesses of the Bible are trustworthy, Biblical teachings could be considered more credible than scientific speculations. Witnesses are a key component for determining truth. Many of the authors of the Bible claimed to have actually witnessed the events they recorded. The "witnesses" for the Theory of Evolution are the scientists in each respective field of study. In the fray of the heated argument between these two ideologies, one must not forget that witnesses exist for many other religions. When seeking after the truth one must consider as many options as possible. To write off any religion without properly examining its claims might lead one to miss out on the truth altogether. Discerning truth from reality is necessary for anyone who desires to formulate a coherent worldview. The process of discernment involves questions. For some people the questions are merely trivial but to others their answers determine the manner by which one ought to conduct his or her life.

Regardless of one's religious convictions, every worldview seeks to answer three key questions: Where did everything come from? This question sets the groundwork for understanding the nature of the universe. Why is the world in its present condition? Through this question, a person can understand how he or she can improve the condition of his or her current situation. What will the world be like in the future? Understanding the fate of all things helps a person determine what is and is not important throughout the duration of his or her life. These are the questions that have entertained the minds of countless souls. Understanding one's origin, path, and destination are the very elements of a person's intellect that define life's purpose. The most defining factor of the three is one's understanding of where he or she came from.

Where did everything come from? A person strives to understand not just where he or she came from, but where everything came from. Did all things naturally evolve? Is there some sort of supreme intelligence that has designed every aspect of the universe? Is the universe itself some sort of living force that guides the creation of matter, life, and all of the processes that are involved in nature? The answers lie in the fact that all things were created by one of two means: either they were created supernaturally or through natural processes.

It is well known that the belief in the supernatural dates back to ancient times, but many neglect the reality that naturalism, or materialism, dates back almost as far. The evolution of the universe was postulated by humanists that date back at least to ancient Greece. Even though materialists claim no supernatural events have ever occurred, they often spend much time trying to rationalize supernatural claims of certain religious groups. For instance, materialists will often claim that some of the healings that Jesus performed were psychosomatic in nature. They do not always deny the healings, but they might attribute the healing of a leper to a longing for physical contact and compassion. The healing would therefore be a matter of one's own will opposed to supernatural causes. Even though materialists are typically heralds of the Big Bang Theory and Darwin's Theory of Evolution, there are many other theories concerning the universe and life's origins that certain elite scientists grant more credibility than the popular theories. The majority of such theories have only been postulated in modern times and most are unheard of among the general population.

In contrast, most people are familiar with the antiquity of supernaturalism. There is an even greater variety of supernatural tales that describe the universe's origins than there are natural explanations. Many times throughout history, natural processes have been mistakenly labeled as supernatural events due to scientific ignorance. One of the most popular fallacies was the belief that the sun was the god Apollo riding his chariot from one end of the horizon to the other. There are problems that face theists and atheists alike when it comes to proving one paradigm over the other. Answering the question of origins makes it easier to answer the next question.

Why is the world in its present condition? Once again, the two possible answers derive from naturalism and supernaturalism. The naturalistic explanation is that everything evolved into its current state from a primordial starting point. A supernatural explanation suggests that death and suffering are real problems and not just natural consequences of life. The traditional supernatural explanation for today's broken world is that something went wrong with the Creator's original creation. The deviation from God's created design is known as "sin." Most religions believe in some sort of original sin. Different legends and myths regarding the original sin will be discussed in later chapters, but for now it will suffice the reader to know that sin altered the relationship between God and the natural world. The severance of this relationship has resulted in grave consequences. Thus, the world as it exists today is a result of the internal conflict between the sinful behavior of the creation and its inherent longing to restore itself to the Creator. Understanding the condition of the world as it currently resides helps one to understand what will become of the world in the future.

What will the world be like in the future? The naturalist can only speculate about what tomorrow may bring. Many believe that the world is heading toward disaster, while others believe that it is heading toward utopia. Many naturalists see mankind as the enemy of nature. Mankind must return to a natural way of living or else succumb to a world that has been depleted of its natural resources. The health of the planet is their highest priority because it is the only thing that is sacred. After all, nature is what brings forth and sustains life. Some people believe that the universe is an everlasting cycle. Sometime in the distant future the universe will collapse on itself and start over from scratch. In their minds, the universe is the only thing that is truly eternal.

On the other hand, those that believe in an eternal God typically believe that there will be a day of reckoning for the entire world. If the world is in a broken condition caused by its rebellion against its Creator, the world deserves some sort of judgment. No two religions agree on how the world will end, in fact people with the same religious affiliation often disagree, but most believe that it will be a cataclysmic event unlike any other. Because it is impossible to sum up every religion's beliefs, this subject will not be given much attention. Heaven, hell, nirvana, and other eternal dwelling places are closely related to end time matters. The actions of individuals on earth affect one's final judgment and final destination in the afterlife. It is vitally important to understand the nature of the Creator so that the appropriate preparations can be made to spend eternity in paradise.

The question of origins, if answered correctly, directs a person to a desirable end and a profitable afterlife. If there are no gods, a person might find it most beneficial to live life however he or she sees fit with no structured rules or particular worries. If a god of some sort exists, it would be most beneficial to discover how to earn his or her favor. This might require a person to live a life by a particular code of conduct. The question of origins has become so important that scientific organizations have devoted their entire existence to unlocking the mysteries of the universe's beginning. The urge to discover where all things came from is not a vain pursuit. It is actually an urge to discover how people ought to behave during their lives on earth.

John Courtney Murray wrote, "God is not a proposition but an Existence. . .Similarly, godlessness is not a proposition but a state of existence. The knowledge of God is not an affair of affirmation alone; it is a free engagement in a whole style of life."[1] The mystery of origins poses a problem far greater than curiosity. One who understands the origin of the universe also understands the created order. One who has been enlightened in such a way has a responsibility to live in a manner that is acceptable to the created order.

Scholars today wage war over this vitally important topic. Three main parties are actively engaged in this battle: Evolutionists, Creationists, and those who believe in Intelligent Design. Each possesses a unique worldview that requires practical application. The debate is not just about whether God exists or not; it is about how a person should live his or her life. Just like the question of origins, the presupposition of a person or group on that topic greatly influences every aspect of his or her life.

Evolutionists advocate an atheistic worldview. Atheist literally means "no God." Most, if not all atheists, claim that their disbelief in God is purely scientific. That which is supernatural is not readily observable. Scientific observation is rooted in duplication. Science deduces laws and theories through tests and experiments. Experimentation allows for scientists to duplicate

---

[1] John Courtney Murray, *The Problem of God* (London: Yale University Press, 1964), 77.

conditions and phenomena that regularly occur with the intention to better understand the natural world. Needless to say, supernatural phenomena are impossible to duplicate because they have divine origins. Under such a premise, the atheistic conclusion that God did not create the universe sounds reasonable enough. They believe that everything had strictly naturalistic origins. They have a variety of different beliefs concerning where the universe came from and how life emerged, but all of their theories share one common element: God played no role in the creative process.

Just because atheists reject the existence of God does not mean they lack morality. There are many evolutionists that believe in morality. Most attempt to derive morality from a progressive evolutionary model. For example, this typically means they believe murder and stealing are wrong. At one time in evolutionary, history they believe that these actions were necessary, but today they believe that the evolved individual should be able resolve conflicts without resolving to primal solutions. Regardless of common sentiments there is truly no way to discern good from evil according to an evolutionist's worldview. Many actions they would consider moral are detestable to other worldviews. Of the three parties this is the most unrestrained because their view on morality changes over time.

Creationists are perhaps the most restrained of the three main worldviews because they believe that the God of the Bible created the heavens, the earth, and all life. Most creationists would be defined as Christians and many of them would be deemed fundamentalists by the mainstream culture. Creationists can be split into two main categories: old earth creationists and young earth creationists. An old earth creationist concedes to the popular scientific teaching that the world is billions of years old. Young earth creationists disagree. Instead, they trust that a literal interpretation of the Bible can be used to deduce the age of the earth. Most young earth creationists believe that the world is between six to ten thousand years old. Ultimately, creationists trust in the authority of the Bible when interpreting the surrounding world.

Creationists believe that God is the basis for all morality. The Bible is viewed as the inerrant and infallible Word of God. Pleasing and honoring the God of the Bible is the highest priority for a creationist. Moral issues that warrant no thought from evolutionists might actually stir up creationists. Their strict belief in a black and white God makes them zealous over issues that others might not take as seriously. Not everyone who believes in God is a creationist, and not everyone who gives credit to an Intelligent Designer see "God" as black and white.

Advocates for intelligent design are the most ambiguous of the three parties. Those who profess belief in intelligent design do not hold to any particular religious tradition. Many people in this movement claim that they are in no way religious. A good number of people with this worldview could be classified as "agnostics" (which means "no knowledge," as in someone who is unsure if God exists). Nonetheless, people from various religious traditions have joined hands with the intelligent design movement to pursue the notion that some supremely intelligent being designed life and maybe even the entire universe. Morality seems to be one of the undertones of intelligent design. Despite their longing for moral absolutes, the intelligent design movement has no single document or ideology that determines right or wrong. It is possible that a strict code of ethics may be formulated one day, but the basis for intelligent design is that life and the systems that sustain life are far too complex to have happened by accident. The Designer is very mysterious. In fact, according to this worldview, the Designer is not necessarily a god. This worldview allows for the possibility that life was seeded on earth by an extraterrestrial.

There is much mystery to life and it is quite possible, and even likely to intelligent design advocates, that life evolved. Under the premise that God created life, most intelligent design advocates regard life as a precious gift. Nobody can really conclude anything about the Intelligent Designer's character or authority, though. Not knowing who or what the Designer is makes for a very complicated worldview. Their lack of knowledge of the Designer is because they only try to draw conclusions about the Designer's nature through scientific observations. Science is taken seriously by the intelligent design advocate, while religion is either secondary or disregarded altogether.

Because intelligent design does not have a strict religious affiliation it is often able to poke its head into the classroom whenever the topic of origins is brought up. Regardless of whether intelligent design is allowed in the classroom or not, evolution is the primary teaching of nearly all science classes in relation to origins. It is considered inappropriate to teach creationism in school, so creationists often take a back seat to evolutionists and intelligent design advocates in the realm of public debate. It seems as though the expectation is that evolution must be taught as fact in the public classroom and understood as fact by the common person. Although intelligent design is scoffed at by many atheists, they at least appreciate that it allows for the possibility, and even probability, that evolution took place. Those in opposition to creationism often do not consider it creative enough to be taken seriously and have ostracized it when given the opportunity. What this really means is that the other two camps think that creationists take the Bible too literally. The two perspectives that get the most public attention are intelligent design and evolution.

Of the books on the topics of atheism and intelligent design, two epitomize their respective arguments: Richard Dawkins' *The God Delusion*[2] and Michael Behe's *Darwin's Black Box*.[3] Richard Dawkins is an atheist that believes in evolution, while Michael Behe is a Catholic who believes in intelligent design. Although they will both go down in history as pivotal works of this era, their arguments against one another display the futility of the scientific debate over God's existence.

Richard Dawkins has devoted his life to disproving the existence of God. He has written several books in an attempt to prove that there is no need for an intelligent individual to believe in God. He believes that there is enough evidence in the natural world to conclude that God does not exist. *The God Delusion*, thus far, has been his magnum opus. He also makes room in his book to aggressively attack the concept of irreducible complexity,

[2] Richard Dawkins, *The God Delusion* (New York: Mariner Books, 2008).

[3] Michael Behe, *Darwin's Black Box* (New York: Free Press, 2006).

which was a major theme in *Darwin's Black Box*. An organism is considered to be irreducibly complex when it is composed of vital parts that depend on one another to provide itself with life and function. Supposedly, it would be impossible for the parts to evolve separately in the organism because it cannot function or live without one or the other. The only solution from an evolutionary perspective would be for the parts to evolve at the same time, which would be nearly impossible without some sort of intelligent guidance. So when an organism, when it is reduced to its most basic elements, is too complex to evolve one step at a time it is considered irreducibly complex. In *The God Delusion*, Dawkins does his best to prove that the belief in God is ignorant, irrational, and dangerous.

To Dawkins, creationism is foolish and intelligent design is not a reasonable alternative. He views intelligent design as nothing more than a last ditch effort to preserve the belief in God. He believes that there is no reason to give credit to God for any of the processes that are observed in nature.

Dawkins wrote about Behe's book, "Without a word of justification, explanation or amplification, Behe simply proclaims the bacterial flagellar motor to be irreducibly complex. Since he offers no argument in favour of his assertion, we may begin suspecting a failure of his imagination."[4] Dawkins asserts that people like Michael Behe automatically resort to God as their explanation whenever they observe a process that they do not currently understand. He wants to make it clear

[4] Richard Dawkins, *The God Delusion* (New York: Mariner Books, 2008), 157.

to his reader that if one gives the evolutionary process a sufficient amount of time, it can indeed assemble highly complex biological "machines." Dawkins seems very concerned about Behe's "imagination" and not so much about the information he provided. One who reads *The God Delusion* ought to read *Darwin's Black Box*, as well. Strangely, Dawkins' claim that Behe's argument for irreducible complexity is not backed by any sort of logic or proof is an outright lie. Behe goes into great detail to show his reader that there are systems of life that are irreducibly complex.

Michael Behe brilliantly explains the components and functionality of the bacterial flagellar motor. He does not argue that it could not have evolved. He makes the case that "Darwinian evolution" could not have produced the bacterial flagellar motor in all of its complexity. "Darwinian evolution" is evolution through purely natural processes with no involvement by God. The case that Behe makes is that certain parts of it would have needed to evolve at the same time in order for it to survive. Logically, this means that either the necessary parts evolved at the same time or were already set in place when it was created. The option that the essential components evolved separately is not possible, according to Behe.

Behe thoroughly explains the irreducible complexity of many biological systems. Irreducibly complex systems baffle critical observers almost as much as the layman. How on earth could these systems have evolved without an Intelligent Designer? The bacterial flagellum was Behe's most famous example of an irreducibly complex system. It was for this reason that Richard Dawkins chose it in his attack against intelligent design. Ironically, Behe did not intend to disprovc the evolution of the flagellum. He indicated that it was unlikely for it to have evolved through a natural process, not that it did not evolve. He placed a disclaimer at the beginning of his book in which he informed his readers that he does not doubt the process of evolution nor does he think that the world is any younger than what popular science assumes.

> Evolution is a controversial topic, so it is necessary to address a few basic questions at the beginning of the book. Many people think that questioning Darwinian evolution must be equivalent to espousing creationism. As commonly understood, creationism involves belief in an earth formed only about ten thousand years ago, an interpretation of the Bible that is still very popular. For the record I have no reason to doubt that the universe is the billions of years old that physicists say it is. Further, I find the idea of common descent (that all organisms share a common ancestor) fairly convincing, and have no particular reason to doubt it.[5]

It is clear that Behe believes in evolution and that the world is over ten thousand years old.

In admitting this, he gives credibility to Dawkins' assertion that he simply inserts God when he cannot answer a question about how things evolved. After all, he did not say that the flagellum did not evolve. He was proving that the flagellum is too complex to have evolved

[5] Michael Behe, *Darwin's Black Box* (New York: Free Press, 2006), 5.

naturally. It may have evolved. The implication is that the Intelligent Designer guided the evolutionary process according to some plan or purpose. In other words, God is the mechanism of evolution.

Despite claims by fundamentalist atheists, Michael Behe sets himself apart from creationists. The Bible is not Behe's source of authority. He seems to consider the findings that are published in scientific journals to be the most credible source of information:

> The Nice thing about science is that authority is easy to locate: it's in the library.
>
> Molecular evolution is not based on scientific authority. There is no publication in the scientific literature–prestigious journals, specialty journals, or books–that describes how molecular evolution... either did occur or even might have occurred.[6]

To a creationist, Behe's trust in authority is misplaced. It should not be placed in scientific journals and studies (even though their relevance is not ignored by creationists either), but in the Bible. More importantly, a creationist believes that the Creator of all things was the God of the Bible. Michael Behe claims that he does not know the identity of the Creator:

> Inferences to design do not require that we have a candidate for the role of designer. We can determine that a system was designed by examining the system

[6] Behe, 185.

> itself, and we can hold the conviction of design much more strongly than a conviction about the identity of the designer.[7]

> The conclusion that something was designed can be made quite independently of knowledge of the designer. . .The inference to design can be held with all the firmness that is possible in this world, without knowing anything about the designer.[8]

Behe is a scientist and must attempt to approach every situation as though he is a non-biased observer. Scientists that believe in God are often scrutinized by their peers. It is nearly impossible to be a scientist without disowning one's religious beliefs. Political pressure within the realm of mainstream science has created this reality. Given this problem, Behe should be credited as a free-thinker for believing that nothing could have evolved without a divine hand. But a theist confessing that the Theory of Evolution is true is highly problematic. It is as though they are saying, "Yeah, your theory is false, but I am going to build my theory starting with your theory as its foundation." If the first theory was false, how can you build anything upon it?

There is simply no authority behind the arguments of either Behe or Dawkins. Their source of authority is derived from human opinion and observation, both of which have been frequently wrong in the past. Because there are many ways to interpret scientific observations,

---

[7] Behe, 196.

[8] Behe, 196.

determining which scientific source is authoritatively true becomes a matter of one's own opinion. Scientists, therefore, become their own authority. For instance, in *The God Delusion* Dawkins cites his own work from *Scaling Mount Improbable* as proof for his assertion. In *Scaling Mount Improbable* he tried to explain the "easy" process of evolution:

> One side of the mountain is a sheer cliff, impossible to climb, but on the other side is a gentle slope to the summit. On the summit sits a complex device such as an eye or a bacterial flagellar motor. The absurd notion that such complexity could spontaneously self-assemble is symbolized by leaping from the foot of the cliff to the top in one bound. Evolution, by contrast, goes around the back of the mountain and creeps up the gentle slope to the summit: easy![9]

Rarely, if ever, in the field of science has anyone claimed that evolution is "easy." Dawkins seems rather confident that it was simple. There are fundamentalists in every religion, and it is fitting to label Richard Dawkins as a "fundamentalist humanist."

A fundamentalist, in the derogatory sense, is a person who overlooks reality for the sake of holding tight to a personal belief. In this case, Dawkins qualifies as a fundamentalist because he overlooks reality when formulating his illustration. In a world full of ultra-violet rays, torrents of water, molten lava, earthquakes, tornadoes, hurricanes, and the countless other factors that make planet

[9] Dawkins, 147.

earth dangerous today, it probably would have been many times more chaotic and dangerous in the pre-life world of Dawkins imagination. Would it be far-fetched to say that, under these conditions, the emergence of life would have been *miraculous*? Dawkins started with his presupposition that God never existed and automatically concluded that the path of jumping straight to the top of Mount Improbable was impossible. If one believes that there is no God, leaping to the top of Mount Improbable in a single bound is impossible. Walking up a steady incline would make it very easy.

But if one decides to scrutinize another person's theory, he or she ought to do so with the allowance that the opposing theory could be true. Allowing God into the scene would make Dawkins' argument just plain stupid. Christians, along with other religions, believe that God is all-powerful. All things are possible for an all-powerful deity! His probability for success would be 100%, making the leap from the foot of the mountain to its peak child's play.

In *Darwin's Black Box,* Behe used an illustration similar to that of Dawkins. Instead of a mountain, he used the analogy of leaping across a giant ditch.

> If the 'ditch' were actually a canyon 100 feet wide, however, you would not entertain for a moment the bold assertion that he jumped across. But suppose your neighbor – a clever man – qualifies his claim. He did not come across in one jump. Rather, he says, in the canyon there were a number of buttes, no more than 10 feet apart from one another; he jumped from one narrowly spaced butte to another to reach your

> side. Glancing toward the canyon, you tell your neighbor that you see no buttes, just a wide chasm separating your yard from his. He agrees, but explains that it took him years and years to come over. During that time buttes occasionally arose in the chasm, and he progressed as they popped up. After he left a butte it usually eroded pretty quickly and crumbled back into the canyon. Very dubious, but with no easy way to prove him wrong, you change the subject to baseball.[10]

What Behe is saying is that it is easy to provide a reasonable explanation for anything, if one is "imaginative" enough to come up with a process that could make sense of a seemingly impossible task. Richard Dawkins makes some wonderful observations, but he honestly misses the fact that although he used good logic, starting from his presupposition, he failed to recognize that he could not prove any of his hypotheses. That is not to say that Behe's arguments are any more compelling or productive in answering the question of origins.

Neither argument matters. Behe still gives credit to the Theory of Evolution and allows Dawkins a foothold. Dawkins then proceeds by pulling the rug out from under Behe with rude insults and childish comments that are laced throughout *The God Delusion*. If evolution is observably true, then how could Dawkins be wrong? If life forms evolve naturally over time, then certainly, given the appropriate amount of time and chance, highly complex organisms could evolve even under unlikely

[10] Behe, 13-14.

conditions. Under Dawkins' premise, Behe's suggestion that Darwinian evolution has never been observed is irrelevant because nobody would be able to live long enough to observe the noticeable changes through Darwinian evolution. All Dawkins is required to do, in such a situation, is to say, "Just wait a little longer." Because they both presuppose evolution, their arguments literally go nowhere. This is why a view on creation that is strictly in line with what the Bible teaches is necessary.

Many people claim that old earth creationism is a viable alternative to intelligent design. Old earth creationists accept mainstream science in regards to the age of the earth, but typically reject the notion that mankind evolved from primitive primates. Young earth creationists greatly disagree with them regarding the age of the earth. They believe that old earth creationism is not an alternative that honors the authority of Scripture. There are several old earth creationist theories that have attempted to reconcile the accepted scientific age of the earth with Scripture.

Many people consider old earth creationism to be a reasonable alternative to intelligent design. Perhaps the most appealing aspect of old earth creationism is that it allows for people who believe in the Bible to also accept the proposed scientific age of the earth. Some old earth creationists allow for the possibility of evolution, while others do not. The majority of creationists uphold the doctrine that mankind was created in the image of God and therefore reject the notion that humans evolved from a primitive primate ancestor. There are two old earth creation theories that are accepted by the evangelical community: Day Age Theory and Gap Theory. As secular interpretation became more popular in the scientific realm, old earth theories were devised to defend the authority of Scripture and reconcile evangelicals to the mainstream world. When old earth theories are compared to secular science, it is clear that old earth creationists had to put forth serious effort to satisfy both scientific and theological concerns.

Day Age Theory embraces a pretty broad range of accepted models. Some models embrace the Theory of Evolution, while others do not. The premise of Day Age Theory is that the days described in Genesis were not twenty-four hour days, but were long, indefinite, periods of time. The theologian who is most associated with this theory is Saint Augustine, although his interpretation of the days was significantly different from the modern interpretation. To Augustine, the days represented different ages in history in which the seventh day would be history's final movement. Around the time that science began interpreting geology in terms of millions of years, his theory was remembered, revised, and popularized within the religious community.

The other major old earth proposition is Gap Theory. Gap Theory was popularized by a man named Thomas Chalmers. There are at least two different ways that Gap Theory is proposed. One interpretation is that Genesis 1:1 is a description of the "first creation" and Genesis 1:2 is the "second creation." The interpretation is that Genesis 1:1 only accounts for the "second creation" and the "first creation" is unmentioned in Genesis. Regardless, between the first creation and second creation, proponents of this theory believe that there were millions of years. During this time angels lived on the earth and Satan rebelled. His rebellion resulted in the destruction of the first creation. Although the late Bible scholar, Merrill Unger, believed in the Bible and the Gap Theory, he admitted that the Gap Theory did not originate from a straightforward reading of Scripture. He conceded that it was created as a means to reconcile Scripture to science. Unger compromised a thoroughly straightforward understanding of Scripture to make way for the millions of years proposed by science.

Nonetheless, Unger saw the conflict with the "first creation" of 1:1 and the "second creation" of 1:2. He believed that 1:1 was an account of a new creation and that the previous age, which included millions of years and the rebellion of Satan, were simply not meant to be included in Scripture. He believed that, "The original earth created *ex nihilo* was brought into being by the hand of God *before* sin entered God's moral universe (Ezk 28:13-14; Isa 14:12) and was designed to be the habitation of God's first sinless angelic creatures (Job 38:4, 7; cf. Isa 45:18)."[11] Biblical evidence for the Gap Theory is not derived from a clear understanding of Scripture. One must reinterpret key passages in a creative manner in order to arrive at the Gap Theory's conclusions. Gap Theorists place the rebellion of Satan before the creation of mankind to develop a coherent chronology of events that accommodate for the proposition of millions of years. It will be displayed in later chapters that such an accommodation, in both respects, is unnecessary.

Since Merrill Unger's day, much progress has been made in Christianity regarding the interpretation of

---

[11] Merril Unger, *Unger's Bible Handbook* (Chicago: Moody Press, 1980), 37.

natural processes. Before the challenge of evolution became serious, creationists either relied on poorly constructed scientific models to support the idea of a young earth, or simply ignored the scientific debate altogether and trusted the Word of God. Today, creationists acknowledge that the challenge from evolution does not derive from the evidence that evolutionists provide, but from their interpretations of the evidence. Several organizations have been established to point out these interpretive errors in mainstream science and to even conduct their own research in relation to the topic. The most prominent force in promoting the idea that the world is not millions of years old and that the natural world can be reconciled with the Bible is the creationist organization Answers In Genesis. Answers In Genesis has employed a team of scientists and Bible scholars with the intent of disproving the proposition that the earth is millions or billions of years old. In other words, they intend to prove the authenticity of God's Word from Genesis to Revelation.

Most young earth creationists do not force the doctrine of a young earth as a necessary prerequisite for salvation. In fairness to Merrill Unger, he faithfully interpreted the Bible using his knowledge of science and archaeology to prove its authority. He even wrote, "Authority resides in God's inspired Word, the Bible, interpreted by God's Spirit operating through Spirit-taught human agents."[12] The difference between Merrill Unger, liberal theologians, atheists, and agnostics was that he approached the Word of God as inerrant and

[12] Unger, 6.

infallible. Most people that reject a literal interpretation of the Genesis creation account reject the Bible as a historically reliable document. Once one denies the historic reliability of the Bible, it is only a matter of time before he or she denies Scripture altogether.

Chapter 2
Establishing Authority

> For this reason I, Paul, the prisoner of Christ Jesus for the sake of you Gentiles – Surely you have heard about the administration of God's grace that was given to me for you, that is, the mystery made known to me by revelation, as I have already written briefly. In reading this, then, you will be able to understand my insight into the mystery of Christ, which was not made known to men in other generations as it has now been revealed by the Spirit to God's holy apostles and prophets. This mystery is that through the gospel the Gentiles are heirs together with Israel, members together of one body, and sharers together in the promise in Christ Jesus.[13]

These words were written by the Apostle Paul in one of his letters to the Ephesians in the first century A.D. Back then, the implications of these words were profound. The Apostle Paul was known as Saul among the Jewish people and was an esteemed religious leader of his day. When Christianity arose, Saul became extremely

[13] Ephesians 3:1-6

zealous in his legalistic tradition and decided to rile up crowds of people to murder anyone who taught in the name of Jesus Christ. One day, when he was traveling, he was blinded by an incredible light and the resurrected Jesus came to him:

> As he neared Damascus on his journey, suddenly a light from heaven flashed around him. He fell to the ground and heard a voice say to him, "Saul, Saul, why do you persecute me?"
>
> "Who are you, Lord?" Saul asked. "I am Jesus, whom you are persecuting," he replied. "Now get up and go into the city, and you will be told what you must do." The men traveling with Saul stood there speechless; they heard the sound but did not see anyone. Saul got up from the ground, but when he opened his eyes he could see nothing. So they led him by the hand into Damascus. For three days he was blind, and did not eat or drink anything.[14]

Paul then realized the truth of the Gospel and was healed of his blindness by a disciple of Jesus known as Ananias. Afterwards, he began to preach the Gospel that he once hated. Despite his hatred toward Christians, he eventually became one.

As a result of this experience, Paul realized that Jesus was the messiah that the Holy Scriptures predicted. Since he was a great scholar of the Old Testament, he was able to make the connection in his mind between

[14] Acts 9:3-9.

the ancient prophecies regarding messiah and how Jesus fulfilled them. He often referred to these Scriptures when he wrote to the New Testament churches. Although many of the people of that day, Jews and non-Jews alike, were familiar with the writings of the Old Testament, not everyone that Paul preached to was familiar with the Old Testament's teachings. He had to use another method to communicate the Gospel to the people who were not familiar with the Jewish faith.

Even though he did not consider foreign religions to be authoritatively true, he recognized that their teachings could sometimes be used to forward the message of the Gospel. The pagan religions taught that the world was created by some great supernatural entity. In the Greek creation myth, mankind was fashioned in the likeness of the gods. Despite this reality, they also believed that mankind had experienced some sort of a fall and, as a result, were not looked favorably upon by the deities that ruled over them. Paul was able to see these elements of truth amid the plethora of lies and superstitions held by the Gentiles. He was able use these foundational truths to reach a culture that was significantly different from his own. At times he even referenced teachings of the non-Christian world to enforce the idea that Christ was not just the messiah of the Jews, but the savior for the entire world. For instance, the Apostle Paul gave a sermon in Athens where he preached,

> As some of your own poets have said, "We are his offspring." Therefore since we are God's offspring, we should not think that the divine being is like gold or silver or stone – an image made by man's design

> and skill. In the past God overlooked such ignorance, but now he commands all people everywhere to repent.[15]

The mystery of Christ has existed since the dawn of creation. The first prophecy concerning Christ was written in the book of Genesis. The idea of a messiah has always existed, and not just in Jewish tradition but in other religious traditions as well. Nearly every religion realizes that there is something wrong with the condition of the world and this problem desperately needs fixed. Many stories have been written about an exceptional individual that would one day change the way the world operates. The Hebrew title for this individual is the "Messiah." Because of the abundance of "Messianic" prophecies, one must wonder if any one religion is correct concerning the identity of the messiah.

The existence of messianic characters in other religions propagates the notion that the truth is relative. It goes back to the idea that if one messianic story sounds similar to another, then one of the stories is a forgery of the other. This means that either one is true and the other is a lie, or both are lies. To many spectators, this reality nullifies the possibility that one individual could be responsible for the salvation of the entire human race. As a result, people believe that all religions are the same and that salvation is a matter of opinion. Who can blame the world for reaching this conclusion?

All one needs to do is read the stories from different cultures to realize that there are many similarities

[15] Acts 17:28-30.

between religions. It would be ignorant to simply say that the stories in the Bible are totally unique to any of the other traditions formulated by religious groups around the world. That does not mean that the truth is relative. It is possible that a single religion contains the entire truth independent from other traditions. Jesus confronted this issue directly when he spoke to a Samaritan woman at Jacob's Well in Sychar.

Judaism (Jesus' upbringing) and the religion of the Samaritans had similarities, but their differences were enough to create a bitter hatred between the two peoples. Jesus and the Samaritan woman, whose name was not given, debated back and forth until their conversation brought them to their religious differences:

> "Sir," the woman said, "I can see that you are a prophet. Our fathers worshiped on this mountain, but you Jews claim that the place where we must worship is in Jerusalem."
>
> Jesus declared, "Believe me, woman, a time is coming when you will worship the Father neither on this mountain nor in Jerusalem. You Samaritans worship what you do not know; we worship what we do know, for salvation is from the Jews. Yet a time is coming and has now come when the true worshipers must worship in spirit and in truth."[16]

The woman was intent on justifying her people's method of worship. Jesus was intent on declaring the true method

---

[16] John 4:19-24.

of worship. Telling the Samaritan woman that her people worshiped what they did not know declared that the worship they engaged in was not honoring God according to God's standard. He then said that salvation came from the Jews. He informed the woman that the tradition that she was mocking was the official worship order of God. The Jews were right and the Samaritans were wrong.

However, he then told her that the traditions of temple worship and mountain worship were coming to an end. After the coming of Jesus, worship was only acceptable to God when it was accomplished through spirit and truth. Jesus had come to reveal to this woman that there was an acceptable way to worship, and neither the Jews nor Samaritans could accomplish it merely through their traditions. The mystery of the Gospel was revealed to her. It did not matter whether she was a Jew or a Samaritan; it only mattered that she accepted the Messiah's testimony concerning the truth.

The truth is not relative. A statement is either true or it is false. Good and evil are either real or make-believe. Either there is a Supreme Being or there is not. Those who are wrong and those who take the middle-ground are not upholding the truth. They would be considered liars, whether lying is their intention or not. The truth must contain something in substance that distinguishes it from fairy tales. The difference between Christianity and every other religion is the God that it worships and his disclosure of himself through his Son, Jesus Christ. Jesus is real and through his life, teachings, and miracles, we know that the God he worshipped is also real. Despite how similar the teachings and the stories of other religions may be to the Bible, the character of the God of the Bible is totally unique compared to the other religions.

The primary objective of this book will be to prove the importance of a sound Biblical worldview opposed to an alternative worldview. This will be accomplished by surveying the first eleven chapters of the book of Genesis. The first eleven chapters of Genesis explain how the world became what it is today. The world was created by God, destroyed by God, and repopulated by the grace of God. The Biblical stories contained in Genesis will then be compared to those of other cultures. This will help the reader to understand how ancient people viewed the world in which they lived. After comparing these stories, the uniqueness and superiority of the God of the Bible will be exposed.

The majority of this survey will be describing a pre-flood world. Most religions have myths that describe a catastrophic flood that engulfed the entire earth and supposedly altered the course of history. It is almost impossible to know anything about the pre-flood world aside from the testimony contained in the Bible and other religious traditions. A small portion of the survey will be devoted to a post-flood world and will explain where all of the variances in the flood account came from. Ultimately, it will be proven that the Bible accurately describes the world in its early stages in Genesis chapters one through eleven.

The second objective will be to paint a picture of what the pre-flood world looked like and why it was destroyed. This will be accomplished by using the Biblical creation account, pagan myths, and even the Theory of Evolution. After the informational portions of the book have accomplished their purposes, a fictional narrative will be provided to help one visualize the message that is being presented. As the book progresses it will be increasingly evident that the world today is not what it was created to be. Even though God created a world that was free of sin, the entrance of sin resulted in horrible acts of evil. As evil infiltrates the world more and more, the closer the world brings itself to divine judgment.

The third objective is to establish a Biblical worldview based on the teachings of Jesus Christ. The Apostle Paul saw that it was not only necessary to instill in the Gentiles a fear of the Lord, but also to introduce them to Jesus. Jesus is the central figure of the Christian faith, but is also highly revered among other religions. Understanding the truth behind the world's origins is futile if one fails to see Jesus' role in it all. Although the teachings of Jesus transformed the world, many people today have disowned the Gospel for alternative religions and beliefs.

The Bible is the most historically accurate book ever written. It has been scrutinized for centuries and has stood the test of time. Unfortunately, no source can be proven to be one-hundred percent accurate beyond a shadow of doubt. Nonetheless, the Bible seems to accurately depict what the ancient world was like as verified through many archaeological findings. Even though it may be impossible to prove the accuracy of every event described in the Bible, it is impossible to prove any one event in the Bible to be false, which is more than can be said for any other source of ancient literature. This is because the Bible is rooted in reality; the history it describes is true history, and the supernatural phenomena it describes were not just misunderstandings of natural events but were truly signs that the hand of God was at work. The central character of the Christian Bible, Jesus, is acknowledged by non-Biblical sources as being a true historic figure.

Many noteworthy people have acknowledged Jesus' holy nature. Albert Einstein once said:

> As a child I received instruction both in the Bible and in the Talmud. I am a Jew, but I am enthralled by the luminous figure of the Nazarene. . .No one can read the Gospels without feeling the actual presence of Jesus. His personality pulsates in every word. No myth is filled with such life.[17]

Mahatma Gandhi, who practiced Hinduism, said Jesus was, "A man who was completely innocent, offered himself as a sacrifice for the good of others, including his enemies, and became the ransom of the world. It was a perfect act."[18] Even Bill Maher, an out-spoken atheist, comedian, and the star of the 2008 documentary *Religulous*, acknowledged Jesus' uniqueness! He said, "Jesus, as a philosopher is wonderful. There's no greater role model, in my view, than Jesus Christ."[19] How can

---

[17] Liberty Tree, liberty-tree.ca, (http://quotes.liberty-tree.ca/quote/albert_einstein_quote_c07c [accessed September 27, 2011]), from an interview with George Sylvester Vierek, "What Life Means to Einstein," The Saturday Evening Post, October 26, 1929, Curtis Publishing Company.

[18] M. K. Ghandi, *Non-Violence in Peace and War*, vol. 2, (Ahmedabab-14, 1949) 160, as cited in Peter J. Hadreas, A Phenomonology of Love and Hate, (Burlington, Vermont: Ashgate Publishing Company, 2007), 108

[19] Wikiquote, Wikiquote.org, (http://en.wikiquote.org/wiki/Bill_Maher [accessed September 27, 2011]), from an interview on *The O'Reilly Factor*, September 26, 2006, Fox News.

a figure such as Jesus, who is so tightly associated to a particular religious movement, receive as much praise from people who are critics of the faith he founded? If any man's words were ever truly alive, Jesus would have been the one to utter those words.

The ethical teachings of Jesus transformed the world. He taught that the poor are people who are greatly loved by God and often stand a higher chance of getting into heaven than rich people! The laws of the Old Testament taught that order must be upheld by justice. Jesus taught his believers to uphold justice through mercy. Jesus is the authority for the Christian Church and many people who are not Christians acknowledge that Jesus does have a special type of authority in his words.

The reason that Jesus is acknowledged by many non-Christians as the greatest figure in all of history is because of his credibility as a moral teacher. He never claimed that he desired to change what was moral and what was immoral; instead, his purpose was to fulfill the moral code of ethics that was understood by the people of his culture. He would accomplish this by living out this code while preaching and teaching about how everyone who follows him could fulfill this code as well. Some of the teachings that are widely acknowledged by the modern world that were popularized by Jesus are: do unto others as you would have them do unto you;[20] love your neighbor as yourself;[21] and giving to those who are in need.[22] As the founder of a religious movement, he

---

[20] Matthew 7:12

[21] Luke10:25-28

[22] Matthew 6:2

was totally unique. Some religious leaders have tried to forward their agenda through pacifism. Other religious leaders have tried to force their agenda through violence. Of all of the religious movements in history, Jesus not only taught that his words were truth; he boldly declared it despite opposition. Yet he remained gentle. He bravely rebuked his opposition without causing them any harm. He believed in his own teachings so much that he gave himself up to be killed by those who hated him.[23] With this sort of integrity, one must wonder why Jesus believed so strongly in the words that proceeded from his mouth.

It was because of his identity as the Messiah that he preached with authority. This identity was defined by the entire Old Testament. The Old Testament explained the dilemma that mankind created. From a human perspective, it can be concluded that Jesus believed that God created a world that was good. Through sin, that world went bad. Whether Jesus was truly God or not, he clearly believed that he was God's chosen Savior that would rid the world of the curse of sin. Therefore, Jesus was not silent when it came to the topic of creation.

Jesus seemed to interpret the Bible quite literally. If Jesus was a mere human, this would not be a dilemma because humans are fallible. But, Jesus claimed to be God. This claim creates a problem. If Jesus is God that means that he has more than just a special authority on any given topic. It means that he is *the* authority on any given topic. If Jesus is God, as Christians believe he is, there is nothing foolish about believing in the literal interpretation of the Genesis creation account. He would

[23] Romans 5:6-8

be the only person that would know how the world was truly created. That is why atheism and intelligent design do not provide reliable answers to the question of origins.

There are many different ideas concerning where life came from. Some say that life evolved naturally, while others insert God into the equation as a special Creator. The truth is that nobody can know beyond a shadow of a doubt how everything came to be unless someone had witnessed life's origins firsthand. This goes to show how futile the human quest for knowledge has become. It is no wonder that God had to reveal himself in the flesh through the man Jesus Christ.

To Paul, Jesus removed the mystery of God and revealed him openly and fully to whoever would listen. To early Christians, the Holy Scriptures and the letters from apostles revealed the true identity of Jesus Christ. By acknowledging Jesus as God, they could know that the Creator of all things loves his entire creation and humanity above all else. Because of the condition of this present world, we are in many ways like the early Christians that Paul preached to two millennia ago. It appears that those early believers relied on the Scriptures as being both inerrant, meaning that it contained no informational errors, and infallible, meaning that it always conveyed its desired message. As you read further into this study, I hope that you discover the inerrancy and infallibility of the Holy Scriptures which stand true even in the fields of science, history, and religious studies today.

Chapter 3
God is the Creator

In the beginning God created the heavens and the earth.[24] The civilized world faces a unique situation today. There is a rapid increase in the number of atheists, and for the first time ever they are considered among the intellectual elite. This is because of the emergence of empiricism which says that all things that are real can be measured and understood in a material way. But, God is not a being that can be measured or understood in an empirical sense. In ancient times the world was understood in terms of mystery. Knowledge of the natural world had to be acquired before it could be understood and subdued. Philosophy was perhaps the most important field of study. Most logical thinkers of the ancient world could not imagine a world that came into existence through random chance; atheists were truly a minority.

It is thought that ancient man was not sophisticated enough to grasp the complexity of the Theory of Evolution and had to cling to legends of deities in order to make sense of the world. One who studies philosophy can attest to the truth that the exercise of logic is just

[24] Genesis 1:1.

as complex as studying the natural world. Logic has never made room for a creation that lacks a Creator. Before empiricism became popular, the idea of a godless creation was considered foolish and illogical. What mechanism could have unified particles that operated in a state of utter chaos? A natural solution was not a result of man's ingenuity; rather, it was formulated because of the availability of a larger body of knowledge. Facts can always be interpreted in a way that flatters the eye of the beholder. The naturalistic process of creation has come to be known as "evolution."

The predecessors to the Theory of Evolution held beliefs that are not at all foreign to those of the modern evolutionist philosophy. One of the oldest recorded evolutionist theories proposed that random collisions between microscopic particles eventually formed matter, from which all things came into existence. These microscopic particles were called atoms. Many ancient thinkers despised this theory because it was highly illogical. They knew that the probability of atoms colliding and creating in sort of matter, especially life, were slim to nonexistent.[25] Something or someone had to have guided such a process in order for it to have been taken seriously in the academic world.

A more commonly held truth was that a god, or several gods, existed and directed the process of creation. There are many diverse creation stories that have preserved this belief since ancient times. Archaeology and anthropology are marvelous fields of study that often observe the beliefs of our ancient ancestors. One common mistake made in these fields, however, is that people often assume that the oldest

[25] Bill Cooper, *After the Flood* (Norfolk, England: New Wine Press, 1995), 22.

stories that have been uncovered to date are indeed *the* most ancient and therefore are the originals. As a result, many scholars assume that there are many stories that predate the Biblical accounts. Such assertions are unwarranted, unnecessary, and ignorant. The most ancient stories are always considered to be the most ancient stories until a story is uncovered that is more ancient. Not only is this true, but there may be countless more creation stories that predated the traditions that have been uncovered to date. Oral tradition was a more popular form of transmitting information than carving stories in stone, so some ancient stories may have been totally eradicated and impossible to rediscover. Regardless, most outspoken critics regard all of the stories as nothing more than myths. This is a mistake.

The Bible has preserved an account of creation that harmonizes the common elements of many different creation stories. There are remarkable similarities between the Biblical account of creation and pagan accounts. One does not have to concede the truth of the Bible to concede this point; it is simply a fact. What is remarkable about the Bible is that it has preserved and popularized these stories for several thousand years and has even attempted to explain why many of the ancient stories contained their own unique elements. The Bible explains that there used to be one common language throughout the world and that it was confused when the world gathered in a common location.[26] This would explain as the people travelled away from their common location, why the various creation stories retain similarities but

[26] Genesis 11:1-9.

contain deviations as well. As a result, the truth of God was preserved throughout the world.

The truth of God is spoken of in Taoism. Taoism is defined as, "the search for the Tao, the Way of Nature which, if you could become a part of it, would take you to the edge of reality and beyond."[27] Lao Tzu was one of the founders of Taoism. He was credited for having said, "Before time, and throughout time, there has been a self-existing being, eternal, infinite, complete, omnipresent. . .Outside this being, before the beginning, there was nothing."[28] Despite the fact that Taoism is more of a philosophy than a religion, the truth of God is still present in its doctrine. The profound truth in Lao Tzu's statement was that there were people in the ancient world who were not Christian or Israelites, and these people believed in one being that transcended time and space. There was knowledge of the One who is self-existing. The knowledge of this being did not derive from the Judeo-Christian philosophy. Lao Tzu was not the only ancient thinker who postulated God.

An ancient text from Heliopolis in Egypt states: "I am the creator of all things that exist. . .that came forth from my mouth. Heaven and earth did not exist, nor had been created the herbs of the ground nor the creeping things. I raised them out of the primeval abyss from a state of non-being."[29] Notice the incredible similarities between this account and the Biblical account. The "heaven and

---

[27] Martin Palmer and Elizabeth Breuilly, *The Book of Chuang Tzu* (New York: Penguin Arkana, 1996), xiii.

[28] Cooper, 16

[29] Cooper, 17.

earth did not exist, nor had been created the herbs of the ground nor the creeping things." The Biblical account declares that God created all things, and it mentions some of the specific creations that the Egyptian account pointed out. The first verse in the Bible established the creation of the heavens and the earth by God. On day three, the author of Genesis wrote that God created all of the green plants of the earth. On day six, the creeping things of the earth were created. There are remarkable similarities between the Biblical text and the Egyptian account.

Perhaps the most definite link between the Egyptian text and the Biblical text is the phrase, "that came forth from my mouth." The Creator in the Bible speaks all things into being. The New Testament reveals even more as it states in John chapter one, "In the beginning was the Word, and the Word was with God, and the Word was God. He was with God in the beginning."[30] God the Son is portrayed as the "Word." So the tradition of the New Testament is consistent with the Old Testament's teaching that it was "the Word" that brought all things into existence. John continues, "Through him all things were made; without him nothing was made that has been made."[31] This alludes back to Lao Tzu's statement about how the world came into existence and how nothing existed before God had started creating.

Even the modern myth of the Big Bang shares similarities with the Biblical Creation Account. The Big Bang is the premier "scientific theory" that is used to explain how everything came to be. Jim Holt, a *Wall*

---

[30] John 1:1-2.

[31] John 1:3.

Street Journal science writer, stated, "The universe suddenly exploded into being. . .The big bang bears an uncanny resemblance to the Genesis command."[32] It is interesting to note that even though scientific conclusions are contrary to what the Bible says, scientists cannot escape the evidence that the Bible is accurate in its account of creation. Even more interesting is that "science expresses the universe in five terms: time, space, matter, power, motion." Genesis accounts for all five of these components of the universe within its first two verses: "In the beginning [time] God created [power] the heavens [space] and the earth [matter]. . .And the Spirit of God moved [motion] upon the face of the waters."[33] Even the most contemporary creation theory, which attempts to remove God, explains the creation of the universe in terms that echo the Creation account found in the first chapter of Genesis. But what distinguishes the Biblical creation account from the other accounts of the universe's origin?

The Creator himself separates the Biblical creation account from the others. He discloses his personality throughout the narrative of the Bible and especially in the Biblical creation account. The average readers of English translations miss the theological depth contained in the Bible's first verse. The word used to identify the person of God, in the original Hebrew language, reveals much to the reader about his nature. The Hebrew word for God in this context is *Elohim*. Surprisingly, it is a plural form of the word "God" and is not the Hebrew's

---

[32] Ray Comfort, *Hidden Wealth Series: Scientific facts in the Bible*, (Gainesville, Florida: Bridges – Logos Publishers 2001), 24.

[33] Comfort, 27.

personal name for God, "YHWH" (possibly Yahweh or Jehovah; it is technically unpronounceable). Despite the claims of "higher critics," the reader must understand that the person who wrote the first verse of Genesis also wrote, "The LORD our God, the LORD is one."[34] So Genesis 1:1 does not mean that "gods" created the earth but that a being of high authority was at work. In certain languages, people of higher status are referred to in a plural form. This is called the "plural of majesty." Therefore, the word for God is plural. But whys does a "majestic" title take upon a plural form? Could it be that the first "majestic" authority, God, has a plural nature?

The New Testament reveals that God is a Trinity. He is three persons that exist as One unified Being. From the very beginning, God referred to himself in a plural form. This is strong evidence that God progressively reveals his nature. Some of the Old Testament truths could not be fully understood until Jesus revealed them throughout the New Testament.[35] In fact, in the light of Genesis 1:1, God's decision to become a man in the form of Jesus makes sense as well.

The word Elohim is a masculine form of the word "God." Even though God is not specifically male or female, he chose to be identified with the male gender. This is seen throughout the Bible, especially in the New Testament. God is represented as "Father" and is even incarnate as a man, the "Son of God." Perhaps God chose a male identity because he is apart from his creation the same way that a father is apart from his offspring. A father

---

[34] Deut 6:4; which uses both God's formal and informal names.

[35] Gary Staats, *Christological Hebrew Grammar: A Study of Creation: Genesis 1:1-2:3* (Austin, Texas: WORDsearch Bible, 2001), 2.

plays a major role in the procreative process but relates to his offspring differently from a mother. An infant grows inside of his or her mother and becomes a part of her until she gives birth. In contrast, the infant is not a part of his or her father. Likewise, creation is not a part of God even though it bears his image. He is not the "Mother" of creation. A father takes part in the creation process in a different way. He does not give birth to something that is of his body but instead provides the "seed" necessary for life to begin. God identifying himself in the masculine sense reveals that he does not want to be identified as a part of his creation. He wants to be recognized as the "Transcendent Creator," or the "Father of Creation."[36] God does not seek reconciliation with the world for the sake of his own salvation, but because he is above his creation he loves it passionately and unconditionally.

The character of God in Genesis is unique compared to other ancient gods.

> Emphasizing solely the similarities to other ancient literature produces a misleading impression that they are the most distinctive features of the material in Genesis. The situation is just the opposite. The reader is first impressed with the unique features of the biblical accounts. Only a trained eye discovers the similarities.
>
> In contrast to the exalted monotheism of Gen. 1-11, the Mesopotamian accounts present gods which are embodiments of natural forces. They know no

[36] Gary Staats, 2010, OT 501 Pentateuch Lecture (Winebrenner Theological Seminary, Findlay, OH, June, 8 2010).

> moral principle. They lie, steal, fornicate, and kill. Moreover, humans enjoy no special dignity in these accounts. They are the lowly servants of the gods, being made to provide them with food and offerings.
>
> The biblical narratives present the true, holy, and omnipotent God. The Creator exists before creation and is independent of the world. God speaks and the elements come into being. The divine work is good, just, and whole. After the human family rebels, God tempers his judgment with mercy. Even when an account shares common elements with the thought forms of nearby cultures, the distinctive nature of the Creator shines through the narrative.[37]

It is a shame that modern scholars have tried to lump the Genesis creation account together with common myths and fairy tales. Too many people focus solely on the wrath of God in the Old Testament instead of his mercy. Such a picture of God would make him no different from the pagan accounts. The God of the Bible has a powerful love for his creation.

In the beginning God created the universe as an act of love. Although the faults of this world are obvious to most observers, enough good still lingers from the original creation that mankind can clearly observe the loving nature of God. The good of nature is so prevalent that certain Greek philosophers concluded that the universe was supernaturally created by love. The writers

---

[37] William Sanford Lasor, David Hubbard, and Frederic Bush, *Old Testament Survey* (Grand Rapids, Michigan: William B. Eerdmans Publishing Company, 1996), 21-22.

of the Bible transformed this concept, the creative force known as "love," into a personal Being. Giving love a living personality is the only logical and rational way that it could have become a creative force. Love cannot be love without its personal qualities, just as love without personality cannot truly be love.

Historically, mankind has known that the God of the Bible is the true God. Ancient documents from various cultures have acknowledged the existence of a transcendent being that fits the description of the God of the Bible. These sources have acknowledged that God is eternal, beyond his creation, spoke everything into existence, and is the very embodiment of love. The God of the Bible is indeed unique from the gods of other religions. The Holy Spirit testifies to the truth of the one true God throughout the Holy Bible. The truth of God can only be realized by one who opens his or her heart to the beckoning of God's Word.

Chapter 4
The Age of the Earth

In the beginning, God. . .[38]

Everything was created by God. When man was created, he knew how old the earth was because God revealed it to him. In the Bible, the lineage of the first people was traced through an extensive genealogy. To calculate the age of the earth, creationists start with Adam, who was created on the sixth day of creation. They trace Adam's descendants through history to a figure that can be dated relatively accurately; typically this figure is Moses. From that reference point, it is fairly simple to track the number of years from Moses to Jesus, and the years from the time of Jesus to today. According to a young earth creationist's worldview, this is how the age of the earth is calculated. Most young earth creationists believe that the age of the earth is somewhere between six and ten thousand years old. Creationists frequently debate scientists concerning the age of the earth.

Creationists claim that the earth is thousands of years old while most scientists believe that the earth is billions of years old. Most people today do not accept

[38] Genesis 1:1.

the creationist's method of dating the earth's age. The majority of people err on the side of evolutionists because it is perceived that their conclusions are solely based on unbiased scientific information. To assume that only one side of the debate is biased is, in itself, a very biased perspective. When creationists are given a chance to elaborate on their perspective, it appears much more reasonable than how it is portrayed by popular sources. Those who are unfamiliar with the creationist's side of the debate typically dismiss it without much consideration. In fairness, their acceptance of the evolutionist's perspective is not because they are intentionally disregarding Biblical authority. Many people that believe in a world that is billions of years old profess to be Christians. Most Christians in this category question the intent of the language in the Genesis account.

The question is: when the Bible says day one, day two, day three, etc. what does it mean by a "day?" The common argument is that the Hebrew word for day, *yom*, can also mean an indefinite period of time.[39] For instance, a passage from 2 Peter states that, "With the Lord a day is like a thousand years," giving validity to this statement. However, what is oftentimes ignored is that the second half of the statement says, "and a thousand years are like a day."[40] For the sake of this argument, the intent of this Scripture must be called into question.

Inside of its context, 2 Peter 3:8 is saying that God does not operate under the restriction of time. Most people would concede that a day is not a very long span

[39] Staats 2001, 13.

[40] 2 Peter 3:8.

of time while most people would also concede that relative to a day, one thousand years is a very long span of time. God does not perceive time the same way that people do. What a human may perceive as a long time is like the blink of an eye to God, and what a human may perceive as a blink of an eye may be like an eternity to him. God is not a prisoner of time. He is beyond time, which is the point being stated in this passage.

In the context of Genesis, the word *yom* appears to take a literal meaning. In other words, "day one" was intended to mean "day one."[41] From a literary perspective the author could have used other phrases to describe an indefinite period of time. Instead of saying *b*^{e}*reshit bara Elohim* ("in the beginning God created"), the Holy Spirit, through the author of Genesis could have inserted the word *tol*^{e}*dot* or, "in the generations of," to get across the point that this was not meant to be a literal six day creation account but an indefinite period of time.[42] To state it plainly, if the author wanted to convey the idea that each "day" was an indefinite period of time it would have made more sense if he would have said, "These are the generations of when God created the heavens and the earth." Such a statement would have added an artistic hint to the text and cleared up the meaning of the word used for "day." It would have made even more sense if

---

[41] Francis Brown, S. R. Driver, and C. A. Briggs, *Hebrew and English Lexicon of the Old Testament* (Oxford: Oxford University Press, 1951) 398.

[42] A. Phillip Brown II and Bryan W. Smith, *A Reader's Hebrew Bible*, from A Phillip Brown II, Bryan W. Smith, Richard J. Goodrich and Albert L. Lukaszewski, *A Reader's Hebrew and Greek Bible*, (Grand Rapids, Michigan: Zondervan, 2008), 1, 3.

the author would have simply wrote, "God said let there be light, and there was light. . .and this took 35 million years." If one simply reads the Biblical text without considering outside sources, the most orthodox view on creation would be a literal six day creation order with a seventh day Sabbath.

The Biblical Age of the Earth

The age of the earth from a Biblical perspective is much simpler to obtain than, say, the scientific/evolutionist way of guessing the age of the earth through natural observations. The way that the age of the earth has been traditionally obtained through a Biblical understanding has been by adding up the ages of the people given in its genealogies. From a Biblical perspective, the age of the earth is an important topic because it verifies the Messianic bloodline by tracing it from Adam to Jesus. The Genesis narrative is a very straightforward story that links all of its events together chronologically through the use of genealogies.

The dating method used by Biblical creationists is often mocked as being too simplistic by evolutionists. The Biblical dating method is not necessarily directly confirmed by scientific data; nonetheless, it cannot be said that creationism lacks tangible evidence. Although an abundance of evidence exists to prove a young earth, the primary source of authority for a Bible-believing Christian should not be physical evidence. Physical evidence does not speak for itself. It is left to the eye of the beholder to interpret evidence. The Bible is the lens that Christians should use when interpreting physical evidence. Nobody observes evidence without the biases of his or her worldview. Even though a Christian and an atheist observe the exact same evidence, they interpret it from two different worldviews.[43] Creationists try to interpret the age of the earth by starting at the beginning of time and tracing it to today. Evolutionists try to interpret the age of the earth by starting with uniform natural processes observed today and tracing them backward through time.

The problem evolutionists have is that their method relies on many assumptions, especially on the assumption of uniformity of natural processes. Uniformitarianism is the belief that all processes in nature have continued at a fixed rate throughout time. Radioactive decay rates, erosion, and the speed of light are some of the processes that they assume are fixed constants. They do not allow for the possibility that the rate of natural processes has changed over time. The silence of the material world poses an even greater obstacle than even the necessity for historically uniform natural processes.

The only definite way to know anything is through firsthand experience or the testimony of a witness. Science has acknowledged this truth, which is why the scientific method is a popular way to gather data. The problem is that nobody existed to observe the first cause or the evolution of the universe, which is why scientific theories of origins are constantly evolving. The Bible gives an account of creation that could have only been recorded by the Creator who was supposedly there in the beginning. Other than God, "the only really reliable

[43] Henry M. Morris and John C. Whitcomb, *The Genesis Flood* (New Jersey: Presbyterian and Reformed Press, 1961), 213.

recorder of time is man himself! In any kind of natural process that might be used to determine past time, there is always the possibility that the rates have changed as well as uncertainty regarding its initial condition."[44] Morris and Whitcomb's work, *The Genesis Flood*, exhaustively argues from scientific and Biblical perspectives that the world is much younger than what evolutionary scientists claim. Given the fact that no human records have been discovered that predate 3200 B.C. it is difficult to solidify a claim that mankind has existed for over ten thousand years.

On the other hand, most early cultures agreed that the world was created nearly six thousand years ago and that a global flood occurred approximately four thousand years ago. Although consensus is not the deciding factor when it comes to determining truth, testimonies from diverse sources that are all in agreement should be taken seriously. If mankind has existed since the earth's infancy, it is reasonable to believe that early cultures would have retained some sort of knowledge through stories and other traditions to remind them of the earth's young age. When taken literally, the Bible testifies to an earth that is much younger than what science teaches.

Deception by "the Appearance of Age?"

A theory that has recently emerged among creationists is that God created the universe with the "appearance" of age. This theory has been formulated under the assumption that God created a mature creation. In this

[44] Morris and Whitcomb, 393.

case, even though it would have taken certain elements a long time to evolve through radioactive decay, God could have created them in a mature state early on in creation. Certain Christians turn this theory against creationists. They claim that such a theory paints God as a liar. Where does this accusation come from? The accusers believe that the "appearance" of age is deception. If God created everything with a false appearance of age, God lied about the earth's age. The young earth creationist's claim to a young earth is, therefore, disregarded. However, this accusation is riddled with problems.

What young earth creationists truly believe is not that God created the earth with an "appearance" of age but that he created everything in a mature state. For example, how old was Adam when he was created? The Scriptures highly imply that he was created as a full grown man. So was he 25? 50? 75? Regardless of his physical appearance, the Scriptures are very clear: Adam, on the day he was created, was not even a day old yet. He was "0." Was God lying about Adam's age? The very thought is ridiculous! God did not deceive Adam by creating him in a mature state because Adam knew how old he was. Adam knew that he was created on day six. The problem today is that mankind dismisses Biblical authority. Throwing out the authority of the Bible allows Christians to feel at ease about accepting the proposition that the world is billions of years old. The intellectual community makes many strong arguments that science cannot be directly reconciled to the Bible in this area. One of the most common arguments used by mainstream science is in regard to radioactive decay.

Creationists that understand the debate know that there truly is no conflict between radioactive decay rates and Biblical authority. If decay rates have remained a constant, nobody is aware of when their decay began. Under the assumption that everything evolved naturalistically, one could only assume that the decay of the elements would need to be traced back to a common source. Such an extrapolation would take the formation of elements back billions of years. This, however, is only an assumption. There is not enough evidence to show that decay rates have remained constant throughout earth's existence. In a universe as delicate as the one that currently exists, one cannot assume that everything has made a steady stream of progress with no hindrances whatsoever. Over the course of time, it is likely that decay rates have changed, especially if some global disaster happened that altered the earth's atmosphere.

Even if decay rates have remained constant it does not prove that the earth is old. Genesis chapter two reveals that there was gold in the Garden of Eden. In other words, on day six there were already elements in existence that supposedly could not have evolved for millions or even billions of years after the formation of the universe. Morris and Whitcomb wrote in their book *The Genesis Flood*, "This creation must have included all the chemical elements already organized in all the organic and inorganic chemical compounds and mixtures necessary to support the processes of the earth and of life on the earth."[45] When one adopts a Biblical worldview, the authority of the Bible trumps secular

---

[45] Morris and Whitcomb, 344-345.

interpretations of scientific evidence. That is not to say that one who believes in the Bible should ignore challenges from the secular world against Biblical authority; rather, a Christian should be aware of the evidence and understand it in the context of a Biblical framework. One might claim that such an approach is ignorance, but atheists do the same thing by ignoring the possibility of God. If the Bible is the authoritative Word of God, all evidence discovered should point to the fact that either 1) God created the earth in a specific way, or 2) something happened that changed the original created order. Both of these concepts are Biblical and reasonable. Christians have no reason to accept the secular teaching on the age of the earth.

Martin Luther had to combat a similar false teaching in his day, except that he was combating a teaching that claimed that God created the world in one day opposed to six. The people he was arguing against were intelligent theologians, but he countered their intellectual pursuit by saying:

> How long did the work of creation take? When Moses writes that God created heaven and earth and whatever is in them in six days, then let this period continue to have been six days, and do not venture to devise any comment according to which six days were one day. But, if you cannot understand how this could have been done in six days, then grant the Holy Spirit the honor of being more learned than you are.[46]

[46] Martin Luther, *What Martin Luther Says*, (St. Louis, Missouri: Concordia Publishing, 1986) 1523. Quoted in Ken Ham. *Answers...With Ken Ham: Did God create in 6 literal days?*

Despite the fact that the theologians were arguing in the opposite direction of what the modern world argues, they were still teaching a heresy. Martin Luther had the wisdom to know that even though God was powerful enough to create the universe in a day, the Bible clearly states that he took six days to create everything.

The perception of the earth's age is relative to one's starting point. If a person's starting point is secular science, the earth is clearly billions of years old. If one's starting point is the Bible, the earth is calculated to be about six thousand years old. When one understands the Biblical age of the earth it helps him or her link the first events of the Bible to the rest of its story. The claim that an "appearance of age" is deceptive is flawed. And yet, well-intentioned individuals still beg the question, "What does God *really* mean by a day?" If the Bible is the story of creation and redemption, it needs to fit together coherently. In order to have a coherent story Genesis chapter one must be literal.

Produced by Mark Looy and Jim Kragel. Recorded at Cedarville University, Ohio: Answers in Genesis in Association with Cedarville University.

Section 2
The Creation Week and the Two Creation Accounts

The main focus of this section will be to compare the Biblical creation account to the secular theory of the world and life's beginnings. The creation account will be assessed from Genesis chapter one, considering the events of each respective day. Since the secular theory is supposedly rooted in facts, any common elements it would share with the Biblical account would be noteworthy.

Chapter 5
Day 1

> Now the earth was formless and empty, darkness was over the surface of the deep, and the Spirit of God was hovering over the waters. And God said, "Let there be light," and there was light. God saw that the light was good, and he separated the light from the darkness. God called the light "day," and the darkness he called "night." And there was evening, and there was morning – the first day.[47]

The Big Bang is the evolutionist's hypothesis that explains how the universe came into existence. This supposed theory explains that a very long time ago nothing existed except for a tiny, nondescript point in which the universe was condensed. But the Big Bang was not really an explosion. An explosion presupposes that pieces of something are blown outward into the surrounding space. There was no space before the Big Bang, thus it would be impossible for something (actually nothing, in this case) to explode. The Big Bang was the actual expansion of space itself, resulting in the

[47] Genesis 1:2-5.

universe. Somehow, through the rapid expansion, it is believed that gases were produced and were somehow compressed into solid matter and gradually evolved into everything else that exists. Thus the entire universe came into existence.[48]

One can only speculate what such a Big Bang would look like. Even though the Biblical account disagrees with the Big Bang theory, the two accounts sound very similar in regards to the "first event." One moment, there was nothing but darkness. Not even blackness existed back then. The primordial heaven and earth existed in a state of invisibility. The next moment a radioactive burst invaded the primordial universe resulting in the creation of light. This light illuminated newly created universe. From this vantage point, the two descriptions sound so similar that it is hard to distinguish them. Perhaps one of the most frightening things for the naturalist is that even if the Big Bang and all of the evolutionist theories were to be proven beyond the shadow of a doubt, there would still remain one problem. The evolutionist's theory of the birth of the universe sounds remarkably like the Genesis account. The Biblical first day is perhaps one of the biggest similarities that the Bible has with the Theory of Evolution. Unfortunately for atheists, the Big Bang is one of the events in which the evolutionists are most certain, regardless of the fact that evidence continues to accumulate that disproves the Big Bang Theory.

One piece of evidence often cited in support of the Big Bang model of creation is background radiation:

---

[48] Douglas C. Giancoli, *Physics* (Upper Saddle River, New Jersey: Pearson Prentice Hall, 2005), 933.

> In 1965, two scientists accidentally discovered the universe's background radiation – and it was only 3.7 degrees above absolute zero. There's no explanation for this apart from the fact that it is a vestige of a very early and a very dense state of the universe, which was predicted by the Big Bang model.[49]

Given the reality of background radiation one must ask, "Is it *really* evidence for the evolutionary Big Bang theory or is it evidence of the Biblical creation account?" This passage, taken from *The Case for A Creator*, jumps the gun with its conclusion. It is foolish to claim that a particular phenomenon can only be explained one way. How could anyone make such an outrageous claim about a phenomenon that nobody really knows anything about? However, one might fire back by saying that the belief in a supernatural God is a less practical conclusion than the Big Bang Theory. Since God cannot be physically observed, should he be ignored by scientists?

The Biblical creation was a supernatural occurrence. Does that eliminate the possibility that there could be physical evidence that God was the Creator? Perhaps background radiation is residue from the first day, when God created light. One must also accept the fact that the Big Bang theory would have to overcome the laws of physics in order to operate properly. Defying the laws of physics is, by definition, "supernatural." Therefore, the Big Bang model is no less religious of a belief than the Biblical creation account.

---

[49] Lee Strobel, *The Case for A Creator* (Grand Rapids, Michigan: Zondervan, 2004), 105.

Light

After the foundations of the heaven and earth were established, God created light. Why did he choose light? Light has a mysterious nature. Science has not been able to unravel all of light's mysteries. It is a substance that composes of both wave and particle qualities.[50] Nothing else in the known universe behaves in the same manner as light. Light moves so fast that it has been theorized that if one were to match its velocity, everything surrounding him or her would appear as though it was standing still. There may be a day when light is finally deciphered, but people will always marvel at its incredible nature.

Among its remarkable qualities, light is invisible. No one has ever "seen" light. Its components can be observed, but it is very difficult to contain light so that it may be observed. Even though it is invisible, it reflects off of the objects it comes into contact with and enters the eye in a manner that allows things to be seen. To say the least, this is miraculous. Light is not seen, but it allows for things to be seen.[51]

It is the same with the nature of God. He is invisible, he is uncontainable, and he makes it possible to see the universe for what it really is. The Bible symbolically refers to Jesus as light.[52] The book of Revelation says that in God's eternal kingdom the sun will not exist anymore

---

[50] Giancoli, 759.

[51] C. S. Lewis, *Mere Christianity* (San Francisco: HarperCollins, HarperSanFrancisco, 1980), 39.

[52] 1 John 1:5.

because he will be the light that illuminates everything.[53] The sun and moon are not essential in God's universe for providing light. In fact, God intentionally did not create the sun or moon until three days after he created light. The sun and the moon were often worshipped as gods in pagan cultures, and science teaches that light from the sun is what sustains plants so that they may carry out photosynthesis. The plants were created before the sun and moon, yet light was still present to sustain the earth and the plants for a brief period of time so that the sun and moon could not be credited for sustaining life by their own power.[54] Neither the sun nor the moon is the source of light. God is the source of light. At the beginning of time he was the light-bearer. He placed the sun and the moon in charge of governing day and night. Some say that God is literally light. It is idolatrous to claim that light, is God. The Bible clearly states that God created light when he spoke the words, "Let there be light."[55]

Conclusively, God's light is what brings life. The sun and the moon are just governing bodies. The sun was taught by God how to shine, and the moon was taught by God how to reflect light. As a result the earth has a "greater light" and a "lesser light" that shine upon it twenty-four hours a day, three hundred sixty five days a year.[56] God did not require an outside energy source to aid Him in the creation of all things. The first day he

---

[53] Revelation 21:23.

[54] Gary Staats, *Short Meditative Thoughts on the Bible and Life* (Findlay, Ohio: Dr. Gary Staats. 2010), 47-48.

[55] Genesis 1:3.

[56] Genesis 1:16.

created the heavens, the earth, and light. He alone dictated night and day. After he established the boundary between day and night, he could properly order the rest of his creations.

Chapter 6
Day 2

And God said, "Let there be an expanse between the waters to separate water from water." So God made the expanse and separated the water under the expanse from the water above it. And it was so.[57]

In the very beginning of earth's history, this planet was a giant, red hot, roiling, boiling sea of molten rock - a magma ocean. The heat had been generated by the repeated high speed collisions of much smaller bodies of space rocks that continually clumped together as they collided to form this planet. As the collisions tapered off the earth began to cool, forming a thin crust on its surface. As the cooling continued, water vapor began to escape and condense in the earth's early atmosphere. Clouds formed and storms raged, raining more and more water down on the primitive earth, cooling the surface further until it was flooded with water, forming the seas.[58]

---

[57] Genesis 1:6-7.

[58] "Extreme Science," ExtremeScience.com,http://www.extremescience.com/zoom/index.php/geolo.gic-earth-history (accessed July 17, 2010).

Did you ever notice that the formation of the atmosphere is explained in the Bible? So many people get caught up inside of the religious aspects of the Bible that they miss profound scientific truths. This particular truth would have been impossible for the ancient world to conclude on their own because they did not have the understanding of the world that people today often take for granted. The Biblical account says that the two waters were separated; one was placed above the expanse (the "expanse" refers to the air around us) and the other was placed beneath. Is it coincidental that "Extreme Science" describes a "separation" of the two waters to explain the formation of the atmosphere?

As you already read, "Extreme Science" claims that, in its primordial state, the earth was a molten mass. When it began to cool, water vapor escaped into space. The water vapor cooled while in space and then rained down to the earth. The earth was cooled due to the raining down of the cold water. The process of evaporation and precipitation went on for so long that it eventually flooded the earth. This is very reminiscent of the separating of the waters below from the waters above in Genesis 1:6-7.

True, the Bible makes it appear as though the division happened in one day, while the evolutionary model claims it took millions of years, but the stories remain incredibly similar. What are the odds that a scientifically ignorant people, writing about supernatural beings, would accidentally write an account that nailed the scientific process by which the atmosphere was formed? Perhaps there is validity to the evolutionist's claim on how the waters were separated. The Bible specifies that God spoke the division between the waters into existence, but it does not explain how the waters were separated as he spoke. Does "Extreme Science" outline the method by which God created the atmosphere and the oceans?

In *Enuma Elish*[59], the Babylonian creation myth, the creation of the atmosphere and oceans were vastly different. It was the result of a struggle. Two gods, Marduk and Tiamat, did battle. Tiamat had a hand in creating the other gods and was enraged when her mate was killed. As a result of her rage, she began to kill off the other gods. Marduk was selected by his peers to do battle with Tiamat. At the conclusion of their battle Marduk blew wind into Tiamat and shot her with an arrow. Tiamat was defeated and Marduk split her into two parts. Part of her was used to make the waters above and part of her was used to make the waters below. This Babylonian myth claims that the oceans and the atmosphere were made out of the body of a slain deity. Is there anything in science that could confirm this? Certainly other myths would attest to similar stories, but these other myths seem to lack credibility, given the knowledge of the universe mankind now possesses.

Nonetheless, all three of these accounts agree that at some point in the past the waters below had to be separated from the waters above. It is a mystery as to how some of these myths developed. Some might claim that such a myth came about because of the observance of natural occurrences, such as rainfall. Most myths were created to explain natural events. Since water falls from

---

[59] Stephanie Dalley, *Myths from Mesopotamia: Creation, the Flood, Gilgamesh, and Others* (Oxford: Oxford University Press, 2000).

the sky, some of these myths may have been formulated to explain why rain falls to the earth.[60]

In terms of truth, one must conclude that the most rational explanation should be conceded. Science agrees with the Bible that the two great waters were created from non-living materials. The main difference is that science does not suppose that God had a hand in this event. When considering the possibilities, both accounts say that the earth was void and without form. Both accounts hint that all of the earth's elements were, at one point, mixed together. And finally, out of some sort of necessity, both agree that the waters had to be separated. If not for the separation of the two waters, the world as it exists today would not be possible.

[60] Staats 2010, 45-46.

Chapter 7
Day 3

> And God said, "Let the water under the sky be gathered to one place, and let dry ground appear." And it was so.[61]

> It is theorized that the true age of the earth is about 4.6 billion years old, formed at about the same time as the rest of our solar system. The oldest rocks geologists have been able to find are 3.9 billion years old. Using *radiometric dating* methods to determine the age of rocks means scientists have to rely on when the rock was initially formed (as in - when its internal minerals first cooled). In the infancy of our home planet the entire earth was *molten* (melted) rock - a *magma* ocean.[62]

When the topic of rocks is mentioned, one cannot avoid discussing the earth's age. Not a geology class across the world speaks about the different sorts of rocks and minerals without referencing the supposed

---

[61] Genesis 1:9.

[62] Extreme Science, (accessed July 17, 2010).

ages of their elements of interest. The appearance of dry land was a highly significant event in the history of the world. It literally paved the way for the emergence of land dwelling creatures. The Bible and science have their opinions on how dry land appeared, but instead of discussing dry land (which I find to be a *dry* topic), this chapter will discuss the age of rocks (not to be confused with the Rock of Ages).

Whenever rocks are mentioned in relation to the age of the earth, good students are quick to mention radiometric dating methods. Unfortunately for good students, they are taught never to question their teachers because their teachers are smart, unbiased, and almost never wrong. Unfortunately for their teachers, a student eventually graduates and learns that teachers too are humans and humans have many flaws; one of which is that their teachers once had teachers that they also never questioned. The organization *Answers In Genesis* (AIG) has broken this cycle and has sought to prove that radiometric dating, in relation to the age of the earth, is a flawed method.

AIG has employed a team of scientists, known as *RATE (*Radioisotopes And The age of the Earth), to prove that radiometric dating methods are inconsistent. One of their experiments took volcanic rock samples from Bass Rapids in the Grand Canyon and applied several different radioisotopes to see what the results would be. Between the youngest date obtained, from potassium-argon which was 841.5 million years, and the oldest date, samarium-neodymium which was1,379 million years, there was a difference in the dating of the respective methods of 500 million years! There are possible factors, which have been accounted for by the *RATE* research team, which could have caused this difference.

Nonetheless, this does not relieve radiometric dating from scrutiny. The exact reason for these differences is still unclear. Popular teachings on the age of rocks do not mention the problems with the scientifically accepted model. By analyzing this rock layer through radioisotopes, one conclusion could be reached: Radiometric dating is not a reliable method for determining the age of the earth, let alone the age of rocks. For more information on this topic visit www.answersingenesis.org or pick up the book *Thousands. . .Not Billions*[63] or *The Genesis Flood*.[64]

Rocks cannot tell us the age of the earth. On the contrary, they can tell us how old that it is not, because it cannot be any older than the oldest date given by radiometric dating methods. According to this logic, the earth could be significantly younger than what radiometric methods show. There are holes in both theories, but no theory is without its complications.

Creation of plant life.

> Then God said, "Let the land produce vegetation: seed-bearing plants and trees on the land that bear fruit with seed in it, according to their various kinds." And it was so.[65]

---

[63] Dr. Don DeYoung, *Thousands...Not Billions* (Portland, Oregon: Master Books, 2006).

[64] Andrew Snelling, Answers in Genesis, http://www. answersingenesis.org/articles/aid/v2/n1/radioisotopes-earth (accessed July 17, 2010).

[65] Genesis 1:11.

Before the fish, the birds, the cattle, or mankind walked the earth, there were plants. Both evolutionists and creationists believe that plants probably existed before animals emerged. Evolutionists view animals as being the next logical step from being inanimate to fully animate. Plants, although they have tremendous reproductive ability, cannot uproot themselves to seek after food. Evolutionists would suggest that plants were among the world's earliest living creatures, but a Biblical perspective would be at odds with referring to plants as "life."

In a Biblical sense, plants are not living. Among the different organisms mentioned in Genesis, the plants were the only ones that did not possess the breath of life. Scientifically speaking, the creatures that were given the breath inhaled oxygen and exhaled carbon dioxide. Plants "inhale" carbon dioxide and "exhale" oxygen. Even though this might seem like a silly point, it has great theological implications.

According to the Bible, there was no death until after original sin had taken place. A common question among skeptics is, "what about plants?" This is a reasonable question because God told the creatures that they may eat the plants. If God created a world without death or suffering, but plants were considered to be "living organisms," either the Bible infers that God ordained death and suffering before original sin or that plants were not categorized the same as the animals. According to God's created order, if animals did not eat something they would die.

Certainly, if one is to take the Biblical creation account as a historic retelling of true events, God must have defined plant life differently. According to a biology textbook, "Life can be viewed as a constant flow of energy, channeled by organisms to do the work of living. . .Deprived of a source of energy, life stops."[66] In order to sustain life, God had to create a food source that had a reproductive system and contained all of the elements that life needed to survive. This had to be accomplished without creating an organism that could suffer or be killed. Plants were God's solution for this problem.

Life without a source of energy cannot survive. The evolutionist's model of life's cycle is rather barbarous. The emergence of life could be viewed as more of a curse through their perspective than anything. Life emerged and had to find something to provide it with energy. What was the first organism's source of food? Regardless of the answer to that question, life would have eventually evolved cannibalistic tendencies in order to evolve higher. Through atheistic logic, this practice would have been commendable for the first organisms. After all, if it were not for primordial savagery, mankind would never have evolved. The Bible provides a much more satisfying answer to the emergence of plants and of life.

God created plants before he created all of the living creatures. This provided an immediate source of food so that the animals would not starve for a couple of days, nor would they resort to savagery. According to the Bible everything was supposed to get its energy from feasting on plants: "'and to all the beasts of the earth and all the birds of the air and all the creatures that move on the ground – everything that has the breath of life in it – I

---

[66] George Johnson, Jonathan Losos, Peter Raven, and Susan Singer, *Biology, 7th edition* (Madison, Wisconsin: McGraw Hill Higher Education, 2005), 143.

give every green plant for food.' And it was so."[67] Only later did God permit mankind to feed on other animals, and that was a result of the warped nature of creation brought upon by the Fall.

The Bible suggests that God did not intend on "survival of the fittest." He intended all creatures to exist in a state of peace and harmony. Even the most carnivorous beasts that are observed roaming the earth today used to eat plants in the Garden of Eden. God wanted all of life to enjoy the universe that he created. Plants were the perfect food source for the living creatures. Even today they remain the healthiest alternative to a sin-cursed diet.

[67] Genesis 1:30.

Chapter 8
Day 4

God made two great lights – the greater light to govern the day and the lesser light to govern the night. He also made the stars.[68]

According to the ancients, the stars, except for the few that seemed to move (the planets), were fixed on a sphere beyond the last planet. The universe was neatly self-contained, and we on earth were at or near its center. But in the centuries following Galileo's first telescopic observations of the heavens in 1610, our view of the universe has changed dramatically. We no longer place ourselves at the center, and we view the universe as vastly large. The distances involved are so great that we specify them in terms of the time it takes light to travel the given distance.[69]

Many ancient people believed that the earth was the center of the universe and that the stars were fixed in place at a distance. Ever since Copernicus' assertion

---

[68] Genesis 1:16.

[69] Giancoli, 915.

that the earth revolves around the sun, the scientific community has blamed Christianity for teaching that the universe revolves around the earth. The idea that the universe revolves around the earth actually has a pagan origin. It is true that certain Bible-believing Christians have believed and taught that the stars and planets were on a fixed sphere and that they all revolved around the earth. The problem is that the Bible does not teach such a doctrine. It is mostly silent concerning where the earth resides in relation to the rest of the universe. Because Christianity is the largest religion in the world, it often faces scrutiny for teachings and actions of other religions.

However, it is true that certain Christians are responsible for committing some of the atrocities that other religions or ideologies would promote. In the past few years, the Roman Catholic Church has faced much criticism for priests that have sexually abused children. A vast minority of the priesthood is responsible for this evil; nonetheless, Christianity as a whole has been deemed responsible for the deviant behavior of these select individuals. Other cultures and religions would not condemn the actions of these priests. In fact, such abuse would be considered a rite of passage for boys in certain cultures. The actions of these priests were clearly contradictory to the moral code promoted by the Bible. If it were not for Christianity, and in all fairness Judaism and Islam, these crimes would not be considered evil. A few bad apples should not be allowed to blemish the Church as a whole. Such logic should be applied to all of the inconsistencies between Scriptural teachings, contrary actions, and false doctrines.

It is evident that the Biblical creation account attempts to refute the teachings of other creation accounts. For instance, elements of nature are deified in pagan religions. Two major culprits of such deification are the sun and the moon. Many of the ancient religions worshipped the sun and moon as though they were gods. Genesis was written so that God, the Creator, would be worshipped and not objects of his creation.[70] Genesis refutes the idea that the sun and moon are deities.

In the Hebrew language, the word used to describe both of these objects is *ma'or*. This literally means "light-holder." The names "sun" and "moon" are never mentioned in this account. When objects are given names they are also given identity. Identity usually includes personality. Since the sun and moon were often worshipped by pagan cultures, God may have seen it fit to not give them names in his creation account.

The Psalmist tells us that "the heavens declare the glory of God."[71] Instead of being worshipped, the sun, moon, and even the stars were set in place so that people would know when to worship God. The sun awakens the day and God's creatures are to rise from slumber. During the daylight hours, all of the creatures are to worship him every moment. The stars helped the Israelites determine the seasons so that the festivals of worship could be arranged according to God's commands. The moon comes out at night to prepare God's creation for a time of rest.[72] The two lights are faithful governors over God's creation.

---

[70] Romans 1:25.

[71] Psalm 19:1.

[72] Staats 2010, 47-48.

Star Light

Science largely disagrees with the idea that God created all of the stars, and the earth's sun and moon, in one day. There are too many stars for God to have created them all so quickly, the universe is too big for God to have created them all, and it is possible that the expanse of the universe is limitless and that the number of stars is also limitless. How could God create something like that? For an infinitely powerful God, such a work would be child's play. Scientifically, though, there are significant objections that would challenge the existence of a young universe and the creation of all of the stars in one day. First, according to science, a phenomenon known as "red shift" is claimed to prove that the stars are moving away from the earth, just as the Big Bang theory predicts. Second, scientists point to the fact that it would take light millions or even billions of years to reach the earth from outer space. Can Scripture stand up against the scrutiny of these theories?

In reality, there is no problem with the idea that the stars are moving away from the earth. The Bible clearly states that the heavens and the earth were created first and it was not until the fourth day that the sun, moon, and stars were created. Certain Scripture passages suggest that the heavens have been "stretched out,"[73] thus it is possible that they are still being stretched away from the earth. Could this stretching out of the universe imply that the Bible agrees with the notion that the universe is expanding? Such a notion may be more of a problem for a secular scientist than for a believer.

---

[73] Isaiah 42:5.

Another problem that may exist for the secularist is that if all of the stars and planets are moving away from the earth, then earth may actually be in or near the center of the entire universe! That is not to say that everything revolves around the earth. After the sun was created, the earth was set in orbit due to the sun's gravitational pull and the other planets completed the galaxy in which earth now resides. Nonetheless, it is rather peculiar that in a chaotic universe, all of the stars would be moving away from the earth and creating red shifts. Whether the earth resides near the center of the universe or not is inconsequential. If the universe were to be infinitely large, its center would be a matter of opinion. If earth is the only planet in the entire universe that possesses life, who could claim that the earth is not the center of the universe? Supposing that the universe has boundaries, though, could provide logical answers concerning why, in a relatively young universe, star light can be observed from the earth.

Albert Einstein's Theory of Relativity suggests that gravity and speed directly affect the passage of time. This is called "gravitational time dilation." If such a principle were true it would not take light billions of years to reach earth from distant stars. Relative to itself, if light were conscious, it would feel like the passage of time was billions of years. But for an outside observer the passage of time would have been extraordinarily less. Such a phenomenon, however, could only be possible if the universe were contained within some sort of a system. This notion would fit well with the idea that a Creator designed a well-structured universe. Evolutionary presuppositions have led to mainstream scientists rejecting

Einstein's theory about gravitational time dilation, but if Einstein was correct (if he was the genius everyone thought he was) this phenomenon would validate the theory that the sun, moon, and stars were created in one day, around six thousand years ago.[74]

Unfortunately, nobody has observed the universe in its entirety. Forming conclusions about an unimaginably large universe is very difficult. It is just as likely that the universe could be infinitely large! Such a circumstance would also fit the notion that an infinitely large Creator designed the universe. The observations mankind attains through studying the stars should be pursued further. If the heavens declare God's glory, it is an act of worship to study the heavens. This enables us to announce God's glory with the sort of wonder and awe that characterizes his name.

---

[74] Mark W. Cadwallader, *CREATION: Spelled Out for Us All* (Conroe, Texas: CTS Publications, 2007), 48-49.

Chapter 9
Day 5

> And God said, "Let the water teem with living creatures, and let birds fly above the earth across the expanse of the sky." So God created the great creatures of the sea and every living and moving thing with which the water teems, according to their kinds, and every winged bird according to its kind. And God saw that it was good.[75]

> The question of how life originated is not easy to answer because it is impossible to go back in time and observe life's beginnings; nor are there any witnesses. Testimony exists in the rocks of the earth, but it is not easily read, and often it is silent on issues crying out for answers. There are, in principle, at least three possibilities: special creation, extraterrestrial origin, and spontaneous origin.[76]

The Bible bears witness that living creatures were created on day five. As already mentioned, there is

---

[75] Genesis 1:20-21.

[76] Johnson et al., 64.

a distinction between the living things in this verse and the plants that were created on day three. These creatures swarmed and moved about the earth. Plants reproduce so that they are plentiful but they do not have cognitive thought processes or complex feelings like animals, nor are they able to move about the earth. As different of a perspective as creationists and evolutionists have, it is interesting to note that both believe life originated in the same place.

According to evolutionists, life originated in the water. The evolutionist correct, but it is important to understand that their reasons for believing life originated in water are flawed. Their assumption is: "When life was originating, water provided a medium in which other molecules could move around and interact without being held in place by strong covalent or ionic bonds. Life evolved in water for two billion years before spreading to land."[77] They suppose that water was a good medium for evolutionary processes. In their minds, this resulted in the development of life. There is no evidence that water played an important role in life's development. The assumption derives from the fact that without water, life could not exist. Although this is true, it will never be proven that water can produce life out of inanimate materials. Such a notion would suggest that the creatures of the sea are lower on the evolutionary scale and land animals are higher.

Following the same kind of logic, proponents of evolution suggest that birds developed much later than the creatures of the sea. Evolutionists believe that avian

---

[77] Ibid, 27.

life took hundreds of millions of years to develop and some even believe that birds evolved from reptiles, particularly the dinosaurs. Ironically, the creationist model says that birds were among the first created animals. The Bible says that on day five God created the fish of the sea and the birds of the air. Strangely enough, this statement is commonly misunderstood by most scientifically-minded readers.

The classification system for living organisms in the Bible is much broader than that of modern science. When the Bible says that God created the birds of the air and the fish of the sea, it does not mean the scientific definitions of birds and fish as people today understand them. It seems that the Bible classifies animals into broad categories and defines them according to their abilities, habitats, and anatomical features. According to Mosaic Law, bats are a type of bird.[78] What constitutes a bird? A bird, by scientific definition, typically has feathers and wings. A bat does not have feathers but does have wings. This, of course, enables them to fly. Therefore, bats were created at the same time as birds. Anything that was able to fly was probably created on day five of creation. Likewise, all sea creatures were created on day five of creation, which actually reveals a very interesting truth.

The first water dwelling reptiles, such as plesiosaur and ichthyosaur, were created on the same day as birds. They were not created millions of years apart. On day five God created what some English Bibles refer to as the whales. What English Bibles miss is that the word used for whales, *tannin* (singular) or *tanninim* (plural),

---

[78] Leviticus 11:13-19.

is a word used for dragons in the Hebrew language. The word *tanninim* is a term that contains a broader definition than the English word for whales. In regards to Biblical classification, this word refers to the "great creatures of the sea," specifically dragons. So not only did God create the great whales of the sea, he also created the great dragons of the sea.[79]

In this passage, the author of Genesis was probably trying to put the menacing sea dragons into perspective. "If we go back to the Ugaritic literature, the sea monster was constantly in conflict with Baal; Yahweh creates it and controls it."[80] In Psalm 75, it is shown that God created the great sea monster and put him in the water. God does not see him as menacing or as an adversary, but as one of the playful creatures that he created. Although Leviathan would appear as a terror to man, the terror of Leviathan was God himself. In the book of Job, the beast known as Leviathan is described as a great and terrifying creature that rises up from the sea. He causes the waters to churn and boil as he breathes fire and smoke departs from his nostrils. God used Leviathan as an illustration for Job. Only God could approach Leviathan with a sword and overcome him. Man, which God created in his own image, trembled in fear at the very thought of confronting Leviathan.[81]

A variety of animals were created on day five, and each was after its own kind. No doubt, God did not just

---

[79] Steve Golden, Tim Chaffey, and Ken Ham, *Tannin: Sea Serpent, Dinosaur, Snake, Dragon, or Jackal?* August 8 2012. www.answersingenesis.org/articles/aid/v7/n1/tannin-hebrew-mean.

[80] Staats 2010, 49-50.

[81] Job 41.

create the scaled fish and the feathered birds; rather, he created a variety of animals that could fly and swim. The words used in Genesis signify a broad category of animals, not a specific scientific classification. Along with birds and fish, certain mammals, reptiles, and amphibians would have been created on day five. The creation of all of these animals was for the glory of God and he accomplished this by making sea creatures and aerial creatures that were both great and small.

Chapter 10
Day 6

> And God said, "Let the land produce living creatures according to their kinds: livestock, creatures that move along the ground, and wild animals, each according to its kind." And it was so.[82]

Day six was the day that all land animals were created. There are many different ideas where terrestrial life came from but the Bible makes it simple. God molded animals from the dirt of the ground and told them to go forth and multiply. When he was finished, he created man in a like manner, out of the dust of the earth. Evolutionists acknowledge that creatures evolved from the particles of the earth, but not in this manner. They believe that life originated in the ocean and eventually adapted to live on land.

> Most scientists tentatively accept the hypothesis of spontaneous origin – that life evolved from inanimate material as associations among molecules became more and more complex. In this view, the

[82] Genesis 1:24.

> force leading to life was selection. As changes in molecules increased their stability and caused them to persist longer, these molecules could initiate more and more complex associations, culminating in the evolution of cells.[83]

A spontaneous origin from nonliving material, called abiogenesis, is what the preceding quote is proposing. Such a process has never been observed, but evidence of such an occurrence has certainly been anticipated. People used to believe that flies spontaneously generated from rotting meat. Needless to say, this theory was proven wrong a long time ago. Just the mention of spontaneous origins should make scientists cringe. And yet, evolutionists maintain faith in purely naturalistic origins through spontaneous generation. They assert that living things have far too many similarities to not have a common origin.

Homology is the study of structural similarities in different kinds of animals. Homologous structures are anatomical links between one kind of animal and another. The argument from homology is that one can track the evolutionary history of an organism based on homologous structures. According to a college level biology text, "Comparative studies of animals have provided strong evidence for Darwin's theory. In many different types of vertebrates, for example, the same bones are present, indicating their evolutionary past."[84] The argument is intriguing, but flawed.

---

[83] Johnson et al., 64.

[84] Johnson et al., 13.

Many college level biology labs teach their students about the evolutionary process and homology through a certain exercise. The exercise is conducted in such a manner: The class is split into several groups. Cards with the image of a make-believe organism are distributed among the groups. There are typically between ten and twenty cards with either slight or extreme variations of the creature. Each group is assigned the task of arranging the organisms chronologically in a manner similar to the Evolutionary Tree of Life. The Evolutionary Tree of Life is a concept used by evolutionists to chart the evolution of a given organism and is typically traced through homology and the geologic column. At the bottom of the tree is the least evolved organism and at the top is what that organism evolved into after a long period of time.

The point of the exercise is to show the class that no two groups will agree on the evolutionary history of the assigned organism. It shows that many versions of the Evolutionary Tree of Life exist. Therefore, the assignment does not prove that creatures are evolutionarily related through homology. For all the student knows, the variations of the creature may have co-existed and had no relation to the others. In one case, an evolutionist may suppose that a human descended in the order of an amoeba, a fish, a newt, a rat, a sloth, a primate, and then to its present form. In another case, one might argue that humans actually descended from an amoeba, to a fish, a dolphin, a canine, a kangaroo, and then into its present form (why do most people have to include a primate? Why are kangaroos excluded from mankind's evolutionary tree?). Evolutionary steps cannot be deduced through homology. Evolution must be presupposed in order for this exercise to prove its point. Homology is not proven to be evidence for evolution in this exercise, as it is intended. Instead, the argument from homology is clearly falsified because nobody can construct an exact evolutionary tree through using homology alone. The only true purpose of this exercise is to teach students to blindly accept the Theory of Evolution.

The Bible says that God created the different kinds of animals after their kind. He created all creatures in broad categories, as previously discussed. These broad categories are how the Bible classifies the different creatures. For instance, certain birds by human classification may have been created on day six. Why? These birds could be classified as cattle by the definition in Genesis. Under scientific definitions, not all birds fly and not all water-dwelling creatures are fish.

When observing the vast diversity of life on this planet, it is important to notice the incredible similarities between creatures that are totally unique. Not all birds fly; some walk on two feet and others prefer to swim. There are certain fishes that can walk on land and others that can "soar" out of the water (but they cannot be called birds because they live under water). Reptiles are also diverse. They can be found on land, in the ground, in the water, and some can even glide through the air. Even though many of these creatures share similar abilities, there are very few evolutionists that would argue that they descended from a common line.

Evolutionists typically do not conclude that creatures sharing common abilities evolved one from the other. Their conclusions on common descent involve a lot of speculation and imagination. It is a romantic thought to think that life's history could be traced through a neatly organized geologic column in which each step in the evolutionary process is laid out definitely and conclusively. This thought is widely rejected by evolutionists who approach the topic with a truly scientific mind. Much of the evolutionary propaganda attempts to simplify the process of macro-evolution, but fails to accurately represent the Theory of Evolution. The truth is that the relationship all creatures share is that they have a common origin, which is through a common Creator. God, by designing similarities into creatures, left his "signature" on his creations just like an artist. Homology is not proof of common descent. It is proof that the Creator God created all that is living.

Furthermore, these similarities and differences show that the Creator values both uniformity and diversity. He created life to consist of males, but also of females.[85] He created flying reptiles, fish, birds, mammals, and insects. He created land walking fish, mammals, birds, insects, and reptiles. He created swimming reptiles, mammals, fish, birds, and insects. He created burrowing creatures and climbing creatures of all sorts. He created nocturnal creatures and day walking creatures. He even created types of animals that we classify as amphibians because they can live on land and in water. God is strange and wonderful.

God loves diversity but brings about order. Even though men and women are significantly different, they are also remarkably similar. The similarities in the two indicate unity, but their differences indicate a difference in the intended function of each gender. If animals were

[85] Genesis 1:27.

not originally supposed to prey on one another, this makes sense. They would all serve the same God and a sense of unity would need to exist. The differences would give each animal a specific function in God's creation.

Man and Woman

> Then God said, "Let us make mankind in our image, in our likeness, so that they may rule over the fish in the sea and the birds in the sky, over the livestock and all the wild animals, and over all the creatures that move along the ground." So God created mankind in his own image, in the image of God he created them; male and female he created them.[86]

Mankind is a special creation. Certain creation stories, however, ignore the significance of mankind in relation to the rest of the world. According to Babylonian mythology, Marduk, the god who defeated Tiamat, created "savage man." The purpose of mankind was to be a servant to the gods.[87] According to the Theory of Evolution, the first real humans evolved nearly two million years ago from a primeval species of human that was called an australopithecine. Both of these myths claim that at man's origin, he was a savage. But the Bible's creation account elevates man above the level of a mere animal. Genesis 1:27 says that God created man in his own image. In other words, to understand the intention God had for humans, one has to look at the being of

[86] Genesis 1:26-27.

[87] Staats 2010, 50.

God himself. From this, it can be deduced that man was meant to be a loving, creative, intelligent, and reasonable creature. According to Psalm 8:5, man was created just a little lower than the angels. According to *Enuma Elish* and the Theory of Evolution, man is not much higher than the animals.

The Theory of Evolution derives its conclusions on human origins from fossils and skeletons of "primitive humans." Even though evolutionary scientists have had some strange conclusions regarding ancient man, their evidence may be more useful for proving the Biblical model of man's origin than for supporting their own theory. So far there have been no conclusive transitional forms between primates and humans. There have been many alleged missing links, but none of them have stood the test of time and were eventually proven to be frauds. What has been proven, though, is that primitive humans were not much different from modern humans. Because of this unexpected phenomenon, articles detailing new discoveries often include a phrase along the lines of "This new discovery forces scientists to reconsider their former assumptions about human evolution." Theories concerning human evolution have evolved much since Darwin's day.

To aid the general public in understanding the premise of evolution, images have been created to condition evolutionary thoughts into their minds. The purpose of these images is to provide an easy to understand visual of how life evolved from a primitive life form into the many diverse species of animals that exist today. One of the most popular images is a diagram of the progressive evolutionary changes that occurred from chimps up to their human descendants. One would be challenged to find a person in the civilized world who is not familiar with this famous depiction of human evolution. It is a "parade" of primates by which a chimp step-by-step evolves into a modern man. The proof for this progression, as portrayed by the artist, is that the chimp starts off hunched-over and gradually erects until he is fully upright and evolved into the modern human being. College textbooks protest that this model is misleading:

> Another misconception is to think of human evolution as a ladder leading from an ancestral ape to *homo sapiens*. This error is often illustrated as a parade of fossil species that become progressively more like ourselves as they march across the page. If human evolution is a parade, it is a very disorderly one, with many groups breaking away to wander other evolutionary paths. At times, several hominin[88] species coexisted [89]

The above quote is taken from a textbook that is a proponent of the Theory of Evolution. Even the authors of such a text realized the deception portrayed in such illustrations. Zoos, museums, textbooks, and other popular media use this diagram to promote the Theory of Evolution. Many evolutionary scientists actually want people to understand that evolution is not an orderly process. Their theory is a lot more confounded,

---

[88] Hominin: A species on the human branch of the evolutionary tree.

[89] Neil Campbell, Lisa Urry, Michael Cain, Steven Wasserman, Peter Minorsky, and Robert Jackson, *Biology* (New York: Pearson Benjamin Cummings, 2008), 728, G-18.

confusing, and inconsistent than the image showcases. Given this deception, why do the evolutionary "experts" refrain from correcting this misleading portrayal? This is because it effectively communicates the evolutionary ideology. To portray evolution as a tree is confusing, but more accurate. These depictions make it seem logical enough for the average person to understand. If the truth were exposed, many people would realize that the Theory of Evolution is based on speculation, not facts. Few people would conclude that all of mankind evolved from an ape-like creature in light of such a revelation.

This same text book goes on to say, "The fossil record indicates that hominin diversity increased dramatically between 4 million and 2 million years ago. . .With the discovery of more fossils, it became clear that *A. africanus* walked fully erect (was bipedal) and had human-like hands and teeth."[90] An article that AOL News posted on February 26, 2009 gave more insight about the fossil evidence of ancient humans:

> Early humans had feet like ours and left lasting impressions in the form of 1.5 million year old footprints. . .They. . .help tell an ancestral story of humans who had fully transitioned from tree-dwellers to land walkers. . .The researchers identified the footprints as probably belonging to a member of Homo ergaster, an early form of Homo erectus. Such prints include modern foot features such as a rounded heel, a human-like arch and a big toe that sits parallel to other toes.

---

[90] Campbell, et al., 729.

> By contrast, apes have more curved fingers and toes made for grasping tree branches. The earliest human ancestors, such as Australopithecus afarensis, still possessed many ape-like features more than 2 million years ago – the well-known "Lucy" specimen represents one such example.
>
> Anthropologists continue to debate whether these older footprints from an earlier "Lucy" type hominid show that Australopithecus walked about easily or awkwardly on two legs.[91]

This, in light of the rest of the article, revealed that the theory of human evolution contained serious inconsistencies. Specifically, these footprints made evolutionists have to rethink how long ago primitive man transitioned from a tree-dweller to a land-walker. The problem with this article is that the researchers took evidence that clearly exemplified that primitive humans had feet like ours and mixed it up with hypothetical evolutionist mumbo jumbo. These footprints do not hint at anything in regards to human evolution. In fact, they show the lack of evolution in human feet from whenever these footprints were created. The researchers in this article, despite the evidence that was uncovered, insisted that the creatures that made

---

[91] http://news.aol.com/article/earliest-human-footprints-found-in/360312 [Last accessed on February 26, 2009. Access to the article only exists in a paper printout from the original article on the day it was published on AOL News. This link no longer exists, but to read about this topic check out the following link: BBC News, http://news.bbc.co.uk/2/hi/7913375.stm (accessed July 4, 2011).

these footprints were not *Homo sapiens*, but were yet another type of hominid, perhaps related to the infamous Lucy (*Australopithecus afarensis*), known as *Homo ergaster*. While Lucy possessed many ape-like features, *Homo ergaster* looked nearly identical to modern humans. The fossils indicate that the proportions were comparable, the brain size was comparable, and the structure of its skeleton was nearly identical.[92] It is ridiculous, outside of the religious presuppositions of humanists, to think that these creatures were anything less than human.

The same thing goes for the species known as the Neanderthal. Despite the fact that "they had a brain as large as that of present-day humans, buried their dead, and made hunting tools from stone and wood,"[93] they were considered to have gone extinct 28,000 years ago. According to scientists they were not directly related to *Homo sapiens*. The history of the discovery of Neanderthals shines light on the distinction between *Homo sapiens* and Neanderthals. Marvin Lubenow, a professor of Bible and apologetics, wrote one of the few prevailing creationist works regarding the skeletal remains of primitive humans. His book, *Bones of Contention: A Creationist Assessment of Human Fossils*, goes in depth to describe how evolutionists have historically misinterpreted the remains of ancient humans. Concerning Neanderthal, he details its discovery and how scientists manipulated it to make it seem less human.

The scene he describes took place in La Chapelle-aux-Saints, France in 1908. Marcellin Boule was called upon

---

[92] Campbell et al., 731.

[93] Campbell et al., 731.

to reconstruct the remains of a Neanderthal recovered in a cave in the Dordogne River Valley. Lubenow notes, "Not for a moment did Boule believe that the Neandertalers, with their low, wide skulls and their sloping foreheads, deserved a place in the direct history of humans."[94] Imposing one's worldview on a discovery is natural, but when it is taken as far as Boule's construction of the Neanderthal, it becomes a crime against science. Lubenow details Boule's meddling with the discovery:

> Boule, who made the first detailed description of the bones of the Neandertalers, emphasized what he felt were simian (apish) features – based on his preconceived ideas of evolution. Although there was evidence that the vertebrae were severely deformed because of arthritis, and rickets, Boule ignored the pathological evidence. He claimed that the spine lacked curves that enable modern humans to walk erect. He placed the head in an unbalanced position on the neck, thrust far forward, so that the individual probably would have sprained his neck had he looked at the sky.
>
> Boule also decided that this man could not extend his legs fully, but walked with a bent-knee gait. He made the foot only slightly arched, resting on its outer edge, with toes pointing in. Hence the man would have walked like an ape, pigeon-toed. Boule formed a wide separation between the big toe and the other toes, making the big toe like an opposable thumb – such

[94] Marvin L. Lubenow, *Bones of Contention: A Creationist Assessment of Human Fossils* (Grand Rapids, Michigan: Baker Books, 1992), 26.

> as monkeys and apes have. Under those conditions, if Neandertal Man walked at all, he would have looked like a shuffling hunchback. His center of gravity was located so far forward of his center of support that he probably would have fallen flat on his face.
>
> Using casts of the inside of the La Chapelle-aux-Saints skull, Boule felt that the brain of Neandertal, although larger than the average brain size of modern man (1620 vs. 1450 cc), resembled the brain of the great apes in organization. Boule concluded that the Neandertal was closer to apes than humans in brain-power, had only a trace of psychic nature, and had only the most rudimentary language ability – possibly not much more than a series of grunts.[95]

Boule's report was written between 1911 and 1913 and his reconstruction of the Neanderthal skeleton remained mainstream science's perspective on primitive man for over forty years! Clearly, for a renowned scholar of paleoanthropology, mistakes as elementary as overlooking pathological impairment should not have been made. This should have been an obvious clue that Boule's interpretations of the Neanderthal's remains were horribly biased. History is still struggling to correct the false images Boule had impressed on society of Neanderthals. What is even worse, Boule tried to conclude that Neanderthal was stupid, could not speak intelligibly, and lacked morality. All of this was determined from the bones of a person who was long dead. Over forty years

---

[95] Lubenow, 37.

later William L. Strauss and A.J.E. Cave re-examined the La Chapelle-aux-Saints skeletons.

They discovered that there were not profound differences between modern humans and Neanderthals in regards to their anatomy. When Neanderthals were healthy, they walked upright and they probably had a brain capacity not too different from that of modern humans.

> Their low, wide cranium and heavy brow ridges caused people to think of them as "savage," even though there is nothing in the anatomy of a person to indicate his morality, behavior, or degree of culture. Since the average cranial capacity of the Neandertalers is almost 200 cc higher than the average for modern humans, that should have helped their image. But thanks to Boule's prejudice, it did not.[96]

As time goes on, more evidence arises that links what scientists call *Homo sapiens* to Neanderthals, but how much evidence is needed before the scientific community finally concludes that they are merely variations of the same creature?[97] Thanks to Boule, the perception of the Neanderthal skeletons will continue to be spun in favor of the evolutionary perspective on man's origins.

Although the mistakes were eventually corrected, the image conveyed by Boule's work on Neanderthals continues to be used as evidence for human evolution. "It is a case where the entire evolutionist community allowed those mistakes to persist for forty-four years,

---

[96] Lubenow, 38.

[97] Campbell et al.,732.

failing to correct them."[98] How can a worldview that endures so little scrutiny be overturned by another worldview that faces much scrutiny? Because of the lack of scrutiny placed upon Boule's analysis, Neanderthals have become just another "sub-species" of primitive human that is not directly related to *Homo sapiens*. To consider a Neanderthal to be a different species from a modern human is a problem, especially since modern man cannot even determine the proper meaning for the word "species."

The definition of "species" is so loose that there truly is no accepted definition. One textbook defines a species as, "A population or group of populations whose members have the potential to interbreed in nature and produce viable, fertile offspring, but do not produce viable, fertile offspring with members of other such groups."[99] Another textbook defines a species as, "A kind of organism."[100] These authors chose this definition because they were aware of the ambiguity and the disagreement concerning the word species. They simplified the word to have a very broad definition so that not much attention would be paid to it as it was used throughout their text. By this second definition, is every organism that is born its own species? Some would lead you to believe this is true. For example, all humans have slight genetic differences from one another. *Webster's Dictionary* makes it no easier to determine what a species really is as it defines it

[98] Lubenow, 39.

[99] Campbell et al., G-34.

[100] Johnson et al., G-14.

as a "sort, kind. . .class; subdivision."[101] The lines are not clearly drawn concerning where one species ends and another species begins. Charles Darwin was correct when he wrote that, "each species had not been independently created, but had descended, like varieties, from other species."[102] Each species was not independently created, because a species is a human system of classification. God created each broad category of animal with the genetic capability to produce a wide variety of offspring that would display unique phenotypic (expressed) traits. A unique individual is not a distinct species until others are produced that bear its likeness.

The standard biology textbook attests to the diversity of life that exists in the fossil record. Is it possible that, if every skeleton of living humans were observed today, much diversity would be uncovered just from person to person? The answer would most certainly have to be a resounding, "YES!" When considering genetic defects, deformities, variances, and, yes, even natural selection, the form of human skeletal structures from one person to another would almost have to be different. And these differences, even in rare occurrences, would probably be pronounced enough across the globe that one could actually categorize each as a unique species. The problem becomes that nobody today was present to observe what the people looked like before their fossils had taken form. Did they look mostly like *Homo sapiens* or would they have resembled something more like an ape-man?

---

[101] *Webster's Dictionary,* s.v. "Species." New York: Harper Collins, 2003.

[102] Charles Darwin, *The Origins of Species*, (New York: Barnes and Noble Classics, 2004), 13.

The problem with the definition of species in regards to humans becomes, if there are multiple human species, is there one that is superior to all others? If one were to hold humans to the same standard of speciation as animals, there would probably be dozens of species of humans in existence today! If one were to remain faithful to the Theory of Evolution, certain species of humans have probably risen to the top of the evolutionary ladder. If there is not yet a dominant human species, it is likely that there will be interspecies competition to determine which is the fittest to move forward into the future. Sadly this ideology has often been reflected in the world. Whenever a nation proclaims its superiority over other nations, the principle of survival of the fittest goes to work. This principal usually results in genocide. The question of "What is a species?" is vital, indeed.

Perhaps an honest definition of species is, a group of organisms, within a kind, that share similar genetic traits that are displayed through its phenotype, and have the potential to produce viable offspring with others of its kind and/or group. This definition upholds a strict standard of what a species is while allowing some room for ambiguity. In regards to humans, people from different ethnic backgrounds are able to reproduce and bring forth viable offspring, when they clearly do not look the same. There is no problem, given a strict definition for species, saying that there are different species of humans. If the Theory of Evolution is not upheld as a viable theory, differences between human beings would be rendered irrelevant because no one species would be considered better than another. Instead, it would be easy to say that all humans were created equal under God, the Creator.

The problem with paleoanthropology is that it only interprets human fossils from the lens of evolution. Artists have been given much power by the evolutionary world. Whenever a new fossil or skeleton is uncovered, it is given to an artist and he or she is expected to create an accurate representation of the creature. But an artist can only accomplish such a task by being informed by a scientist. Supposedly, the scientist already knows what such a creature looked like. He or she merely relies upon an artist to put their thoughts into pictures for the sake of the public understanding of science. Ultimately, in the case of a fossil or skeleton that appears humanoid, the final product will be a creature that shares the characteristics of both an ape and a man. These are not unbiased portrayals of conclusive evidence. These are people with an agenda.

To prove this, Mark Lubenow posted an article through Answers In Genesis in 1993 describing a project he assigned to the students of his college apologetics class. He would assign them each a fossil that is accepted by the greater scientific community and he wanted them to conduct research concerning their assigned fossil. The rules were:

1) The student is to spend a minimum of eight hours of research on each fossil.
2) He must use only evolutionist sources.
3) He is to determine the date the evolutionist has assigned to the fossil.
4) He is to determine the category (australopithecine, Homo erectus, Neandertal, etc.) assigned to the fossil by evolutionists.

5) He is to write a one-page paper outlining his findings and make copies for distribution to the class.
6) The paper must contain at least five documented sources.[103]

The purpose of this project was to show his students the incredible number of inconsistencies in the Theory of Evolution's model for human evolution. He wrote that ultimately all of his students became frustrated because none of their sources agreed with one another. All of the experts had different opinions regarding the fossils they were studying. In this article, he implies that the Bible accounts for all of the fossils found in the geologic column. The evolutionary model failed to accomplish this in Darwin's day and has failed to do so ever since. There are far too many contradictions from expert to expert to take the model for human evolution seriously.

Evolutionists so desperately want to construct a timeline for human evolution that they often neglect the facts for the sake of their theory. Because of their loyalty to the Theory of Evolution, they commit a cardinal sin of scientific inquiry: they apply their conclusions to the evidence without first properly analyzing the evidence.[104] Their theory ultimately trumps the evidence. This is not to say that Bible-believing Christians first observe the rocks, the fossils, and genetics before concluding that God created everything, but nobody starts with a blank slate and then forms conclusions from a neutral

---

[103] Marvin Lubenow, *The Human Fossils Still Speak*. http://www.answersingenesis.org/creation/ v15/i2/fossils.asp (accessed July 4, 2011).

[104] Lubenow *The Human Fossils Still Speak*.

position. Not even God himself could develop an unbiased perspective on evidence because he already knows its proper interpretation. The only person who could accomplish such a miracle, as observing evidence with no preconceived biases, is a person who does not exist.

Nonetheless, one of the greatest strengths of the Biblical model is that it actually starts with the idea that mankind originated from a common ancestor: Adam and Eve. Evolution does teach that humans descended from a common ancestor, but the common ancestor was ultimately not human. The Bible teaches that mankind's common ancestors were human. None of the evidence presented by science truly suggests that humans descended from anything other than humans. The New Testament declares that God, "hath made of one blood all nations of men for to dwell on all the face of the earth, and hath determined the times before appointed, and the bounds of their habitation."[105] The beauty of this statement is that God created all humans on an equal level, not showing favor to one group or another.[106] Getting wrapped up in the idea of humans descending from different species could cause a division in the human race. In fact, it already has! This New Testament reminder teaches that all humans descended from one bloodline.

Diversity across the human spectrum in the fossil record is evidence that God, through two people, created an entire race of humans that possessed unique physical characteristics. The scientific community needs to see the light and realize that they are not uncovering missing

[105] KJV Acts 17:26.

[106] Acts 10:34.

links, but the fossils of humans. If the feet look human, the hands look human, the skeletal structures look human, and the skulls look human, the logical conclusion would be that the fossils that have been discovered must have been from humans. Fossils do not come with name tags or photos. One must call a spade a spade. To do anything different would be dishonest and would certainly not be science.

Chapter 11
Day 7

> Thus the heavens and the earth were completed in all their vast array. By the seventh day God had finished the work he had been doing; so on the seventh day he rested from all his work.[107]

Simply put, God set aside a day for people to rest. The origin of this day of rest was the day after God finished creating the universe. On the seventh day God rested, which, in Hebrew, literally means that he was "re-souled." Was this process of creation exhausting for God? It is difficult to tell for sure, but at the very least, God set an example for the people he created. The example was for them to work six days and rest on the seventh.[108]

The disconnection between the idea of "a day of rest" and any other worldview is more with practice than with belief. It is easy to understand that everyone needs a break or vacation from time to time. What most people do not believe is that it is good to take one day a week to do nothing except rest and enjoy the Lord. The

---

[107] Genesis 2:2-3

[108] Staats 2010, 94.

cultural practice in America is to work oneself into the ground until it is absolutely necessary to take a vacation for at least a week. This could arise from an evolutionary perspective on life.

Evolution teaches that this life is all that exists. After life is over, there is nothing else to look forward to. With this sort of worldview, it would be very difficult to be motivated to take one day a week to rest. Instead it would seem more efficient to accomplish as much as possible before one dies. Or it might encourage one to never work a day in his or her life. If life is a fleeting moment with nothing to look forward to afterwards, why work? Both perspectives go against God's Word.

The Biblical worldview encourages rest. The world's destiny does not depend on humanity. The saving grace of the entire universe is Jesus Christ. Even though the rest of the world is too busy to slow down and enjoy the good work that Jesus has accomplished, Christians are encouraged by Jesus himself to give him their burdens, for his "yoke is easy" and his "burden is light."[109]

The Difference

These past few chapters have compared and contrasted many elements of the Biblical creation account with the Theory of Evolution. There are some very distinct differences between today's scientific model of how the world evolved and the Biblical creation account. With some of the similarities being as clear as what they are, some people might feel led to conclude that God did

[109] Matthew 11:30

indeed use an evolutionary method to create the earth. Do not make this mistake. Despite the number of similarities between the two respective models the philosophical conclusions of each are totally different.

Those who truly believe in the Theory of Evolution embrace an absolutely horrendous perspective on reality. First of all, God is removed from the picture. Once God is eliminated, purpose is non-existent. Evolution stands alone as an unguided process. Once purpose is eliminated, morality vanishes. Morality is based on virtues that guide mankind toward a desired end. In other words, purpose helps establish the goals for a person's life and morality creates a system of ethics to guide one in accomplishing those goals in the most acceptable manner. Without morality there can be no civility. Every living organism struggles to survive. However that is accomplished is acceptable, but not always desirable.

The animal world displays acts of brutality that are condoned by the evolutionary worldview. Some animals eat their young. When taking on a new mate, some animals kill off the younglings that their new mate created with their old mate. Many birds push their young out of the nest before they are ready. When they are not strong enough to fly, they hit the ground and die. Only the strong will survive. Many of the people that believe in the Theory of Evolution promote the idea that these things are necessary for the survival of each respective species. If they believe that it is acceptable in nature for these things to happen, why would they believe that it is wrong for humans to behave in a like manner?

The only authorities that uphold the Theory of Evolution are teachers and scientists. Neither one has endured the totality of earth's existence. Science has somehow been hijacked by those who mindlessly believe in evolution. Many teachers do not question the Theory of Evolution because the board of education says that it must be taught. The teachers that rebel against their superiors often end up fired for teaching "religion" in the classroom. The hypocrisy of it all is that the evolutionists once fought against a system that oppressed opposing viewpoints.

Those that truly believe in the Bible have a different outlook on life. They believe in God. The very existence of God establishes that there is purpose to life. The purpose to life is found in Paul's letter to the Ephesians, which states, "For we are God's workmanship, created in Christ Jesus to do good works, which God prepared in advance for us to do."[110] Purpose is automatically linked to morality in this case, because the purpose of mankind is to do "good" works. If good works exist, then there must be evil works that exist as a counterpart. The next task is to determine what is good and what is evil. Fortunately for the Bible believer, he or she has an entire book that explains what is good and what is evil. The establishment of good and evil, or right and wrong, is foundational to the code of humanity, which is known as civility.

The truths contained in the Bible are not meant to be abstract; rather, they are meant to be interpreted according to the purpose and context for which they

[110] Ephesians 2:10.

were written. The Bible is meant to be read as a historic document. Many of the events in the Bible have enough archaeological evidence and scientific credibility to verify its reliability as a historic document. That is why the critics of the Bible must try to discover contradictions in order to prove that it is not the Word of God.

Chapter 12
Are There Two Creation Accounts?

Ever since the Bible was written, critics have mocked the Scriptures saying that it has contradictions and inconsistencies. Students of the Bible used to be told that in situations where someone claims that the Bible is inconsistent, the best defense is to take the Bible, hand it to them, and say, "Show me." The critics of the Bible eventually became bold enough to take on the challenge of the Bible student. Unfortunately, Bible students did not anticipate that the critics would start reading the Bible simply to come up with arguments. When the Bible student hands their Bible over to the skeptic, they immediately turn to Genesis chapter two.

There is an apparent problem in Genesis chapter two. This problem, according to the skeptics, is that it presents two separate and different Creation Accounts. They say that it is not just a different perspective on the account; it is entirely unique to the first account. In Genesis chapter one, there is a definite structure. First God created light, then he separated the waters, created dry land, and so forth until he finally created man and woman. But in Genesis chapter two, after the first three verses, it appears as though it returns to a world that was formless and empty.

It reads, "and no shrub of the field had yet appeared on the earth and no plant of the field had yet sprung up, for the LORD God had not sent rain on the earth and there was no man to work the ground."[111] Before this chapter mentions the creation of anything else, God creates man, breathes life into him, and places him in a garden where he makes plants and animals spring up before his very eyes. The literalist who reads the creation account and holds the Bible as the authoritative Word of God would struggle to defend the notion that the earth was created in the order that Genesis chapter one describes. It would then become difficult to harmonize Genesis chapter one with chapter two. Are there two creation accounts in the Bible? One must look at the intent of the first chapter of Genesis versus the intent of the second.

The first chapter of Genesis is a broad, impersonal overview of the entire creation. God is portrayed as the King commanding his creation to come into being. It almost seems as though he was somewhat detached from the creation process. He would speak and creation would commence. After he commanded something into existence he would then tell it what to do. In this chapter, God is on his throne effortlessly commanding the work of creation to be completed. It gives a very transcendent view of God.[112]

In chapter two, a different perspective is given. God dug into the dirt, sculpted the form of a man, and then

[111] Genesis 2:5.

[112] Staats 2010, 137.

breathed life into him. This time he is not emphasized as being a transcendent King. He is much more personal. He is like a potter, molding his creation. A potter is intimate with the work of his hands. Shaping a vessel out of clay dirties the hands of the potter. He must have close contact with his creation as it molds and takes shape. Chapter two is more of a detailed account of day six of creation. Day six required specific attention because it was on that day God chose to form his most important creation: man.

It can be observed in chapters one and two that man was a very special creation. Man was created in the image of God! Having created man in God's image, the Holy Spirit found it necessary to expound on what it meant to be created in the image of God. Chapter two contains a beautiful narrative of how God fashioned man, taught him how to live by giving him authority over creation, and then created a help mate that was both suitable and desirable for him. Learning about the creation and intention of man provides valuable insights into the nature of God. In chapter one, he is untouchable in relation to his creation; in chapter two, he reaches out and touches his creation. These are two characteristics of God that are consistent throughout the Bible. God is holy and transcendent, but God is also personal and intimate.[113] And yet, the literary question still remains: Why does there seem to be a contradiction between Genesis one and Genesis two? The answer is that there is no contradiction. This is made more evident when the Scriptures are analyzed for what they really say.

---

[113] Staats 2010, 138.

> This is the account of the heavens and the earth when they were created. When the LORD God made the earth and the heavens – and no shrub of the field had yet appeared on the earth and no plant of the field had yet sprung up, for the LORD God had not sent rain on the earth and there was no man to work the ground, but streams came up from the earth and watered the whole surface of the ground – the LORD God formed the man from the dust of the ground and breathed into his nostrils the breath of life, and the man became a living being.[114]

One must pay close attention to the language of the author to understand the incredible consistency between chapter one and chapter two of Genesis. The original intent of the language was to elaborate on the creation account, not to start over. John Sailhamer has presented an excellent explanation for this commonly misunderstood passage. According to him, the reference to the "shrub of the field" and the "plant of the field" are really terms used to anticipate the Fall. It is in no way connected to the "vegetation that was created in Genesis chapter one. This is evidenced by the phrase immediately following it as it says that God had not yet created man nor sent rain upon the earth yet."[115] The earth was already cultivated with plant life and the other creations of Genesis one, but it was sustained differently than the post-flood world. Before the Fall, the land was prepared for man as there

[114] Genesis 2:4-7.

[115] John H. Sailhamer, ed. Frank E. Gaebelein, *The Expositor's Bible Commentary Vol. 2*, (Grand Rapids, Michigan: Zondervan, 1990), 40.

was a stream that flowed from beneath the ground to water the vegetation. After the Fall, thorns and thistles sprouted up and man would have to till the ground and work it in order to get anything to grow:

> To Adam he said, "Because you listened to your wife and ate fruit from the tree about which I commanded you, 'You must not eat from it,' Cursed is the ground because of you; through painful toil you will eat food from it all the days of your life. It will produce thorns and thistles for you, and you will eat the plants of the field. By the sweat of your brow you will eat your food until you return to the ground, since from it you were taken; for dust you are and to dust you will return."[116]

Previously, mankind could eat of any of the plants "on the face of the whole earth and every tree"[117] Genesis 3:17 limits man's diet to the "plants of the field." The fields had to be planted by mankind. The phrases "shrub of the field" and "plant of the field" are surprisingly descriptive in conveying the difference. These specific phrases implied that nothing of the "field" had yet grown. In Genesis chapter two, God did not plant a field. He planted a "garden." While gardens require maintenance, fields require toil. The vegetation God created in chapter one was not related to the fields mentioned in chapter two.

---

[116] Genesis 3:17-19.

[117] Genesis 1:29.

The reference to the rain anticipates the rain waters of the Flood. The Flood occurred long after Adam and Eve had passed away: "On that day all the springs of the great deep burst forth, and the floodgates of the heavens were opened. And rain fell on the earth forty days and forty nights."[118] It is traditionally believed that before the Flood, there was no rainfall. Before sin, man had no reason to plant "fields."[119] The author lived after these events took place and wanted his readers to realize the difference between the sin-cursed world and God's original creation.

No contradiction exists between Genesis chapters one and two. The reference to the crops that had not sprung up indicates that man, after the Fall, had to work the ground to get it to produce food. The rain that had not been sent from God referred to the total lack of rain before the flood of Noah's day. Through God's inspiration, the author of Genesis was aware of the earth's situation before and after sin entered the world. When his words are properly interpreted they leave no room for mockers to claim that he contradicted himself.

---

[118] Genesis 7:11-12.

[119] Sailhamer, 40-41.

Chapter 13
The World That Then Was

A world once existed that neither you nor I could ever imagine. God had completed his work. Everything was very good and set in its proper order. This was a world void of evil. Death was merely a whisper in the wind. God had warned Adam about death, but death was beyond his imagination. Nothing feared death. Death was not yet reality. Not only was death not feared, but there was no such thing as fear! Animals did not fear humans. Humans did not fear animals. Everything ate the produce of the land and enjoyed the blessings of God.

The work that had to be accomplished was solely for the glory of God. There was plenty of work to be done. All living things experienced great joy in fulfilling God's purpose. All of creation operated in a manner that was good and acceptable to its Creator. The sun's rays were not a burden to the life on earth. They were an agent of nourishment and energy. No clothes were needed to shield mankind from the devastating effects of ultraviolet light because God sustained his creation and protected it from harm. The moon was present at night to govern the light of the nighttime. Its bright light would remind all of creation of God's watchful, beneficent eye. Animals of the night would be given sufficient light by the moon to be able to navigate through the darkness. The night was not a time of heightened caution.

Nothing had to seek shelter or sanctuary. Protection was not needed against nocturnal predators. There were no such things as predators in those days. Creatures would sleep out in the open with confidence, knowing that they would wake up the next day unharmed. The night was a serene and peaceful conclusion to a busy day's activities. The high seas were not an obstacle to overcome, as they are today. Water nourished plant life and allowed living creatures to bathe. Waters would travel through underground springs. It would gush up through the ground from geysers to shower the earth. There was no rain and there were no storms. Water posed no threat to life. It was trusted, used, and enjoyed for the glory of God.

The great waters of the earth swarmed with life. The animals of the land did not need to fear being picked off by a shark or snared by a crocodile. One could bathe with sea serpents and not fear being taken under by their menacing coils. The swimming holes were safe and protected by the many creatures that guarded their depths. There was nothing to fear about these creatures.

The creatures of the air soared through the skies with majesty. Great birds would have perched upon the tops of the mightiest of trees. Their nests would have been like tree houses. Chicks would never plummet from their nest to their doom. They would leave the nest when they were ready to fly. Never would a parent push its young out of the nest too early, causing it to fall. God saw to it that this was so. They were all under the protection of their loving Creator.

Insects were not insignificant pests. They were among the most sophisticated and strange creatures of God's creation. Wasps would not swarm against intruders. Bees would allow visitors to enjoy the honey they produced, straight from their hive. Even if their stinging barbs and venomous organs had already been installed by God, they would not need to defend themselves against an enemy. Those that would pass by their nests would appreciate their hospitality and enjoy the fruit of their labor.

The land animals were kin to one another. Harmony and peace existed among all cattle and wild animals. A child could ride upon the back of an untamed jaguar and not be harmed. The bull would not charge those who came too near and the hyenas would not gang up on helpless victims. Even dragons lived in harmony with the different kinds of animals. There was no competition for food and all were fit to survive.

The fruit of the land was delectable. Every creature had its favorite food, but none of the food was poisonous or sedative. As a result of sin, animals must now beware the types of produce they eat from the land. There are many diseases and negative effects that can be experienced by eating the wrong food. Imagine a world where no food was off limits. One could pluck a piece of fruit off of a tree without knowing what it was and consume it without the fear of dying.

Then, there was man. Mankind was in its glory. They walked with God, man and woman, fearlessly. There were few commands and only one law: Do not eat from the Tree of Knowledge of Good and Evil. Good was the natural inclination of man's heart. There was nothing in the world that could corrupt man's good nature outside of one tree. There was one entity, however, that was not so fond of man. His jealousy would one day prove to be the undoing of paradise.

Section 3
The Fall

Introduction

> The first millennium was the age of gold: Then living creatures trusted one another; People did well without the thought of ill: Nothing forbidden in a book of laws, no fears, no prohibitions read in bronze or in the sculpted face of judge and master. . .No brass-lipped trumpets called, nor clanging swords, nor helmets marched the streets, country and town had never heard of war: and seasons travelled through the years of peace. The innocent earth learned neither spade nor plough; she gave her Riches as fruit hangs from the tree.[120]

The human mind cannot comprehend a world without suffering. From the day one is born, he or she embarks on a journey that inevitably leads to death. It does not make a difference whether the cause of one's death is illness, tragedy, disaster, or old age, everyone dies. The condition of the world has proven itself so many times that death is one of the only guarantees for

---

[120] Horace Gregory, *The Metamorphoses* (New York: Signet Classic, 2001), 33.

one who is living. The mystery of death has caused many philosophical and religious debates. Nobody has ever been born with the natural inclination to desire death. It is an unfortunate blemish on the world that currently exists. But there was once an "age of gold."

Wickedness was absent from the world and peace reigned. Certainly there was a time when the world existed in such a majestic state. Many religions testify that the world is broken. It was once a place of great peace and is now a place of terrible disaster. The quote at the beginning of this section was written by an author that believed in the Greek and Roman gods. Even in such a culture they could recognize that the world was not behaving the way that it should. Genesis describes how the former world was established:

> Then God said, "Let us make man in our image, in our likeness, and let them rule over the fish of the sea and the birds of the air, over the livestock, over all the earth, and over all the creatures that move along the ground. . .Then God said, "I give you every seed-bearing plant on the face of the whole earth and every tree that has fruit with seed in it. They will be yours for food. And to all the beasts of the earth and all the birds of the air and all the creatures that move on the ground – everything that has the breath of life in it – I give every green plant for food." And it was so. God saw all that he had made, and it was very good. And there was evening, and there was morning – the sixth day.[121]

[121] Genesis 1:26, 29-31.

"It was very good," these words are a stark contrast from how the world would be described today. Today, the creation has abandoned its original order and is travelling a deviant path. It follows a path that is destructive and cruel. One might picture this life as being a cat, toying with a mouse until it finally has its fill of fun and decides to kill and devour its poor victim. Life is the cat and we are the mouse. Could the words "It was very good" have been describing an environment like the one today? Hopefully they were not. Such words imply that a very specific order was established – an order that was conducive for peace.

Mankind was set as the ruler of all creation. Its task was to subdue the animals and the land so that all things might give glory to God. Aside from cultivating the land, it is not revealed exactly how mankind ruled over the animals. It was fitting, though, that God's created image would be the creature that would rule over creation. Such an organism would be able to maintain peace throughout the world. And for a time man was able to uphold the statutes of God. As a result, everything was at peace and harmony.

In Genesis chapter three, mankind brought sin into the world and with it the curse of death: "By the sweat of your brow you will eat your food until you return to the ground, since from it you were taken; for dust you are and to dust you will return."[122] From that point on, the condition of the world deteriorated quickly.

In the very next chapter, the second generation of mankind introduced murder into the world as Cain killed his brother Abel. Man had been corrupted so badly by

[122] Genesis 3:19.

sin that it permeated his nature. Although sin typically involves some sort of disobedient action, the heart of a person prompts him or her to fulfill such a deed. Without a sinful heart, mankind would have no desire to carry out sinful activity. The corruption of man's nature made it possible for him to do unthinkable things including taking the life of one's brother. Sin was so cancerous that God had to judge the world. The worldwide flood was God's instrument of wrath.

Yet, God preserved the family of Noah to repopulate the earth. His goal was to judge those who were wicked and save those who were righteous. Although Noah lived among a wicked and destructive generation, his heart's desire was to serve and honor God. After the flood, God said: "The fear and dread of you will fall upon all the beasts of the earth and all the birds of the air, upon every creature that moves along the ground, and upon all the fish of the sea; they are given into your hands."[123] God then abolished his prohibition on eating meat and animals began to fear man.

Thus the end of the Biblical "Golden Age" was complete.[124] Creation has been incrementally decaying into chaos. Life was meant to be everlasting but after the fall, humans only lived to be a few hundred years old before dying. Now, in the modern day, living to be one hundred is considered to be a blessing. The environment is fallen. The animals are fallen. Man has fallen.

---

[123] Genesis 9:2.

[124] Edith Hamilton, *Mythology* (New York: Warner Books, 1969), 72.

Chapter 14
Philosophy of the Fall

Nothing is easier than to admit in words the truth of the universal struggle for life.[125]

Charles Darwin's complaint against the world is universally recognized as reality. Who can look at the world as it now exists and say, "It is good"? What is more evident than the universal struggle for life? Sure, there are religions that view suffering as the other side of the coin. Many people see that good cannot exist without evil or that sweet cannot exist without bitter. The Bible, however, teaches that good can exist without evil. In fact, God's ultimate goal is to banish evil so that good may reign for all eternity! If that is true, why did Darwin's belief lead him and many others away from the belief in God? Darwin sought after a naturalistic cause for suffering and overlooked the possibility that God and nature were not responsible for its existence.

If God is all-powerful, he clearly has the power to stop evil from happening. If God is so good, how could he allow evil to exist? A "good God" could not possibly

[125] Darwin, 60.

exist because he would not tolerate evil. This would mean that either God was wicked, or that nature is the cause of all suffering. If nature is the culprit, God is dismissed from existence and there really is no such thing as good or evil. Nature carries on as it naturally shall. The death of one may actually benefit another. Darwin overlooked the true culprit for the existence of evil in the world. Mankind, the enlightened beast, is the one responsible for all death and suffering.

Darwin was correct about the universal struggle for life. It is impossible to deny that there is something about this world that is not entirely good. The world is totally different from the way it was created, and creation groans at the recognition of this problem:

> For the creation was subjected to frustration, not by its own choice, but by the will of the one who subjected it, in hope that the creation itself will be liberated from its bondage to decay and brought into the freedom and glory of the children of God. We know that the whole creation has been groaning as in the pains of childbirth right up to the present time.[126]

This was not a world created for predators and disease. Mankind's inmost being knows that the world is broken and strives to discover why it operates in such a carnal fashion. Mythology, like science, has sought to come up with explanations.

Many ancient religions believed that there had to be a multitude of gods. There is so much chaos in the world

---

[126] Romans 8:20-22.

that one God could not be the culprit. The gods must have distinct personalities so that they could behave as they please. Their conflicting wills are what cause disorder. This is how gods are often viewed in polytheistic cultures. Now, as well as in ancient times, they were not regarded as entities that valued the mortal world.

Man reflected the image of the gods to the mortal world. The gods were immortal and wise beyond the capacity of humans. But a portion of the wisdom of the gods was passed down to the mortal world through mankind. Ironically, this would place the blame for the world's dysfunction on man. The wisdom of the divine, when corrupted, always becomes a great source of evil.

God's perfect creation was corrupted because mankind misused or neglected his ability to reason properly. How else could there be pain, suffering, hardship, and death? Why else would humans conduct war, murder, and slavery? None of these things are good. None of these things are reasonable. All of humanity knows that these acts are wrong. Something drastic must have happened to cause them.

There is a force in the world that is undeniably evil. Just as love is embodied in a personality, so is hatred. It is a creature that first devised the concept of sin. He was an entity that was created with the knowledge of good and evil, and he chose evil. He discovered a way to coerce a reasonable creature to do the unthinkable. He is responsible for the entrance of evil into the world. He is known as Satan.

Satan is one of the most misunderstood creatures of all creation. Biblically, some believe that Satan was created to be evil. Others believe that he was once good and became corrupt. One way or another, Satan is a figure that is taken seriously by most religious people. Not every religion believes in a satanic individual, but most, if not all, teach about a satanic force or evil spirits that cause mischief in the natural world.

Chapter 15
Evil Emerges: Part 1

An angel stares into the darkness. He is a marvelous creation that is shrouded in mystery. Nobody knows exactly what he was or how he became what he now is, but this is the story of how this angel went bad. His name was Lucifer.

As Lucifer looked into the darkness, he observed that it had been separated from the light. Apparently, light was from God. But darkness – where did *it* come from? He looked down at the shadow projected by his body as the moon shined down on him. He then understood: light proceeds from a source. Darkness is the void where light cannot shine. For the first time ever he realized that there was existence outside of light; there could be existence outside of God's jurisdiction. God rules all that is seen. So if there is existence outside of God's presence and sight, who rules this void where God is not? A devious thought crossed his mind, the first thought of this kind ever devised. "I could be that ruler."

Doubt crossed his mind: "What do I know about ruling? I am supposed to be a servant!" As the most beautiful of the heavenly beings, he was assigned to humankind, to watch over them and to guide them in appreciating the beauty of God's creation. This would require drastic change. This would require rebellion.

Chapter 16
The Fall of Satan

Who is Satan? There was a time when pop culture turned him into a silly looking, devious icon. One might recall images of a man wearing red pajamas, sometimes with goat legs and a pointy tale, wielding a trident, and sporting his classic goatee. This figure was often characterized by a mild ability to deceive, a tendency to appear on people's shoulders, and the pleasure he took in torturing people for no good reason. This little red guy is sorely missed in today's world.

Today, mistakes are made of either exaggerating Satan's power or eliminating it altogether. Technology, in combination with human imagination, has transformed this loveable little goofball into a hulking, menacing beast. In reality, this image is probably not too far from the truth. However, this present age has upgraded the devil into a super demon that possesses so much power that he rivals God himself. While images of Jesus and angels are meek and mild, the devil overshadows them with ripped muscles, a scaly body, and deadly horns protruding from his head. He has been given too much credit. Exalting him to a near god-like status, though, is not near as dangerous as diminishing him to nothing.

People today have a tendency to say that Satan does not exist. Doing such a thing renders him powerless in one's mind and gives one the sense that there is nothing that he or she can do that will result in condemnation. Unwittingly, this empowers Satan! This rewards him with more power than one could possibly imagine! A healthy fear of giving into Satan's temptations means that one is aware that his or her actions have eternal consequences. Satan prompts unsuspecting human hearts to do despicable, insidious acts. One of his most effective tricks is to help a person justify those acts in his or her mind. Giving in to the notion that Satan is make-believe eliminates fear of eternal consequences, but even worse, it is one step closer to disowning belief in God.

One of the clearest signs that God exists is the existence of evil. Humans see wickedness operating in the world and can discern between good and evil. One might say that it is a mere matter of perspective, but take into account one who studies the human brain. Doctors who observe the human brain have a difficult task. They must determine what structure performs specific functions inside of what appears to be a hunk of mush that happens to be the most sophisticated structure in the known universe. Simply trying to determine how a brain operates by observing a healthy one is not good enough. The most progress has been made by observing diseased brains. By nature, most people are aware of how a fully functioning and healthy person operates. Most people would conclude that something is functionally wrong with an individual if that person has unusual twitches, claims to hear voices, or is hypersensitive to sound. In these instances, it is much easier to compare the dysfunctional brain to one that is mostly healthy to determine the cause of one's malfunction. The function of particular structures can only be determined when they are not functioning properly. It is the same for the condition of the world.

The work of Satan has disrupted the good work of God in different areas of people's lives. He is not able to disrupt all areas at once because he is not God. Because of this, one might see a husband abusing his wife, a bully pushing around a peer, or someone of great status deceiving one who is poor and realize that these things are wicked. One knows that these actions are wicked because a husband has been observed loving his wife, peers are seen engaged in friendship, and the man of noble status has often aided the man who is poor. It is because of evil that one confirms what is good and it is because of good that one knows what is evil. To deny the existence of Satan is one step toward atheism, because denying the existence of evil also denies the work of God's goodness.

The purpose of this chapter is to develop an understanding of Satan. Three key aspects of Satan will be observed: who he is, where he is, and what is going to happen to him. By understanding these things, it will be easier to understand God's grace, mankind's free will, and the logical consequences of denying Jesus Christ. Satan was the first creation to reject God. Aside from lying about his own nature, he also leads people to believe lies about God. Fortunately, Scripture allows people to cut through the lies of Satan and to recognize his true identity.

Three Common Names

Throughout history Satan has been given several names. In part, this is because the Bible has been translated into a multitude of languages and his name must be translated from one language into another. This is also because the Bible gives him several different names. To keep things simple, only three common names will be observed in this book.

"Satan" is one of the most commonly used names for this entity. In Hebrew, the name Satan means "adversary," and the Greek equivalent means "accuser." Satan is the enemy of God and of mankind. He is a narcissist that seeks to dethrone God and take his place as the universe's supreme ruler. He detests mankind and wishes for his demise. He would go before God and accuse mankind of their sins, but he would also take part in tempting mankind to sin. Jesus pointed out both of these roles by telling the Jews, who accused him of evil, "You belong to your father, the devil, and you want to carry out your father's desire. He was a murderer from the beginning, not holding to the truth."[127]

The second name, "Devil," is nearly synonymous with Satan. In Hebrew, the name Devil is almost absent from the Old Testament and is only translated as such a few times. One of the Old Testament words translated as "devils" can also mean "fauns." A faun is a goat legged nymph that is characterized by his mischief, according to pagan mythology. This might be why the devil is sometimes depicted as having goat legs. The faun, Pan, is the most

---

[127] John 8:44.

famous of these mythological creatures and was associated with much cultic worship in ancient times. "Devil" conveys a sense of other-worldly evil. There is evil that is carried out in the mortal realm but demons, a word that is sometimes synonymous to devil or devils, carry out evil that is more sophisticated than that of the physical world.

Demons are evil spirits that seek to cause harm to God's creation, particularly mankind. In the New Testament, the name is frequently in reference to the demonic adversary of God. Devil is an effective term in characterizing the identity of our enemy. He is a demon and despises all that is good. In the fifth chapter of Mark, this is proven when Jesus casts a multitude of demons out of a man and into a herd of pigs. The evil spirits caused the pigs to run off and drown themselves.[128] Demons intend harm and so does the devil.

The third name, Lucifer, is a common name given to the adversary of God that is not originally a Biblical name. Certain translations of the Bible include the name Lucifer in Isaiah 14:12, but in Hebrew, this name is absent. Instead, the word translated as Lucifer, "heylel," actually refers to the morning star. It is believed that the morning star is literally Venus, the brightest star in the sky. Even so, Lucifer is not necessarily a bad translation from the original Hebrew word. In Isaiah 14, the reference to the morning star is actually a prophetic way of describing the king of Babylon. It was believed that this king was divine by his own right, especially since Babylon was a powerful kingdom in those days. It might

[128] Mark 5:13.

fascinate some people to discover that the name given to the pagan god of the morning star was Lucifer.

Therefore Lucifer, the morning star, was an idol. Likewise, Venus was associated with the egotistic king of Babylon who considered himself a god. In 2 Kings 19:10-12, the king of Babylon, also known as the king of Assyria, taunted the forces of Jerusalem:

> Say to Hezekiah king of Judah: Do not let the god you depend on deceive you when he says, "Jerusalem will not be handed over to the king of Assyria." Surely you have heard what the kings of Assyria have done to all the countries, destroying them completely. And will you be delivered? Did the gods of the nations that were destroyed by my forefathers deliver them[?]

The king that said these words was the same person that the prophet Isaiah prophesied against. The Babylonian king thought that he was greater than the God of Israel and was proven wrong. God's adversary can be viewed the same way. Given this context, the morning star can be likened unto the devil. The devil tries to draw praise away from God and direct it toward himself. He terrorizes God's people and attempts to lure them away from their faith in him. Since the name Lucifer is a pagan god that personifies the morning star, it is a worthy title for the fallen angel who plots against God.

The Roles of Satan

Some of the functions of Satan have already been discussed. His names paint a clear description of how he plays the role of a formidable enemy. His primary roles through history have been that of an accuser and the ultimate adversary to God. He teaches those who defy God to be affective weapons against God's people. It is often difficult to recognize the followers of Satan because they often have no clue that they are doing so themselves. The one that they follow is sneaky and he knows that if he is truthful to those who follow him, they will no longer desire to serve him. Satan's number one tool for defying God and his people is deception.

Jesus testified that "there is no truth in him. When he lies, he speaks his native language, for he is a liar and the father of lies."[129] In the Garden of Eden, Satan used the serpent to deceive Adam and Eve and led the entire world into sin, suffering, and death. In reporting to God, he attempted to deceive him by contending for the body of Moses and was rebuked by the archangel Michael.[130] Again, he brought false witness against the high priest Joshua and was rebuked directly by God.[131] After Jesus was baptized, Satan attempted to deceive him by tempting him in the desert.[132] He also caused Peter, Jesus' disciple, to rebuke him concerning his prophesied crucifixion.[133] Satan's hope is that he can get the better of God through deception and lead men's and women's hearts into sin.

The Apostle Paul wrote, "The god of this age [Satan] has blinded the minds of unbelievers, so that they cannot

---

[129] John 8:45.

[130] Jude 9.

[131] Zecharaiah 3:1.

[132] Matthew 4:1-11.

[133] Mark 8:31-33.

see the light of the gospel of the glory of Christ, who is the image of God."[134] Because of Satan's demonic nature, he wishes for the greatest harm upon humans. The greatest harm he can accomplish is to give people blind eyes and deaf ears when exposed to the Gospel of Jesus Christ. Since there is only access to God the Father through Jesus the Son, Satan must make nonbelievers think that the Gospel is death. "For we are to God the aroma of Christ among those who are being saved and those who are perishing. To the one we are the smell of death; to the other, the fragrance of life."[135] Only Jesus can convince people of the devil's true motifs: "The thief comes only to steal and kill and destroy; I have come that they may have life, and have it to the full."[136] Those who are in Christ have the light of Christ to lead them in all righteousness. Those who have been deceived and are without Christ are under the rule of Satan.

Paul wrote to the Ephesian church and reminded them about how they "followed the ways of this world and of the ruler of the kingdom of the air, the spirit who is now at work in those who are disobedient. All of us also lived among them at one time, gratifying the cravings of our sinful nature and following its desires and thoughts."[137] No matter how pure a person's motives, he or she will always fall short of doing good so long as Christ is absent from his or her life. Even those who believe that they are good without God or without Jesus are deceived. "The

[134] 2 Corinthians 4:4.

[135] 2 Corinthians 3:15-16.

[136] John 10:10.

[137] Ephesians 2:2-3.

work of God is this: to believe in the one he has sent."[138] No matter how pure one's intentions may be, a person cannot please God if he or she has rejected his one and only Son, Jesus Christ.

On that note, those who believe in Jesus are still susceptible to Satan's attacks. After all, Jesus taught his disciples to pray, "lead us not into temptation, but deliver us from the evil one."[139] This proves that the believer must constantly be on guard against the evil one. Peter wrote in his first letter that, "Your enemy the devil prowls around like a roaring lion looking for someone to devour."[140] This describes the devil's initiative. He is not afraid of those who believe in Jesus. Instead, being one who is consumed by pride, he seeks out those that believe in Jesus that he may destroy them by whatever means necessary. The Bible even reveals that for a time, the devil will be given power to wage war against God's saints and defeat them.[141] This will contribute to the perception of the nonbeliever that following the ways of the devil lead to life and that God's ways lead to death.

It is not that people truly believe that the devil's ways are superior to God's, but they believe that the devil is a creature that is not in their midst. They believe that they follow God's ways because God intends to make everyone happy in this life. Then, if we are good enough, we might get to enjoy eternity with God where nobody will be judged or condemned. We have nothing to abstain

---

[138] John 6:29.

[139] Matthew 6:13.

[140] 1 Peter 5:8.

[141] Daniel 7:21.

from in this world, for the devil is in hell and we are on earth, right?

The Devil's Biography

It is dangerous to believe that the devil's dwelling place is currently hell. There is no indication throughout the Bible that Satan dances around in hell all day, torturing evildoers. If this was Satan's only function, he might not be considered an enemy of God, but as one who carries out God's justice. In a contrary manner, Satan fears hell because he knows that he will suffer there for all eternity. At this time, he is a creature that is unbound until God determines otherwise. Even though he is unbound, he has been banished from heaven.[142] The Bible shows that Satan came before God on several occasions in his heavenly dwelling and had conversations with him. Because he has fallen, he is no longer allowed in God's heavenly kingdom.

It might frighten some people to realize that the devil's current residence is earth. Revelation 20:9 reads, "He was hurled down to the earth, and his angels with him." Jesus said, "I saw Satan fall like lightning from heaven."[143] Nobody thinks that Satan is currently in heaven. Most people believe that Satan is in hell. Few people understand why he is currently roaming about the earth. Jesus revealed that the eternal fires of hell were prepared for the devil and his angels.[144] If Jesus said that the fires were only

[142] Revelation 12:8.

[143] Luke 10:18.

[144] Matthew 25:41.

"prepared," he meant that the devil and his angels had not yet been handed over to the eternal fires. Satan was once a resident of heaven, was cast down to earth, and is anticipating eternal torment in hell. Satan is not happy that he has been banished from heaven. His dwelling place used to be among the angels. In fact, he is an angel.

One of the best examples concerning Satan's status as an angel is found in the book of Ezekiel: "You were anointed as a guardian cherub, for so I ordained you."[145] The word cherub describes an angelic being. There are people who might dispute the notion that this word actually means an angel, but there is plenty of context in Ezekiel and other books to prove that he is an angel of God. Speaking of context, this is an opportune moment to address this passage in Ezekiel. The full context of this verse is not directly addressing Satan; it is speaking of the king of Tyre. In the same manner as Isaiah 14, this king is being likened to a creation that was once great and became corrupt. This context should not be taken for granted while discussing this matter.

However, the imagery is an allusion to the ultimate good creation gone bad. What greater position can one have than to be a guardian cherub? The angel Michael has a position much like the one Satan had, and the angel Gabriel is God's chief messenger. Both are creatures that are regarded in the highest manner throughout the Scriptures. To put Satan in the same league as them seems unfair, but it is entirely Biblical.

One must understand that one of the primary functions of an angel is to be a ministering spirit. "Are not

---

[145] Ezekiel 28:14.

all angels ministering spirits sent to serve those who will inherit salvation?"[146] The devil was considered a ministering spirit by God. The book of Job even records Satan coming to God and reporting to him: "One day the angels came to present themselves before the LORD, and Satan also came with them. The LORD said to Satan, 'Where have you come from?' Satan answered the LORD, 'From roaming through the earth and going back and forth in it.'"[147] Instead of being a faithful minister, he was an accuser. In this instance, God presented Job to Satan as an example of a person who had not been corrupted by the ways of the world. Immediately, Satan brought accusations against Job.[148] Why would God give the task of ministry to one who was so evil and malicious?

Satan was not always evil. Ezekiel 28 describes him in this way: "the model of perfection, full of wisdom and perfect in beauty. . .You were blameless in your ways from the day you were created."[149] Furthermore, verse twelve says that he was in Eden. This description implies that Satan was created during the creation week in Genesis chapter one. You might also recall that at the end of the first chapter of Genesis, "God saw all that he had made, and it was very good."[150] What happened that caused Satan to become evil? At the creation of the world, a predicament existed that is the exact opposite of ours after original sin and after Jesus' atonement on

---

[146] Hebrews 1:14.

[147] Job 1:6-7.

[148] Job 1:9-11.

[149] Ezekiel 28:11, 15.

[150] Genesis 1:31.

the cross. At the creation of the world, everything was good but was susceptible to corruption. Everything that is good and untested remains good. That which is good and is tested will sooner or later fail. Satan's test was different from the rest of creation.

As an angel he possessed the knowledge of good and evil. The very knowledge of evil tested him. The elements about him that were good were corrupted by his knowledge of evil. He saw his own splendor and marveled. Ezekiel states, "Your heart became proud on account of your beauty, and you corrupted your wisdom because of your splendor."[151] He no longer felt that God deserved all of his worship and all of his praise. He directed his worship and his praise toward himself. The sin of Satan is idolatry, in the form of self-worship.

His love for himself caused him to rebel against the ways of God. Isaiah states, "You said in your heart, 'I will ascend to heaven; I will raise my throne above the stars of God; I will sit enthroned on the mount of assembly, on the utmost heights of the sacred mountain.'"[152] He wanted to usurp God's throne. God's sacred mountain is where the king of Jerusalem sits. Prophetically speaking, Jesus is the King of Jerusalem. Jesus is God, but he is also the new head of the human race and his Church. Therefore, not only did Satan want to usurp God's throne; he wanted to redefine the image of God that is expressed through mankind.

In order to do so, he had to prove that there is inherent fault with mankind. The first fault he found

---

[151] Ezekiel 28:17.

[152] Isaiah 14:13.

was manifest in original sin. Mankind, without the knowledge of good and evil, defied God by giving in to temptation and eating from the Tree of the Knowledge of Good and Evil. Since mankind defied God, its image was immediately corrupted. Because mankind obtained the knowledge of good and evil, he could willfully perform evil deeds. Inevitably, that which is corrupt will do evil despite its knowledge of good. Where mankind used to be good but susceptible to temptation, it became corrupt but susceptible to repentance. Repentance could only be accomplished through the ministry of the angels and God's Spirit. As mentioned before, Satan did not perform the task that God gave him as an angel. He was an accuser of mankind instead of a minister. As one that had power to guide people away from sin, his good influence would have been incredible. But because his hatred toward God was so great he chose to exercise his hatred toward God's image, which is mankind.

Satan does not love mankind, but requires his worship. He sees himself as the only one worthy of praise. The antichrist, a person brought upon by the work of Satan,[153] "will oppose and will exalt himself over everything that is called God or is worshipped, so that he sets himself up in God's temple, proclaiming himself to be God."[154] As Satan's representative, the antichrist will demand that everyone worship and obey him. He will even forbid people from buying or selling goods unless they have his mark and worship his image.[155] Anyone

[153] 2 Thessalonians 2:9.

[154] 2 Thessalonians 2:4.

[155] Revelation 13:11-17.

that worships Satan, or his image, will be doomed to destruction.[156] Is Satan unaware of his fate and ignorant to the fact that he will be defeated by God? His anger and hatred toward mankind is so great, now that his power has already been defeated, that his only desire is to take as many humans as possible with him to hell. Where God desires that all people would repent and be saved, Satan desires this of no one. He initially attempted to destroy man by removing him from his good position with God in Eden. His greatest act against mankind, though, was not in Eden but in a desert.

After Jesus was baptized by John the Baptist, the Holy Spirit led him into the desert to be tempted by the devil.[157] Jesus came to save mankind from his sins, but Satan was not going to stand by and watch as he succeeded. Just as he caused Adam, the first man, to sin and fall away from God, he sought to make Jesus, the Son of Man, sin and fall away from God. If Jesus would have failed to resist Satan mankind would be lost. "The reason the Son of God appeared was to destroy the devil's work."[158]

Jesus' mission was to pay for mankind's sins and reconcile it to God. His march to the cross was a declaration that Satan's power was soon to be destroyed, and the era of God's Church would be established. Jesus foresaw this when he declared to his disciples, "I saw Satan fall like lightning from heaven."[159] This statement was made

---

[156] Revelation 20:10.

[157] Matthew 4:1.

[158] 1 John 3:8.

[159] Luke 10:18.

in the book of Luke sometime after Jesus "resolutely set out for Jerusalem."[160] Many commentators have speculated that everything about Jesus' ministry, after chapter nine of Luke, was focused on his journey to the Cross. His declaration that he saw Satan fall from heaven was prophetic. His triumph over death would hurl Satan to the earth and banish him from heaven forever.

Satan did not suffer any serious consequences for deceiving Adam, Eve, and the serpent in Eden. The latter three paid for their rebellion against God. On top of their specific punishments, death was introduced to the world. Satan maintained his status as an angel and still enjoyed his immortality. His accusations against mankind were not totally without merit, because all of humanity had become depraved. Not a single person could claim to have no sin. Because everyone had sin, everyone could be rightfully accused and condemned. But, Jesus' sacrifice changed everything.

The work of the cross was substitutionary. The Old Testament set up a system of sacrifice through which sins could be covered over. Blood had to be shed by an animal. God declared, "For the life of a creature is in the blood, and I have given it to you to make atonement for yourselves on the altar; it is the blood that makes atonement for one's life."[161] Jesus' sacrifice was superior to the Old Testament sacrifices because it was the blood of a man without blemish. But the sacrifice of a man was not sufficient; this is why God became flesh and accomplished the deed of suffering and dying on a cross. He took upon

[160] Luke 9:51.

[161] Leviticus 17:11.

himself all of the guilt of mankind in its wickedness. If Jesus bore all of mankind's wickedness, on what ground could Satan accuse anyone of sin? If he were to accuse mankind of sin, he would be accusing Jesus, mankind's substitute, of sin. Jesus was found without sin and was one in whom the Father was "well pleased."[162]

Jesus' sacrifice brought upon a war in heaven, for the devil was desperate and knew he only had one shot to overthrow God. Satan and his forces were confronted by Michael and the army of heaven. The devil was defeated and cast down from heaven. Read the song that was sang from heaven as a result of this victory:

> Now have come the salvation and the power and the kingdom of our God, and the authority of his Christ. For the accuser of our brothers, who accuses them before our God day and night, has been hurled down. They overcame him by the blood of the Lamb and by the word of their testimony; they did not love their lives so much as to shrink from death. Therefore rejoice, you heavens and you who dwell in them! But woe to the earth and the sea, because the devil has gone down to you! He is filled with fury, because he knows that his time is short.[163]

He was accusing mankind "before our God day and night" and was overcome "by the blood of the Lamb and by the word of their testimony." The Lamb's blood was that which was shed on the cross, and the testimony was

[162] Matthew 17:5.

[163] Revelation 12:10-12.

the rapid spread of the good news that Jesus was raised from the dead and that sin had been wiped away.

Because sin was wiped away, the devil lost the basis for his accusations and the kingdom that he was establishing through darkness and destruction. Before Jesus, mankind was lost in its sin and would have been condemned to hell. Jesus' sacrifice bought all of mankind back for God, requiring only that man would believe in the Son of God. Although it was futile, Satan had to lead a rebellion against God if he desired to steal his glory. His rebellion was thwarted and he lost his heavenly status. Satan had become cursed. The earth was cursed to suffer and die because of Satan's deception. Satan became cursed because he attempted to steal glory from God, bore false witness against mankind, and led his evil forces against the army of heaven. Revelation puts it perfectly: "He is filled with fury, because he knows that his time is short."[164]

Satan's fall is not yet complete. Because God "is patient with you, not wanting anyone to perish, but everyone to come to repentance,"[165] Satan has been allotted time on earth to work his wickedness until Christ's thousand year reign. That is why one must pay attention to the warning in Revelation: "Woe to the earth and the sea, because the devil has gone down to you!"[166] Satan continues deceiving people, hoping that they will buy into his lie and resist God's grace. As one that was once an angel, he still "masquerades as an

---

[164] Revelation 12:12.

[165] 2 Peter 3:9.

[166] Revelation 12:12.

angel of light."[167] This means that he disguises himself as something that is good, hoping to win the approval of men. These disguises are worn in the forms of false teachings, wrong actions, and in seeking unity through lies. Anything that seems like it is pleasing, but contradicts the word of God, is of the devil.

The Apostle Paul warned in his letter to the Galatian church: "But even if we or an angel from heaven should preach a gospel other than the one we preached to you, let him be eternally condemned!"[168] Experiencing the presence of an angel would convince almost anybody concerning anything, but Paul preached that we should not be fooled. Even if angels present an alternative Gospel, he declared that their message is not truth. Religions have emerged since Paul's words that claimed they bore the authority of angels. One should not be confused by their words. It is quite possible that other religions have been founded upon the testimony of angels. Why should anybody be surprised at such a claim if, indeed, Satan masquerades as an angel of light?

His masquerade, in part, is carried out to disrupt the Church's worship of Christ. All sorts of evils have existed inside of the Church, even since its establishment! People have perverted the doctrines of God, justified their own wicked deeds, taught the tolerance and promotion of unspeakable perversions, and have caused divisions where division is not necessary. Instead of taking God at his word, people manipulate the words of the Bible to suit their own selfish ambitions. Doctrines that were meant to

---

[167] 2 Corinthians 11:14.

[168] Galatians 1:8.

steer Christians away from temptation and sin are now watered down so that sin may be excused for the sake of being politically correct. This is the work of Satan!

One of the common beliefs of today is that everyone must be accepted and loved by the Church. God does want his people to love all people but he does not want us to call that which is evil, good. Groups that feel alienated by the Church constantly push for acceptance inside of the Church. It is not for the sake that they are merely different that they are excluded, but for the sake that they will not submit to God's Word. People who do not profess Jesus Christ as their personal Lord and Savior should be allowed inside of a church. Membership of a church, however, should be based on one's confession of Jesus Christ as Lord and Savior. This does not merely require a verbal confession of faith, but a genuine act of repentance. Once someone has made that confession, the rules change a little.

When a "believer" proudly announces his or her sin and condones it, the church must take immediate action. Satan, in such instances, is in their midst. To continue having fellowship with that person can be detrimental to the rest of the church. After the full process of restoration has been attempted and the one sinning refuses to repent, that person must be expelled until he or she has repented. The Apostle Paul dealt with such a case in Corinth. He wrote, "When you are assembled in the name of our Lord Jesus. . .hand this man over to Satan, so that the sinful nature may be destroyed and his spirit saved on the day of the Lord."[169] Handing a person over to Satan means

[169] 1 Corinthians 5:5.

removing a person from the fellowship of the Church so that he or she may experience the wickedness that Satan was trying to accomplish. In understanding this evil, it is hoped that the person would repent from sin and eventually be allowed back into fellowship. This Scripture does not try to suggest that Satan accomplishes good; rather, it hopes that the believer would recognize the obvious difference between God's goodness and Satan's wickedness. That person would then be compelled by God's love to repent. For the one who does not believe, this difference cannot be recognized.

People that do not believe cannot understand why God declares their ways evil. As noted earlier, Satan blinds the unbelieving mind so that it cannot understand the Gospel of Jesus Christ.[170] Even presenting the good news, "For God so loved the world that he gave his one and only Son, that whoever believes in him shall not perish but have eternal life,"[171] is offensive to one who does not believe. To them, it is a message of condemnation: "If God so loved the world, why should any go to hell? Are you trying to tell me that you believe that I am going to hell?" or, "What about Hindus and Buddhists? Are they going to hell for not believing in Jesus? What about people that have never heard about Jesus? That's not fair!" Such people do not understand the grave consequence of sin, and they remain in Satan's grasp. That is why Christians are to be light to the world, so that the darkness might see light and be overpowered.

---

[170] 2 Corinthians 4:4.

[171] John 3:16.

Someone might suggest that Satan is currently in hell and that he no longer contests against mankind. For instance, Jude 6 says that certain angels left their positions of authority and abandoned their home in heaven. It reveals that these angels are now bound in chains inside of the darkness until the final judgment. Peter also speaks about such a judgment in his second letter, saying that God "sent them to hell."[172] Does this imply that Satan and his minions are already in hell?

Though it may appear that way, two factors make it unlikely. The first factor is that there are too many Scriptures that promote the teaching that Satan roams about the earth and continues blinding people's minds and causes saints to stumble for this to be Peter or Jude's intent. The second factor is that ancient tradition teaches that these Scriptures are actually in reference to Genesis 6. The angels, out of disobedience, took human wives and procreated to give birth to the *nephilim*. A teaching among the Jews was that these disobedient angels were cast into a dark place and bound. In fact, this dark place was not hell. The intent of the original word actually comes from Greek mythology. They believed in a place that was lower than hades, known as Tartarus. Peter used this term to distinguish the "dungeon" from the eternal damnation of hell.[173]

Hell's torment is summed up by the absence of God, not a series of tortures arranged by demons. A serious misconception of hell is that it is a place where God sends

---

[172] 2 Peter 2:4.

[173] Edwin A. Blum and Frank E. Gaebelein, *The Expositor's Bible Commentary: Hebrews through Revelation, Vol. 12* (Zondervan: Grand Rapids Michigan, 1984), 278.

people to be punished for all eternity. It is true that hell is an eternal punishment, but it is consensual punishment. People that refuse God's grace and choose to live their lives as though there were no God are simply granted their wish. Because people want to live independently of God, they choose their destiny to live in a realm that is void of God. There is no conclusive reason to deny the Bible's depiction of eternal fire and worms that never grow full, but their reality is nothing in comparison to an existence that is removed from God's presence. That leads to another serious misconception.

Satan will not be a king in hell. Many people believe that Satan will be the ruler of hell and will conduct its activities. At the present time, Satan is the leader of the forces of hell. Whether or not he goes back and forth between hell and earth is debatable. His fate in hell will be the same as anyone else. His torment will be too unbearable to take pleasure in other people's suffering. All in hell will remain defiant against God just as they defied God in this lifetime.

Satan's rebellion against God is not finished. The world still waits for a great time of tribulation before his final judgment. God will begin a series of judgments against the world that will prepare it for the end. Meanwhile, Satan will be deceiving the world through his antichrist and the false prophet that testifies to the power of the antichrist. Those who choose to follow antichrist will oppose God and bring themselves condemnation. After the tribulation, Satan must be bound. All of the nations of the world will be gathered in one place to make war against God and his people. At this time, Jesus will return to defeat the forces of evil and cast Satan into the pit of fire. He will be bound up and Jesus will rule the earth for a thousand years. After one thousand years, Satan will be released. He will attempt to invade God's kingdom, but he will be defeated by God's own might. At that time he and his followers will be cast into the lake of fire, which is hell, for all eternity.

Satan is very real. He is not a god-like super demon and he is not some goofy little creature prancing around in red pajamas. He masquerades as an angel of light. He is known by many names, all of which describe him as an enemy of God and of mankind. His intention is to deceive mankind, drive people away from God, and bring them to destruction. He currently roams the earth, but will one day be crushed by God, banished from his presence forever, and condemned to fiery torment.

The Fall of Iblis

> "And remember the time when We said to the angels, 'Submit to Adam,' and they all submitted. But Iblis did not. He refused and was too proud; and he was of the disbelievers."[174]

Iblis is the Islamic villain that parallels the Biblical character of Satan. He was a creature that blatantly defied God by refusing his command to submit to Adam.[175] When God decreed that all should submit to man, Iblis

---

[174] Hazrat Tahir Ahmad, *The Holy Qur'an: With English Translation and Commentary, Vol.1, Surah Al-Fatihah – Surah Al-Baqara.* (Great Britain: Islam International Publications Limited, 1988), 83.

[175] Al-Baqara 2:35.

swelled with pride and would not bring himself to his knees. Al-Baqara 7:12-14 elaborates on Iblis' reasoning:

> "God said, 'What prevented thee from submitting when I commanded thee'? He said, 'I am better than he. Thou hast created me of fire while him hast Thou created of clay.' God said, 'Then go down hence, it is not for thee to be arrogant here. Get out; thou art certainly of those who are abased.'"[176]

The dilemma for Iblis was that mankind was created lower than he and those of his kind. To be created of fire meant that he was immaterial and immortal, where a man formed of clay was material and fully mortal. Perhaps this is related to Satan's disdain toward humanity.

Iblis' arrogance was reminiscent of Satan. The angels were meant to be ministering spirits. They congregated before the creature that God called "man" and were commanded to bow before him. Iblis refused to humble himself to such a position. Unlike the angels, Iblis possessed a different sort of nature. He shared in the company of angels, but he was no angel. In all things, according to Islam, angels have to obey God. They have no ability to disobey him. Angels were created to serve the Prophets that God sent to reform the world. Iblis belonged to a secret creation: "He was one of the jinn (a secret creation); then he chose to disobey God's order."[177] Where angels were bound to be obedient, the jinn possessed

[176] Al-Baqara 7:12-14.

[177] Al-Baqara 18:51.

free-will.[178] The jinn, therefore, were held accountable for all of their actions and decisions. One might say that this is a significant difference between Satan and Iblis; others might say that it reveals something about Satan's identity.

The stories of Satan and Iblis are very similar. Both entities were filled with pride and showed contempt toward mankind and God. Is it possible that Satan was a "secret creation"? The Bible does not given an actual account of his creation or the angels. Earlier it was discussed that Satan was an angel and had fallen from heaven. Not everybody accepts this notion, so it is possible that he may have been something different from the angels. Like Satan, Iblis too was alleged to go before God along with the angels. Maybe Satan was another culture's interpretation of the same creature!

Nonetheless, according to Islamic definition, Satan and Iblis are not necessarily the same entities. Satan is more of a title for one who leads another person away from God than a supernatural presence. So Iblis can be "a satan" but he was not necessarily "the Satan." One example of the difference between Satan and Iblis was that he was not the one who was responsible for the temptation of Adam. According to Islam, a satan was responsible for Adam's sin but this satan was not the Devil. Adam was sent to earth to reform evildoers, and it was supposedly one of these people that deceived him and was labeled a "satan."[179] Like the jinn, Muslims

---

[178] Ahmad vol. 1, 84.

[179] Ahmad Vol. 1, 84.

believe that humans also have the ability to disobey God if they please.

The jinn and humankind were the only ones among God's creatures to possess free will. This accounts for why the jinn and humans are held accountable for their actions. All other creatures act exactly as God commands. The other creatures have the opportunity to hear what God says, take it to heart, and say, "You know, God, that does not work for me." Free will is a blessing and a curse. It is a blessing because any good accomplished by a person can be credited to one's personal goodness; it is a curse because any evil accomplished by a person can be credited to that person's wicked heart.[180]

According to Islam, sin does not hold a man in bondage from the day of his birth. When men are born, they are inherently good. It is only through the working of a satan or deceiver that mankind can be fooled into believing the "lies" of Christianity and Judaism.[181] A person's evil begins from the outside, not from within. The great Islamic prophet Mohammad once said, "Every child is born with a good nature (i.e. the nature of Islam); it is his parents who later make him a Jew or a Christian."[182] Islam teaches that one who has fallen away from the truth after being deceived can be called back to belief by listening to a Prophet.[183] Once they have been

---

[180] Ahmad Vol. 1, 85.

[181] Ahmad Vol. 2, 774.

[182] Ahmad Vol. 1, 85.

[183] Ahmad Vol. 1, 85.

spiritually resurrected, it is impossible for Iblis or a satan to deceive him any longer.[184]

The Bible rejects the notion that a person is good starting from one's birth. Genesis says, "for the imagination of man's heart is evil from his youth."[185] Original sin, according to the Bible, tainted the nature of mankind for the duration of the earth's history. The miracle of Jesus, according to certain theologies, was that mankind would not be held accountable for sin because of Jesus' atoning sacrifice on the Cross. The one who was born a sinner would only be held accountable for the sins he or she committed during life. This still leads to all of mankind being wicked, from birth, but does not hold infants accountable for original sin or rejecting Jesus' atoning work. Islam and Christianity greatly disagree on this point.

Despite this disagreement, Christianity and Islam seem to agree that "the evil one" will be punished for all of his sins in the future. After refusing to submit to man, Iblis begged God to withhold his anger until a future time. Since God is far wiser than anything else in existence, he allotted Iblis time on earth before his full judgment would be carried out. As discussed before, Satan is currently waiting for eternal judgment. He has been cast out of heaven but roams about the earth bitter, angry, and full of just as much pride as ever. He must wait until the day that God chooses to fully exercise his wrath against him.

Clearly, Iblis was developed around the Biblical model of Satan. He defied God at man's creation, was

---

[184] Ahmad Vol. 2, 774.

[185] KJV Genesis 8:21.

full of pride, and awaits eternal judgment. Islam was created after Christianity and probably had some strong influence from neighboring Christians or Gnostics that lived at the time of Mohammed. Iblis is a faithful embodiment of evil along with the tradition of Satan. He is a deceiver of mankind that thinks he knows better than God. His disobedience is proof that he is corrupt, and his refusal to repent is proof that he is evil to the core. Even though he is not really Satan and faces mankind under different circumstances, he helps us to understand the nature of entities that are truly evil. He does not openly hate people; he tries to deceive them so that their judgment is their own doing.

Chapter 17
Evil Emerges: Part 2

A new emotion arose in the heart of Lucifer. He became angry. “Why should I be a servant to man?” Mankind was confined by the laws of nature. Man had boundaries that couldn’t be crossed. He was not even permitted to journey into the dwelling place of God. In fact, God had to visit man in order for their relationship to exist.

This world, that God created, was good. It was too good for its own sake. God kept it under lock and key. It was time for one of God’s own to enlighten mankind, so that it might see what it truly was: helpless, ignorant, naked savages. God placed a tree that could accomplish such a task in the midst of the garden. The inclinations of the human heart may have been good, but the Tree of the Knowledge of Good and Evil would change that. It was all a matter of trust and persuasion. A heart that is inclined toward good with no knowledge of evil has no defense against slander.

“These naïve beasts, how could God have made me a servant to them? They should be serving me. I will go to them and make them my slaves. God’s rule will be a thing of the past. I will be like the Most High. I will dethrone God Almighty and take his place as Lord of Creation."

The rest of this story is history. Lucifer, through a serpent, persuaded Eve to eat from the Tree of the Knowledge of Good and Evil. Eve then persuaded Adam to eat its fruit. They were found out by God, all of them, and a curse was placed upon them and all of creation. From that point forward, this mysterious being known as Lucifer would be called by a new name. He would be known as the Devil or the Evil One. But one name truly reflects the character of Lucifer. He is Satan, the Enemy.

Chapter 18
The Fall of Man and Nature

Adam, Eve, and the Serpent

> Now the serpent was more crafty than any of the wild animals the LORD God had made. He said to the woman, "Did God really say, 'You must not eat from any tree in the garden'?"[186]

From a modern reader's perspective, the Biblical account of the Fall may seem like a fairy tale. Modern readers consider the idea of a talking serpent to be absurd. Despite its clear role in the Fall, Christians believe that Satan was the culprit who tempted Eve to eat from the Tree of the Knowledge of Good and Evil. Did the author intend the reader to know that the serpent was Satan? A straightforward reading would suggest that the serpent was just a serpent and nothing more. And yet Christian tradition holds that there was something more to this event than a serpent tempting a woman to sin. What was the message that the author was trying to get across through this story?

---

[186] Genesis 3:1.

Truth be told, the message of Genesis 3 is bizarre but it means exactly what it says. A long time ago, there was a place called Eden, which literally means "paradise." It was perfect until one day a serpent, yes a serpent, spoke to a woman and caused her to eat a piece of fruit from a forbidden tree. She took the fruit, having been convinced that it was good, and she gave it to her husband who also ate the forbidden treat. The message is very simple but has been communicated throughout the ages in different ways.

The serpent, or snake, has become a symbol of deception, which leads to death. The curse placed upon the serpent blemished its reputation beyond repair. This reputation can be summed up in four words: "Never trust a snake." There are many tales that teach this valuable lesson. One such story is the Native American story of the Boy and the Rattlesnake:

> Once there was a boy who was very soft-hearted. One morning, as he was walking he saw a rattlesnake by the side of the road. There had been an early frost the night before and the snake had been caught in it. The snake was stiff with the cold. The boy stopped to look at it, feeling sorry for the snake. Then a wonderful thing happened. The snake opened its mouth and spoke to him.
>
> "Help me," the rattlesnake said in a pitiful voice. "Pick me up, warm me or I will die."

"But if I pick you up, you will bite me," the boy said.

"No," said the snake, "I will not bite you. Pick me up, hold me close to you and warm me or I will die."

So the boy took pity on the snake. He picked it up. He held it close to him so that it would be warmed by his body. The snake grew warmer and less stiff and then, suddenly, it twisted in the boy's hands and – WHAH! It bit the boy on the arm. The boy dropped the snake and grasped his arm.

"Why did you bite me?" the boy said. "You said you would not bite me if I picked you up."

"That is so," said the snake, "but when you picked me up, you knew I was a rattlesnake."[187]

Because of its nature, a snake is cunning and deceptive. A snake is not a trickster because it is evil. It is a trickster because a snake is a snake! The curse has employed the serpent's craftiness to accomplish wicked deeds.

Naturally, Satan would desire the use of an able-minded creature to do his bidding. A crafty animal like the serpent would have been the prime candidate to accomplish his mischief. For its willingness to comply with the pleas of Satan, it became cursed by God. It would be trampled by man's feet to remind it, and humanity, of the day it deceived man and defied God.

---

[187] Josheph Bruchac, *Native American Animal Stories* (Golden, Colorado: Fulcrum Publishing), 61-62.

Observe the curse that was placed upon the serpent after Adam and Eve sinned:

> So the LORD God said to the serpent, "Because you have done this, "Cursed are you above all the livestock and all the wild animals! You will crawl on your belly and you will eat dust all the days of your life. And I will put enmity between you and the woman, and between your offspring and hers; he will crush your head, and you will strike his heel."[188]

Much like a mythical tale, this passage describes why snakes crawl on their bellies and why mankind and snakes are natural enemies. What the serpent had done distinguished it from the rest of the animals in the Garden of Eden and turned it into a despicable creature.

Generally speaking, the serpent was and is a creature that is approached with extreme caution, but there are several instances in the Old Testament where the serpent is used by God to accomplish his purposes. For example, in the book of Exodus, God turns Moses' walking stick into a serpent in an attempt to show Pharaoh God's power.[189] In Numbers, the people had been afflicted with a plague of snakes that bit the Israelites to kill them. Moses fashioned a golden serpent, as God commanded him, so that when the people of Israel looked upon it they would be cured of the snakes' venomous bites.[190] In the Gospel of John Jesus likened himself to the

---

188 Genesis 3:14-15.

189 Exodus 4:3, 7:9.

190 Numbers 21:8-9.

golden serpent that Moses created in the wilderness.[191] The Bible makes it clear that serpents are not inherently evil. Something more had to have happened to cause the serpent to tempt Eve. There was a greater force behind the evil that happened that day than just the guile of a serpent. This evil had to have been Satan. But if the serpent was not Satan and snakes are not inherently evil, what was the connection between Satan and the serpent?

Psalm 58 likens the wickedness of evildoers to the poison of serpents.[192] The poison of a serpent, in this context, can be regarded in two ways. First of all, the bite of a serpent injects venom into its enemy, which results in a slow and painful death. Second, the author hearkens back to the imagery of the Garden of Eden when the serpent led the entire human race astray. The poison of the serpent was not its venomous bite; its poison was its deception. Its deception resulted in suffering and death for all living things. The serpent's "poisonous bite" in the Garden of Eden proved that the devil was in the details that day.

Satan initiated the temptation process that brought sin into the world. A straightforward reading of Genesis will not provide this sort of interpretation, but other Scriptures clearly show that Satan was the initiator of original sin. A more detailed description of Satan has been provided in chapter sixteen and should be referenced if necessary. Afterward, it is necessary to investigate the relationship between Satan and the serpent. For starters, the New

---

[191] John 3:14.

[192] Psalm 58:2-5.

Testament refers to Satan as "that ancient serpent."[193] There are several possibilities concerning the relationship between Satan and the serpent in light of this context.

The first possibility is that the serpent was symbolic of Satan. As previously discussed, serpents were regarded as creatures that were brilliantly deceptive. Satan himself has a nature that can also be classified as brilliantly deceptive. Under this pretense, the first couple of chapters of Genesis would not necessarily describe true historic events. It is not absolutely necessary that one must believe that Genesis is literal, but it dampens one's interpretation of the rest of the Bible to concede such a point. If the early chapters of the Bible are fictitious, what parts of it are true? As a result, it is necessary to consider other options.

The second possibility is that the serpent was influenced by Satan. This would suppose one of two things: either Satan caused the serpent to speak, or Adam and Eve already had an open line of communication with the serpent. The idea that Satan caused the serpent to speak is intriguing because there are Biblical stories that may support this possibility. In chapter twenty-two of Numbers, a man named Balaam was summoned by the king of Moab to pronounce a curse against Israel's army. As Balaam travelled with the princes of Moab, the Lord's angel blocked his course and frightened the donkey he was riding. Ultimately, God allowed Balaam's donkey to speak so that it could warn him about the angel that was preparing to kill them. Balaam spoke back to the donkey

---

[193] Revelation 12:9.

and realized that his life was in danger.[194] God gave the donkey the ability to speak; therefore, it is reasonable to believe that another spiritual being, Satan, may have been able to give the serpent the ability to speak. But that is not the only possible way this could have happened.

It is also possible that Adam and Eve openly communicated with the serpent without any sort of spiritual intervention. At the Tower of Babel, mankind lost its ability to communicate with one another because God scrambled mankind's language. This happened because humans were abusing their ability to communicate with one another by using it to spread evil ideas. In a similar fashion, the serpent used its ability to communicate with man to deceive Eve and to dishonor God. Is it possible that the animal world lost its ability to communicate with humans because the serpent abused its ability to speak?

When Adam and Eve sinned, mankind's relationship with the natural world was damaged. Centuries after the first sin, God brought a flood upon the earth that wiped out every living thing. A man named Noah loaded two of every kind of land animal onto an ark and was protected until the floodwaters receded. After Noah and his family stepped out of the ark, God told them that the fear of man would be placed on the hearts of animals. Is it possible that mankind lost its ability to communicate with animals as a result of this fear of man? If this sounds too absurd, perhaps one should consider yet another possible relationship between Satan and the serpent.

The third possibility is that the serpent was an embodiment of Satan. It seems that most people would like the

[194] Numbers 22:27-30.

serpent in Eden to Satan in a fairly literal fashion. Just the thought of a slimy, slithering snake that has a venomous bite and a rattling tale reminds even the stoutest person of the wickedness of Satan. It is no wonder that Satan would be thought of as a snake. Satan's existence as a serpent could have been accomplished in two different ways: either both Satan and the serpent are one and the same creature, or Satan may have changed his form to resemble a serpent temporarily.

Satan may have transformed into a serpent, like a shape-shifter. The purpose of Satan changing his form would have been to deceive Eve into thinking that she was conversing with a subservient creature. However, it is difficult to know whether the imagery used in the Bible to describe Satan's different forms is for artistic and symbolic purposes, or if it is actually addressing Satan's ability to change his form. The Bible never truly addresses Satan's ability to change his appearance, but it does mention that Satan's image can deceive people. According to the Bible, Satan is an angelic being of some sort. This alone plays a role in Satan's deceptive ability.

According to the Bible, angels typically come down to earth in the form of a human. Sometimes they appear in radiant glory so that people know they come from heaven. Other times they are unrecognizable until they reveal themselves. Satan may be able to transform into an earthly creature the same way that angels appear as humans. It does not appear to be too far-fetched to argue that Satan could change his form to interact with people. For some people, though, this interpretation might not seem literal enough.

The second half of this possibility would be that the serpent and Satan were, and are, one and the same. In an extremely literal fashion this would be a possibility. After all, the serpent is punished for misleading Adam and Eve. In Isaiah's telling of the fall of the morning star, it speaks of the humiliation of Satan. The serpent was changed to crawl on its belly all of the days of its life. This was a sign that the serpent was to be ashamed. Nonetheless, this would imply a general evil about all serpents. Even its descendants would be directly affiliated with Satan. This seems highly unlikely because certain Scriptures do portray serpents in a positive light, as discussed previously. Satan is not actually a serpent and snakes do not have an inherently evil nature.

Considering both the Old and the New Testament, the most likely possibility would be that Satan influenced the serpent, and that the serpent already had the ability to communicate with human beings. Adam, Eve, and the serpent were all punished for sinning. Satan was probably corrupted before this event in history and wanted mankind to lose its position with God and nature. So he interacted with the natural world as a spirit, through influencing one of the creatures mankind was meant to have dominion over, the serpent. Mankind disregarded God's words and gave into the words of the serpent and broke the created order. Man was supposed to be created in God's image, woman was created as his helper, and they were both meant to subdue the animals of the world. The punishment for the serpent was similar to the punishment Adam and Eve faced. It was not that any of the serpents were evil by nature, but this one's sin against God resulted in a curse. The curse that was placed on it was then passed down to all of its descendants for all of history.

The skeptic might ask, "How could Adam and Eve have sinned if all of creation was good?" It is true that all of creation was good. All of the inclinations of Eve's heart were good. That was why it took an animal that was crafty to persuade the woman to eat from the Tree of the Knowledge of Good and Evil. After being tempted, Eve observed the tree and made her decision:

> When the woman saw that the fruit of the tree was good for food and pleasing to the eye, and also desirable for gaining wisdom, she took some and ate it. She also gave some to her husband, who was with her, and he ate it. Then the eyes of both of them were opened, and they realized they were naked; so they sewed fig leaves together and made coverings for themselves.[195]

It was not Eve's ignorance, curiosity, or evil nature that caused her to eat from the Tree of the Knowledge of Good and Evil. She was deceived by the serpent, but the serpent appealed to a desire in her heart to be like God. The desire to be like God was programmed into the human heart. Adam and Eve did not have the knowledge of good and evil programmed into them, so they were probably not aware that the serpent was using their desire to be like God to drive them away from God. The serpent convinced them that God was suppressing their ability to be like him by forbidding them from eating

[195] Genesis 3:6-7.

from the Tree of the Knowledge of Good and Evil. John Sailhamer wrote:

> The thrust of the story, with all its simplicity, lies in its tragic and ironic depiction of the search for wisdom. Ironically, that which the snake promised did, in fact, come about: the man and the woman became "like God" as soon as they ate of the fruit. The irony, however, lies in the fact that they were already "like God" because they had been created in his image.[196]

God was not withholding anything from the people he created. He was allowing them to enjoy him in his purest form. He was allowing them to take care of the very garden that harbored the Tree of the Knowledge of Good and Evil. The serpent confused the woman by showing her that the tree did not lack any of the beauty or goodness of the other trees. The tree was good for food, pleasant to the eye, and it was able to make a person wise,[197] why would someone not want to eat its fruit?

The knowledge of good and evil had not yet been imparted to Adam or Eve, so their only rationality for eating or not eating the fruit would have been obedience or disobedience. They decided to disobey God because they believed he was withholding the truth of the Tree of the Knowledge of Good and Evil. Contrary to popular belief, Adam and Eve were not stupid and the name of the tree they ate from was not "The Tree of Knowledge." It was "The Tree of the Knowledge of Good and Evil."

---

[196] Sailhamer, 52.

[197] Genesis 3:6.

When Adam and Eve's eyes were opened, it did not mean that they became intelligent. It meant that they became aware of evil, and particularly the evil of the sin they had committed. They were also ashamed of their nakedness for this reason.

After eating the fruit of the tree they discovered that they were naked and they perceived that their nakedness was not good. Their reason for being ashamed of their nakedness was not directly stated in the narrative, but it can be rationally deduced from the surrounding Scriptures. One explanation for this is that they realized that their bodies were completely exposed and were ashamed of their vulnerability. Sailhamer, once again, offers his two cents on this subject:

> Their knowledge of "good and evil" that was to make them "like God" resulted in the knowledge that they were no longer even like each other: they were ashamed of their nakedness, and they sewed leaves together to hide their differences from each other. . .they also tried to hide themselves from God at the first sound of his coming.[198]

Man and woman were created to be one organism in the form of two persons, not two separate organisms.[199] Their shame in being different from one another was sinful because it created brokenness in their relationship and their oneness. The brokenness in their "marriage" even harmed their relationship to the God who created

---

[198] Sailhamer, 52.

[199] Genesis 2:24.

them. The world was wrecked because of mankind's failure to obey God.

The entrance of sin into the world involved four individuals: Adam, Eve, the serpent, and Satan. Each was created to be good, but spiritual beings known as angels were created with the knowledge of good and evil. Satan, as an angel, was the one who spiritually influenced Adam, Eve, and the serpent, even though his tempting did not have to result in sin. Ultimately, Adam was the one who was responsible for bringing sin into the world and Satan was the agent who provided him with the opportunity.

Pandora

The famous tale about the first woman, Pandora, is one of the most well-known Greek myths preserved to this day. The similarities that exist between Pandora's story and Eve's are incredible. For a reader who is already familiar with Eve's story in the Garden of Eden, it is easy to understand the parallels between the two stories. Eve was the first woman in the Bible, Pandora was the first woman according to Greek mythology. Eve defied God by eating fruit from a forbidden tree and Pandora opened a box that she was forbidden from opening. Both were made after the creation of their male counterparts and were made in such a manner that men would desire them for their beauty. There are two accounts of the creation of Pandora and how she brought an end to the perfect age. Each account of her creation describes it as a mischievous punishment planned by the gods against mankind.

Men were created by Prometheus and so a race of men already existed on earth before the creation of Pandora.[200] Prometheus was no ordinary god, but a titan. Titans were divine beings that existed before the gods. According to mythology, some of the titans gave birth to the gods. Sometime before the creation of man, the gods and titans were at war. Prometheus defected so that the gods could gain the upper hand against the titans. His brother, Epimetheus, aided him in creating man. Among the titans, Prometheus was the wisest. Epimetheus, on the other hand, was very impulsive.[201]

Epimetheus was originally given the task of creating the world's animals. When he finished, he realized that he had given away all of the best gifts and abilities and left nothing special to give mankind. He sought his brother for assistance and he ultimately took over the project. Prometheus created man in the shape of the gods (bipedal, hairless, etc.) and then went up to the sun, and took its fire. He gave the fire of the sun to man, which was a greater gift than what the wild animals possessed. This caused Zeus, the greatest of the gods, to become angry with Prometheus.

He hated Prometheus for stealing the sun's fire and giving it to man. Zeus' anger escalated as men were also being allowed to keep the best parts of the animal sacrifices. These sacrifices were meant to be for the gods.[202] To get back at mankind and Prometheus, Zeus set out to

[200] Hamilton, 72.

[201] Hamilton, 71.

[202] Hamilton, 72.

create woman. M.L. West's translation of the *Theogony* describes the creation of woman:

> But the noble son of Iapetos [Prometheus] outwitted him by stealing the far-beaconing flare of untiring fire in the tube of a fennel. And it stung high-thundering Zeus to the spirit, and angered him in his heart, when he saw the far-beaconing flare of fire among mankind.
>
> At once he made an affliction for mankind to set against fire. The renowned Ambidexter moulded from earth the likeness of a modest maiden, by Kronos' son's design. The pale-eyed goddess Athene dressed and adorned her in a gleaming white garment; down over her head she drew an embroidered veil, a wonder to behold; and about her head she placed a golden diadem, which the renowned Ambidexter made with his own hands to please Zeus the father. On it were many designs fashioned, a wonder to behold, all the formidable creatures that the land and sea foster: many of them he put in, charm breathing over them all, wonderful designs, like living creatures with a voice of their own.
>
> When he had the pretty bane to set against a blessing, he led her out where the other gods and men were, resplendent in finery of the pale-eyed one whose father is stern. Both immortal gods and mortal men were seized with wonder then they saw that precipitous trap, more than mankind can manage. For from

> her is descended the female sex, a great affliction to mortals as they dwell with their husbands.[203]

In this first account, the very nature of woman was what caused the fall of human decency. The creation of woman hailed the onset of violence and hardship, as she was too much for mortal man to handle. The gods designed her to bring out the worst in man. The second account of her creation does not correlate the entrance of evil to the very creation of woman; instead, it was Pandora's curiosity that brought plagues upon the earth.[204]

After Pandora was created, all of the gods placed something harmful inside of a box and entrusted it to her. While she was left alone, Pandora could not contain her curiosity and opened the box. Out flew all of the plagues which the gods had placed inside and the world has been haunted by them ever since. Nonetheless, it was said that "hope" also escaped from the box.[205] In many respects this sounds much like the creation of Eve and the Fall described in the Bible.

Even though the Biblical and Greek stories have different settings and elements they share some remarkable similarities. Man was regarded as a very important creation, the woman played a serious role in the Fall, and the entrance of evil changed the nature of the entire world. With so much in common, some people have argued that one of these stories may have descended

---

[203] M. L. West, *Hesiod Theogony Works and Days* (New York: Oxford University Press, 1999), 21.

[204] Hamilton, 74.

[205] Hamilton, 74-75.

from the other. Regardless of whether or not this is true, the two accounts are foundational to two totally different worldviews. Each account offers a unique take on who women are in relation to men.

The woman in the Biblical account was not created as an instrument of evil, nor was she inclined toward sin. Woman was created by God as a helper for man. God saw that man was not well-off being alone and introduced him to woman for his own good.[206] The woman was not merely a victim of curiosity, but had been deceived into committing sin. She had actually refused the serpent's initial temptation because God had told her not to eat from The Tree of the Knowledge of Good and Evil. In the story of Pandora, the gods wanted mankind to fall. The gods found mankind detestable. They designed woman so that death, suffering, and evil would enter into the world.

The realization that the gods had it out for mankind would have been frightening to the ancient world. Their gods did not abide by immutable standards, but were subjects of their emotions and egos. But because the gods were higher than the mortal world, Pandora was held responsible for all evil. Woman was responsible for original sin. Despite the deception by divine troublemakers, the mortal world had to suffer for the sake that the immortals were insecure. In the Bible, Adam, Eve, and the serpent were all held responsible for bringing sin into the world. Only one, however, was truly held accountable for the entrance of sin.

Adam, according to the New Testament, was the one held responsible for sinning. Neither the New nor Old

[206] Genesis 2:18.

Testaments blamed Eve for the Fall. One of the few references to woman's hand in the Fall is found in I Timothy, which states that woman had sinned first,[207] but it does not shift the responsibility of sin toward the woman. The book of Romans says that it was through *one man's* sin that death was brought into the world.[208] The one man it is referring to was Adam. He too ate from the Tree of the Knowledge of Good and Evil and he was the one responsible for his family's well-being. Therefore he was the one responsible for original sin. This means that the two stories are actually opposed to one another.

In reality, there are a lot of differences between the two stories. Pandora was intentionally created by the gods to be an instrument of mischief and grief. Eve was created as a partner and lover for Adam. The gods were the initial tempters in Pandora's story, while the serpent was the one who tempted Eve. Pandora was held responsible for sin in the Greek story, but Adam was held responsible in the Biblical account. The differences may appear subtle, but their implications are paramount.

Pandora's tale creates a worldview that makes morality ambiguous because the gods are villains. The God of the Bible is exalted as being righteous and has an immovable standard. The story of Pandora paints a dismal picture of mankind's existence, especially that of woman. A world that is ruled by flighty gods is not a safe place to live. From the beginning, the God of the Bible established a standard for mankind to live by. Unfortunately, man failed to live up to this standard.

[207] I Timothy 2:14.

[208] Romans 5:12.

God informed him of the consequences for disobeying his standard and the repercussions of such a decision. Adam's curse has been plaguing the world ever since.

Evolution

In his earthshaking book, *The Origin of Species,* Charles Darwin wrote, "Natural selection will never produce in a being anything injurious to itself, for natural selection acts solely by and for the good of each."[209] His words set the standard for how future evolutionists would view the world. Evolution does not teach that the world has "fallen." Evolutionists do not believe that the world was ever created to be perfect. They believe that a vacuum of nothingness evolved into chaos and chaos evolved into an orderly system. If the universe started out as nothing and began a process of gradually evolving, the logical conclusion would be that things are getting better.

Darwin also wrote, "The vigorous, the healthy, and the happy survive and multiply."[210] This means that all things will work in accord so that the individual, the species, or the general collective may progress into the next higher level: non-being into being; disorganized into organized; non-life into life; plant into animal; herbivore into carnivore; carnivore into human. It is the "natural" progression from the bottom of the ladder to the top. Nonetheless, humans still take a special seat in the creation order. After all, mankind is the pinnacle of evolutionary achievement.

---

[209] Darwin 2004, 168.

[210] Darwin 2004, 73.

In Stephen Hawking's *Life in the Universe* lecture, he traces the course of evolution up through human history, even into the future! He touts that humans are now totally unique from other animals because they have obtained the knowledge to guide their own evolutionary destiny. This is an excerpt from his lecture:

> An even greater limitation and danger for future generations, is that we still have the instincts, and in particular, the aggressive impulses, that we had in cave man days. Aggression, in the form of subjugating or killing other men, and taking their women and food, has had definite survival advantage, up to the present time. But now it could destroy the entire human race, and much of the rest of life on Earth. . .There is no time, to wait for Darwinian evolution, to make us more intelligent, and better natured. But we are now entering a new phase, of what might be called, self designed evolution, in which we will be able to change and improve our DNA. There is a project now on, to map the entire sequence of human DNA. It will cost a few billion dollars, but that is chicken feed, for a project of this importance. Once we have read the book of life, we will start writing in corrections. At first, these changes will be confined to the repair of genetic defects, like cystic fibrosis, and muscular dystrophy. These are controlled by single genes, and so are fairly easy to identify, and correct. Other qualities, such as intelligence, are probably controlled by a large number of genes. It will be much more difficult to find them, and work out the relations between them. Nevertheless, I am sure

> that during the next century, people will discover how to modify both intelligence, and instincts like aggression.[211]

Hawking believes that it is possible that mankind will cure and eliminate major diseases. Richard Dawkins shares a similar sentiment in *The God Delusion*:

> It is important not to mis-state the reach of natural selection. Selection does not favour the evolution of a cognitive awareness of what is good for your genes. That awareness had to wait for the twentieth century to reach a cognitive level, and even now full understanding is confined to a minority of scientific specialists.[212]

Mankind has never had such an incredible knowledge of its own genome as it does now. It almost seems that mankind's destiny is in its own hands from this point onward. Technology has enabled mankind to analyze the genetic code and it is the hope of many people that technology will also allow for the possibility of genetic modification. Such a miraculous development would be the single greatest achievement of the human race. Is it possible that the ills of society could be done away with through science?

Stephen Hawking, again in his "Life in the Universe" lecture, hypothesized about what would happen when mankind starts guiding its own evolutionary destiny.

---

[211] Stephen Hawking, "Life in the Universe," 1996, http://hawking.org.uk/index.php?option=com_content&view=article&id=65 (accessed July 16, 2011).

[212] Dawkins, 252.

Through much experimentation, many breakthroughs in the advancement of the human race would occur. Ultimately, he believes that a "super human" would emerge. This person would be immune to disease and other detriments brought upon by genetic defects. The quality of life of the first super human would be sought after by the entire world. But not everyone would be happy about such a development.

> Laws will be passed, against genetic engineering with humans. But some people won't be able to resist the temptation, to improve human characteristics, such as size of memory, resistance to disease, and length of life. Once such super humans appear, there are going to be major political problems, with the unimproved humans, who won't be able to compete. Presumably, they will die out, or become unimportant. Instead, there will be a race of self-designing beings, who are improving themselves at an ever-increasing rate.[213]

Efforts to create a race of super humans have been attempted. In the past one hundred years the eugenics movement has sought to bring out the true potential of the perfected human being. The eugenics movement occurred at a time in history when the Theory of Evolution had become popular. Darwin's cousin, Francis Galton, was the man who coined the term "eugenics."[214]

Galton was most famous for developing the statistical heredity-theory. Statistical heredity-theory

---

[213] Hawking, "Life in the Universe."

[214] Erik Nordenskiold, *The History of Biology* (New York: Tudor Publishing Co., 1935), 587.

arose from Galton's previous work to prove Darwin's pangenesis theory that sought to explain why offspring typically resemble their parents. After discovering that Darwin was incorrect in his pangenesis theory, Galton started examining the characteristics of many different families to draw conclusions regarding their inherited features, particularly height. His statistical method for analysing heredity in relation to the Theory of Evolution was popular and it was the first scientific method used to observe the evidence for evolution.[215]

His research concerning heredity gave rise to the notion that the characteristics of the next generation could be predicted based off of the characteristics of the parents. Galton believed so much in this notion that:

> He bequeathed his fortune to an institute for heredity research in London, which afterwards worked in accordance with the principles that he laid down. Galton had human welfare very much at heart; he wanted to create a better human race and desired that all research work should serve that object; he gave to the science that he placed highest of all that name of 'eugenics,' a name that has become universally accepted.[216]

The name "eugenics" was derived from the thought that promoting "good genes" could result in a "better" human race.

Regardless of science's good intentions, eugenics turned into a monstrous abomination that deprived many

[215] Nordenskiold, 585-586.

[216] Nordenskiold, 586-587.

individuals of human rights. "The cure-all proposed for genetic ills was sterilization."[217] During the early 1900's large numbers of people with perceived disabilities were sterilized against their will because of government mandates that sought to promote the greater good of humankind. Such exercises later evolved into Adolf Hitler's Holocaust, which aimed to create the perfect human race by eliminating genetic stragglers. Self-designed evolution is nothing more than the residue of the eugenics movement.

Both methods are mankind's attempt to manipulate the evolutionary process for the greater good of the human race. Eugenics sought to better mankind through calculated breeding. Self-designed evolution seeks to manipulate the genetic code. Does mankind, as it exists today, need to be improved in order to survive? Altering the DNA of an individual could result in more problems than it seeks to prevent.

Such an attempt would be accompanied by a bombardment of ethical questions. Who would determine the genetics of the "super" human? Would the superhuman have a long life or a short life? Would it be both strong and smart, or would this be a dangerous combination? Would the superhuman be asexual, or would the biological reproductive system be done away with in favour of growing humans in labs? Would defective specimens be discarded? Hawking is correct in saying that there would be much opposition in creating a superhuman through self-designed evolution. Even if a superhuman

---

[217] Bruce Wallace, *Topics in Population Genetics* (New York: W. W. Norton Company Inc., 1968), 164.

was created through human ingenuity, what would be the fate of the average person?

Through genetic experimentation, it is possible that the quality of life could improve. On the other hand, the value of life could decrease as a direct result. The scientific community needs to ask itself if it is opening Pandora's box. Mankind needs to be cautious when it boasts of its own greatness. The premise of the Fall was that a perfect creation made a horrible mistake and destroyed a world that was once deemed "good" by its Creator. The arrogance of mankind resulted in the Fall. Perhaps the illusion that mankind is making progress is setting it up for another Fall.

The Curse and Redemption

> So the LORD God said to the serpent, "Because you have done this, "Cursed are you above all livestock and all wild animals! You will crawl on your belly and you will eat dust all the days of your life. And I will put enmity between you and the woman, and between your offspring and hers; he will crush your head, and you will strike his heel." To the woman he said, "I will make your pains in childbearing very severe; with painful labor you will give birth to children. Your desire will be for your husband, and he will rule over you. " To Adam he said, "Because you listened to your wife and ate fruit from the tree about which I commanded you, 'You must not eat from it,' "Cursed is the ground because of you; through painful toil you will eat food from it all the days of your life. It will produce thorns and thistles for you,

> and you will eat the plants of the field. By the sweat of your brow you will eat your food until you return to the ground, since from it you were taken; for dust you are and to dust you will return."[218]

Genesis 3 describes a curse that was placed on the world as a result of Adam's disobedience to God's command. Of all of the chapters of the Bible this, indeed, is one of the darkest. The good world that God created only lasted for a portion of two chapters of the Bible and was immediately thrust into a dilemma that continues from Genesis 3 to Revelation 19. The good news is that it only endures until Revelation 19, because within the narrative of the curse there is also a glimmer of hope. Understanding the Fall and the curse helps one to understand how God intended to bring salvation to the fallen world.

In the Biblical account of the Fall, three creatures are specifically cursed: man, woman, and the serpent. They were cursed because they took part in the original act of sin. Serpents were made to crawl on their bellies and to be at odds with the offspring of the woman. Women were given an increase in birth pains and a longing for their husbands. Men were doomed to work the fields in order to produce food, and their crops would produce thorns to burden them as they tended and harvested them. The greatest consequence for their sin was that they ushered death into the world. On top of the fact that their lives would be full of suffering, their existence would be cut short because they would also die.

---

[218] Genesis 3:14-19.

The concept of death was not experienced until they disobeyed God. Sometime after their sin, Adam and Eve's firstborn son, Cain, killed their second born son, Abel. Afterward, Cain's descendant Lamech murdered a young man and boasted to his wives about his accomplishment. In Genesis 6:11 it is revealed that, immediately before the flood of Noah's day, "the earth was corrupt in God's sight and was full of violence." For nearly a thousand years Adam and Eve suffered through the curse and watched their offspring become wicked before they died. They were forbidden from taking the only cure for their condition, the fruit of the Tree of Life: "After he drove the man out, he placed on the east side of the Garden of Eden cherubim and a flaming sword flashing back and forth to guard the way to the tree of life."[219]

Why did God prohibit man from eating the fruit of the Tree of Life? The text states that if man were to eat from the Tree of Life he would live forever.[220] It was for the good of mankind that it was forbidden from eating the fruit of this tree. If man would have eaten from the Tree of Life, he would have to remain in sin forever. Death was the only way to separate man from his sinful flesh. Mankind would have been forever separated from God had he eaten from the Tree of Life.

In the book of Revelation, the Tree of Life appears in heaven. The fruit of the tree of life would give the person who eats from it eternal life. One day, those who follow God will be allowed to eat from the Tree of Life and they will live with God forever in an environment that is not

[219] Genesis 3:24.

[220] Genesis 3:22.

cursed by sin.[221] If mankind would have been allowed to eat from the Tree of Life in Genesis, it would not have been able to be reconciled to God. Adam, Eve, and the serpent brought sin into the world but deliverance from the curse was promised despite what happened.

The statement that "he will crush your head, and you will strike his heel"[222] was a prophecy. It predicted a day when the curse would be broken and Satan's power, the serpent's head, would be crushed. The Son of the woman would be the one to bring forth salvation. Christians believe that Jesus was the fulfillment of God's prophecy. In Isaiah 53, a servant was described that suffered for people's sins: "By oppression and judgment he was taken away. And who can speak of his descendants? For he was cut off from the land of the living; for the transgression of my people he was stricken."[223] The servant was stricken because he would have to bare the iniquity of his people. His life would be one filled with suffering and sorrow. He would face a bitter end. Thus, the curse of sin is like the bite of a poisonous snake. The suffering servant would crush the head of the serpent, but the serpent would strike his heal. "Surely he took up our infirmities and carried our sorrows, yet we considered him stricken by God, smitten by him, and afflicted. But he was pierced for our transgressions, he was crushed for our iniquities; the punishment that brought us peace was upon him, and by his wounds we are healed."[224] These

[221] Revelation 22:2-3.

[222] Genesis 3:15.

[223] Isaiah 53:8.

[224] Isaiah 53:4-5.

words were fulfilled in Jesus. From before the dawn of time he was appointed to be the one to carry the weight of sin and to heal mankind of its infirmities.

Currently, the world is still under a curse but the work of Jesus was accomplished to remove its power. God has planned a time when all things will be reconciled to him; the faithful people will be rewarded and the wicked will be punished. Jesus has already bought the world back from the clutches of Satan, but there is still a division between those who resist God's grace and receive it openly. Those that resist God's grace seek a peace that cannot be established. Jesus, the Messiah, is the only one who can truly bring peace.

Chapter 19
The Death of Adam

I am the first, but I will not be the last. I was there on the sixth day of creation, named all of the animals, and slept as God fashioned a woman out of my rib. I ate from the Tree of the Knowledge of Good and Evil and brought a horrible curse to the world. You may know me as the Father of Mankind. I am Adam. I am nearly a thousand years old and my strength has faded. My will is broken and I am ready to die. The world was different before the curse of death.

I remember the Garden of Eden. You cannot imagine the splendor of such a wonderful place. All creatures lived in harmony and food grew in abundance. Eve and I spoke with God as he travelled through the garden. We were together during the day and would labor hard. I did not fear work. I did not fear death. I did not fear God. I wish, now, that maybe we had a reason to fear God before the curse. It was for the lack of fear that we ate the tree's fruit. It was through the tempting of the serpent that we lost our trust in God. We were deceived by lies and are now paying the consequences.

I was present at the first sacrifice. God had to slay two animals and use their skin to cover the bodies of

Eve and me. The remains of the animals were laid upon stones as God consumed them with a mighty flame. It was horrifying! It was just the beginning of the terror we would experience. My wife has given birth to many children. Of them, we have wept over Abel the most.

Cain was our firstborn son. We anticipated his birth because God told us that a son would be born into the world that would rid it of the curse. With excitement we celebrated the birth of Cain and exalted him as the one who would become our savior. Then we had Abel.

Abel calmed the excitement that we had for Cain. We still loved both of them, but our love was split between these two children. Both were taught to honor God and both attempted to do so by bringing him offerings. Cain grew crops and Abel raised cattle.

Both of our children made sacrifices to God. But Cain became jealous of Abel because Abel's sacrifices were accepted by God. Cain did not give worthy sacrifices. God's standard for a sacrifice was high. No one could make just any old sacrifice; you had to give your best. In anger, Cain deceived Abel and killed him while they were alone in one of Cain's fields. Oh, the atrocities brought upon by sin!

No man's sorrow can exceed my own. Not only was my second born son murdered by his older brother, I have watched as all of my children have started murdering one another for the sake of making a name for themselves. Even worse, Eve, my wife, has passed. There is no end to my suffering!

She went before me and my heart has known no greater sorrow. Oh, Lord, take me now by the curse of death! I have no desire to live! If there is to be a Savior for this world, he will certainly wear a crown of thorns. There is only death and misery in this life. I pray that my children will find their way. Lord, help them to become a family again!

It is cold and it is dark. Let these be my final words: Adam, the son of God, now lays to rest. May the Lord of all creation have mercy upon all of my children and bring us once again to the place of our salvation.

Section 4
The Flood

Introduction

The Bible makes it clear that the world before the flood was in many ways unique to the world we live in today. The first six chapters of the Bible do not reveal a lot about what the world was like before the global flood. Nonetheless, many cultures have preserved stories of the pre-flood world that are now referred to as myths and legends. Do the myths and legends of other religions actually provide a description of what the world was like during the first six chapters of Genesis? Allow the stories to speak for themselves and let the reader decide if they are merely myths or valid testimonies.

Chapter 20
Men of Renown

And it came to pass, when men began to multiply on the face of the earth, and daughters were born unto them, that the sons of God saw the daughters of men that they were fair; and they took them wives of all which they chose. And the LORD said, my spirit shall not always strive with man, for that he also is flesh: yet his days shall be an hundred and twenty years. There were giants in the earth in those days; and also after that, when the sons of God came in unto the daughters of men, and they bare children to them, the same became mighty men which were of old, men of renown. And God saw that the wickedness of man was great in the earth, and that every imagination of the thoughts of his heart was only evil continually.[225]

Many ancient stories speak of giants that once existed on the earth. Nearly every story describes them as being incredibly strong, incredibly savage, and incredibly skilled in combat. It is hard to believe that such people existed, but many traditions teach that giants once

[225] KJV Genesis 6:1-5.

roamed the earth. If they were real, who or what were they? Chapter six of Genesis opens up by saying, "That the sons of God saw the daughters of men that they were fair."[226]

As a result, the sons of God took the daughters of men as wives and had children by them. "Sons of God" was an expression commonly used to refer to angelic beings and the most common interpretation of this passage is that certain angels took upon human wives. The action of taking on human wives and having children through them was abominable in God's sight and warranted punishment. Many scholars believe that verses like 2 Peter 2:4 and Jude 6 describe the imprisonment of these adulterous angels. Genesis 6:4 describes their offspring: "There were giants in the earth in those days." In its original language the word for giants was *nephilim*.

The *nephilim* were a crossbreed between humans and angels. Apparently they were a freakish race. In the book of Numbers, a race that was referred to as the Nephilim existed in Canaan. They were the reason the Israelites were afraid of taking hold of the Promised Land:

> The land through which we have gone to search it, is a land that eateth up the inhabitants thereof; and all the people that we saw in it are men of a great stature. And there we saw the giants, the sons of Anak, which come of the giants: and we were in our own sight as grasshoppers, and so we were in their sight.[227]

---

[226] KJV Genesis 6:2.

[227] Numbers 13:32-33, KJV.

The Hebrew word used here was, again, Nephilim. A more vivid description exists in this context to give the reader an idea of what Nephilim were. According to this description, Nephilim were men of great stature. An average sized man would be dwarfed in comparison to one of them. They were so remarkable in those days that the Bible testifies that they were the ones that the legends of old were about.

The idea that there were mighty men and giants in the pre-flood world was not exclusively written about in the Bible. Other ancient sources described men of valor that were giants in their time, before the flood. Some of the stories sound significantly more embellished than others. That is not to say that they are necessarily fictional because the pre-flood world was significantly different from the current world. Despite the more fantastic stories of a past race of giants, there are some legends that preserve the memory of such people in a more sober manner. One of the most obvious, in relation to the Biblical text, has gone down in history as a classical literary piece. It is called *Beowulf.*

Beowulf

Beowulf is an epic about a mighty king named Beowulf. Beowulf was a warrior who was capable of accomplishing extraordinary feats of strength and heroism. Aside from its status as one of the greatest epics of all time, it also has some of the most fascinating things to say about the pre-flood world. The most interesting thing about this account was it was written in a culture that was not Christian and not Jewish, yet it referenced a great flood that exterminated a race of mighty giants that existed before the flood.

Beowulf is a historic figure, but many of the details of his epic story are considered to be purely fictional. But because of the authenticity of some of the more historic elements of the story, critics have had to develop explanations to account for Beowulf's fame for slaying certain creatures that are supposed to be mythological.

In this poem, Beowulf entered the land of the Danes and was entrusted with the task of slaying a horrendous beast known as Grendel. He defeated Grendel, but Grendel's mother became enraged. She crept into their villages and wreaked havoc against the Danes. Beowulf then embarked on a quest to hunt down Grendel's mother and slay her. As Beowulf struggled with Grendel's mother, his trusty sword was having no success in penetrating her tough hide.

Fortunately, a break in the action allowed him to discover an ancient relic that would aide him in defeating her: "Then he saw a blade that boded well, a sword in her armory, an ancient heirloom from the days of the giants, an ideal weapon, one that any warrior would envy, but so huge and heavy of itself only Beowulf could wield it in a battle."[228] Whether or not such a weapon truly existed in those days is irrelevant. The statement being made indicates that this culture believed that giants once roamed the earth. If this was referencing the era before the Biblical flood account it was no doubt referring to the Nephilim. The size of the blade, according to this epic, was so large that only the great warrior, Beowulf, was able to wield it and defeat Grendel's mother.

---

[228] Seamus Heaney, *Beowulf* (New York: W.W. Norton & Company, 1987), 108-109.

After slaying the beast, the sword melted because it was spattered in the blood spilt from Grendel's mother. Beowulf brought the hilt of the sword to the king who was waiting for his return.

> Hrothgar spoke; he examined the hilt, that relic of old times. It was engraved all over and showed how war first came into the world and the flood destroyed the tribe of giants. They suffered a terrible severance from the Lord; the Almighty made the waters rise, drowned them in the deluge for retribution.[229]

Not only is it revealed that a tribe of giants used to exist, they existed before a great flood which the Lord caused at a time when war first entered the world. God, in his anger, decided to flood the world to end the wickedness of the Nephilim.

Beowulf testifies of the ancient giants. The mighty warrior-king never encountered any, but his poem claims he used one of their weapons. This weapon supposedly contained a history that revealed wonderful mysteries of the past. The details of the story sound very similar to the Biblical flood account. The giants that brought war into the world were no doubt the Nephilim and they were judged by God through the worldwide flood. Whether or not Beowulf truly discovered a sword that was manufactured by the Nephilim is of no consequence. At the very least, it shows that the author of *Beowulf* believed that giants used to exist.

---

[229] Heaney, 117.

Polyphemus: the Cyclops

Other giants exist throughout mythology, but few, if any, are as popular as the Cyclops in Greek mythology. A Cyclops is a creature that resembles a human but is bigger, stronger, more savage, and has only one eye. They were believed to be an ancient race that existed among the earliest of the world's creations: "All the monstrous forms of life which were first created, the hundred-handed creatures, the Giants, and so on, were permanently banished from the earth when they had been conquered, with the single exception for the Cyclopes."[230] It was not known why Zeus favored them, but for some reason he admired their work ethic and appreciated them because they helped him forge his lightning bolts.[231]

Nonetheless, they were savage beasts. Because of that, it was believed that they had to be secluded to an island by themselves. "Their fierceness and savage temper, however, did not grow less; they had no laws or courts of justice, but each one did as he pleased. It was not a good country for strangers."[232] Heinous acts are often correlated to a lack of governance. People left to their own devices were expected to become nothing more than barbarians. The Cyclopes became even more so since they were already unruly. They were a reminder to the Roman world of how law distinguished mankind from savage beasts. Since the Cyclopes were secluded to their own land, they were ungoverned by the rule of

---

[230] Hamilton, 85.

[231] Hamilton, 85.

[232] Hamilton, 85.

the gods or kings. They behaved as they pleased, which created a land of terror. The environment of an island of lawlessness, giants, savages, and danger, however, was the perfect place for a band of unfortunate sailors to become stranded for the sake of forging a story of gratuitous entertainment.

The most well-known role of a Cyclops was in Homer's *Odyssey*. They encountered a Cyclops by the name of Polyphemus. Before Odysseus' encounter with Polyphemus, it was revealed that the abominable Cyclops was the son of the god Poseidon. Poseidon was the god of the seas and the brother of Zeus.[233] Despite the horrors Polyphemus wreaked upon his victims, harming him would result in great misfortune because of his divine heritage.

It was made known in this tale that Odysseus and his men broke into Polyphemus' cave to loot it of certain goods that they needed for their journey. Instead of immediately leaving after getting what they wanted, they decided to stick around to see if the owner of the cave would offer them a hospitality gift. The Greeks were well-known for their cunning and deceptive natures, and hosts in those days were expected to offer hospitality to strangers. Upon the owner's arrival, Odysseus regretted the decision to remain in the cave because the owner was, "a freak of nature, not like men who eat bread, but like a lone wooded crag high in the mountains."[234] Everything about Polyphemus was awful. They attempted to scare him by reminding him that Zeus protected strangers from those who would cause them harm. The threat did not scare Polyphemus. He did

[233] Stanley Lombardo, *The Essential Homer* (Indianapolis: Hackett Publishing, 2000), 243.

[234] Lombardo, 303.

not fear the gods; he believed that he was stronger than them. He proved his lack of concern by scooping up two of Odysseus' crewmen, one in each hand, smashing them on the ground, and eating them.[235]

Yet, Polyphemus did have a weakness. Odysseus and his men managed to escape by hoarding up all of the fine wine that they could find inside of his home and intoxicating him. After they presented their gift of wine, the impaired Cyclops believed that these doomed sailors were just being good losers. Eventually he passed out because of his alcohol consumption and they poked out his eye. As the story goes on, Polyphemus cries out to his father Poseidon, who hears him. He demanded that Poseidon avenge him. The vengeful lord of the sea complied with the request and proceeded to make life miserable for Odysseus for a long time.

Certain elements in this story may actually reckon back to the memory of the Nephilim. For instance, Polyphemus was a physical descendant of a spiritual being, namely Poseidon. If the Nephilim were physical descendants of the spiritual angels, is it possible that maybe some of them were as freakish as Polyphemus? Could it be that the character of Polyphemus was a reconstruction of the tales of the pre-flood world concerning the giants that once existed? In other stories the pre-flood world humans were more savage, less considerate, and desired only to fill their immediate passions. Polyphemus embodied all of these characteristics. In fact, after Odysseus managed to get him drunk, Polyphemus

[235] Lombardo, 305-306.

expressed his gratitude by telling him that he liked him and he would eat him last as a favor.[236]

There may not have been any real Cyclopes, but perhaps the invention of the Cyclops of mythology was a recollection of the existence of the Nephilim. There are many accounts of humans that exceeded the size limits of average people. Maybe the Cyclops was a way of reminding the ancient world that people used to be bigger and fiercer. Despite the physical advantages spoken of regarding the Cyclopes and Nephilim, their strength was not enough to spare them from their fates. The Cyclopes lived in a land where they were not governed by the laws of men or by the gods. The Nephilim lived at a time that predated the giving of the Law of Moses. Both lived in lawless irreverence toward God and both met a horrible demise. So has it been for every culture that has departed God's ways to pursue lawlessness.

Lycaon

The Greek world believed that mankind was to blame for the Flood. The *coup de gras* of human wickedness was a king named Lycaon. Lycaon was known to be brutally violent and possibly more animal than he was human:

> When Jove from his high seat looked down on earth he sighed aloud: he thought of Lycaon's altar of human flesh, of incident too recent to be well known. . .All who heard trembled and with anxious lips asked who was Lycaon, what breed was he?. . .So Jove

[236] Lombardo, 308.

> was pleased by the anger of his gods. He waved for silence with an easy hand; their murmuring ceased and he resumed his lecture "Lycaon met his fate; here is my story. . .I stepped across rough threshold where Lycaon, bitter tyrant of Arcadian wildness, lived. I raised my hand; peasant and shepherd fell before me to offer prayers at which insane Lycaon looking at them and me began to roar, 'Soon we shall know if this is god or man; I shall have proof of its divinity.' The proof was simple. When I had feasted (So he planned) and heavily asleep, lifted to bed, he hoped to murder me. Nor was this scheme enough; he took a Northern hostage from a cell, slit the poor devilish monster's throat and tossed his warm and bleeding vitals in a pot; the rest he roasted. This was the dinner that he put before me. My thunderbolt struck the king's house to ruins, and he, wild master, ran like beast to field crying his terror which cannot utter words but howls in fear, his foaming lips and jaws, quick with the thought of blood, harry the sheep. His cloak turned into bristling hair, his arms were fore-legs of a wolf, yet he resembled himself, what he had been – the violent grey hair, face, eyes, the ceaseless, restless stare of drunken tyranny and hopeless hate. His house has fallen; others shall follow him; far as the earth reaches. . .[237]

Lycaon was not a giant nor was he the offspring of a god or an angel, but his wickedness was the cause of the flood. Lycaon committed heinous crimes against his fellow man

---

[237] Gregory, 35-37.

and Jove, also known as Zeus. He offered Jove a feast that was composed of roasted human remains, and he had plotted to murder him. Jove was offended. Lycaon's morality had degenerated so far beyond that of any human that he would not even abstain from offending a guest. In the Greek world, such an offense was taboo. To make matters worse, Lycaon suspected that his guest was divine before he proceeded to offend him. This king was so wicked that he could literally take upon the form of a savage beast.

The ancient Greeks highly valued the physical appearance of humans. They believed that man was fashioned in the likeness of the gods. To be transformed into an animal by the gods was a tragic fate. Lycaon's image was altered as he ran away from a furious Jove. In Greek mythology, the gods often transformed certain humans into different creatures. Typically the transformation of a person was a punishment. Losing one's human appearance humiliated the offender for having committed some sort of unholy offense. In this instance, it did not appear that Zeus's condemnation was what caused Lycaon's metamorphosis. Instead, it seemed as though Lycaon's nature was so divergent from that of a human that he could willfully transform into a beast. His beastly nature was the final straw; Jove condemned the entire world because of him.

The Greek tale of Lycaon and the Biblical pre-flood world of the Nephilim expressed the wickedness of the human race before the judgment of the flood. Lycaon had gone so far astray from his humanity that he had the appearance of an animal. The Nephilim were an expression of the wickedness of all creation, as even the angels were committing adultery with the physical world. The form of mankind was tarnished by the interbreeding of the heavenly host with the daughters of men. Nonetheless, in the Biblical pre-flood world God displayed grace to one individual who remained faithful to him. In the story of Lycaon, it was the individual who sealed the fate of the world. Where the God of the Bible spared an individual despite the wickedness of the entire world, Jove condemned the entire world because of the wickedness of one man.

The theological differences between these stories are astounding. Jove, in the Greek story, had been revered by the majority of the people, but was offended greatly by one individual and chose to judge everyone. The God of the Bible was offended at the irreverence of the entire world but extended his grace to one lowly mortal who gave him praise. The Greek gods acted more like petty mortals by condemning the entire world for the sake of one obscenely wicked king. The God of the Bible judged the wicked world righteously. And yet, his personal nature was expressed in the mercy that he showed to one man who, for all that can be known, may have been a nobody. In either case, the world was judged for the sake of its wickedness.

Although Lycaon was not a giant, he was symbolic of the wickedness that existed before the flood. Not only was he deranged beyond comprehension, he could literally transform into a savage beast. A distinct difference between the gods of mythology and the God of the Bible is revealed in this narrative. The Greek gods could judge the world for the sake of one man, while the God of the Bible judges each person for his or her own sins. Wickedness is never ignored, but the gods should be judged for the sake that they condemn the innocent along with the guilty.

The Fate of the Nephilim

The Nephilim were wicked and full of pride. They waged war against mortal enemies and created a world full of turmoil. Not only did they descend from heavenly ranks in an abominable manner, but their nature reflected the character of the perverse angels that took human women for wives. They ran a course of self-destruction. They were already engaged in self-extermination through war mongering, but God saw their evil deeds and judged them. He was displeased with how the world was becoming a place of evil. Mankind was meant to reflect his image and it was acting against his good nature. As their Creator, he chose a fate worthy of their deeds.

Collective judgment was something the world never experienced until that time in history. Adam and Eve were judged in Eden for their sin and Cain was judged for killing his brother Abel, but their judgments were isolated and contained elements of grace. The only grace that God displayed through his worldwide judgment was to preserve certain representatives of the animal kingdom and one human family. God commanded a man to build an enormous ark, because he was going to cover the world in water.

Chapter 21
The Great Flood

The LORD saw how great the wickedness of the human race had become on the earth, and that every inclination of the thoughts of the human heart was only evil all the time. The LORD regretted that he had made human beings on the earth, and his heart was deeply troubled. So the LORD said, "I will wipe from the face of the earth the human race I have created—and with them the animals, the birds and the creatures that move along the ground—for I regret that I have made them." But Noah found favor in the eyes of the LORD. . .

In the six hundredth year of Noah's life, on the seventeenth day of the second month — on that day all the springs of the great deep burst forth, and the floodgates of the heavens were opened. And rain fell on the earth forty days and forty nights. On that very day Noah and his sons, Shem, Ham and Japheth, together with his wife and the wives of his three sons, entered the ark. They had with them every wild animal according to its kind, all livestock according to their kinds, every creature that moves along the ground according to its kind and every bird according to its kind, everything with wings. Pairs of all creatures that have the breath of life in them came to Noah and entered the ark. The animals going in were male and female of every living thing, as God had commanded Noah. Then the LORD shut him in. For forty days the flood kept coming on the earth, and as the waters increased they lifted the ark high above the earth. The waters rose and increased greatly on the earth, and the ark floated on the surface of the water. They rose greatly on the earth, and all the high mountains under the entire heavens were covered. The waters rose and covered the mountains to a depth of more than fifteen cubits. Every living thing that moved on land perished—birds, livestock, wild animals, all the creatures that swarm over the earth, and all mankind. Everything on dry land that had the breath of life in its nostrils died. Every living thing on the face of the earth was wiped out; people and animals and the creatures that move along the ground and the birds were wiped from the earth. Only Noah was left, and those with him in the ark. The waters flooded the earth for a hundred and fifty days. . .

By the twenty-seventh day of the second month the earth was completely dry. Then God said to Noah, "Come out of the ark, you and your wife and your sons and their wives.[238]

Noah's Ark is the most well-known of the flood stories among the different cultures of the world.

[238] Genesis 6:5-8, 7:11-24, 8:14-16.

It contains elements of tragedy, mercy, grace, wrath, law, and love. Most people that are familiar with the story of Noah's Ark are familiar with the general idea of the Biblical flood account: God saw that the world had become horribly wicked and so he commanded the only righteous man alive, Noah, to place all of the animals, one male and one female of each, onto a gigantic boat-like structure known as an ark. Popular knowledge of the story oversimplifies some of the finer details of the account of Noah's ark.

The Bible goes into great depth concerning the details of God's commands to Noah regarding the building of the ark and the animals it would carry. The building of the ark had to be accomplished in a manner that honored God's exact specifications. The New International Version of the Bible says that the ark was to be made of cypress wood and was supposed to be coated with pitch, both inside and out. The ark was supposed to be four hundred fifty feet long, seventy five feet wide, forty five feet high, and the entire vessel was to be finished all the way up to eighteen inches from its top. To cap it all off, God told Noah to include a door on the side of the ark as well as multiple decks.[239] The specifications that God gave to Noah for building the ark were meant to prepare it for the task of safely housing the people and animals on board from the ravages of the flood.

Most people believe that the animals in Noah's ark went aboard two by two, but that was not the case with every kind of animal. Different animals were to be stocked in different quantities. God told Noah, "Take

[239] Genesis 6:14-16.

with you seven of every kind of clean animal, a male and its mate, and two of every kind of unclean animal, a male and its mate, and also seven of every kind of bird, male and female, to keep their various kinds alive throughout the earth."[240] The distinction between clean and unclean animals precedes the Law that was given to Moses in Exodus, Leviticus, Numbers, and Deuteronomy that give precise definitions of what was meant by "clean." How could there have been a distinction between clean and unclean animals before the Law provided a definition? The clear answer to such a question is that the Law existed even before its dictation. In other words, the Law is a result of creation. Jesus declared in the New Testament, "I tell you the truth, until heaven and earth disappear, not the smallest letter, not the least stroke of a pen, will by any means disappear from the Law until everything is accomplished."[241] Carrying more clean animals than unclean animals was in compliance to the Law which already existed and would serve as a foreshadowing of the Law which would later be declared.

The inclusion of both clean and unclean animals in the ark served two purposes. The immediate purpose was for the sake of presenting a sacrifice to God once the ark rested on dry ground. Genesis 8:20 reads, "Then Noah built an altar to the Lord and, taking some of all the clean animals and clean birds, he sacrificed burnt offerings on it." This was not the first example of sacrifice mentioned in the Old Testament. Long before Noah was born, Cain and Abel, the first sons of Adam and Eve, presented sacrifices before

[240] Genesis 7:2-3.

[241] Matthew 5:18.

God. Abel's sacrifice was pleasing to God, but Cain's was not. Because Cain's sacrifices did not earn him favor with God, he murdered his brother Abel.[242] The exact specifications concerning what sort of sacrifices would please God was not specifically written out until Moses recorded God's words in the book of Exodus.

The second purpose for the abundance of clean animals in the ark was for the sake of having food after the flood. Genesis 9:3 commands, "Everything that lives and moves will be food for you. Just as I gave you the green plants, I now give you everything." Even though God commanded that mankind could eat everything that lived and moved, he was setting the stage for the Law to specify to the Israelites which animals were clean and which ones were not. Since not all of the animals on the ark were "clean" it would not make sense to feed upon the ones that were "unclean." Leviticus 12, for example, goes into detail concerning this distinction. A change in mankind's diet was fitting at such a point in history, as the world was experiencing the dawn of a new era.

The flood in the Bible was responsible for a dramatic shift in the course of history. Wickedness prevailed throughout the earth and mankind had become so evil that God was grieved. By his righteous judgment he determined that it was best to destroy those who were wicked and preserve those who were righteous. Eight humans were preserved to repopulate the earth: Noah, his wife, and his three sons with their wives. Although the extermination of the human race was an act of judgment, God remained gracious by sparing a remnant.

---

[242] Genesis 4:5.

After Noah and his family departed from the ark, God saw that the intentions of men's hearts were evil, even from the day of their birth.

One of the first events after the flood story was the drunkenness of Noah. Noah planted a vineyard and became drunk off of its wine. Noah's son, Shem, discovered him naked and unconscious inside of his vineyard. In an attempt to humiliate his father, Shem found his brothers and brought them to see him in his undignified state.[243] Sin continued to exist in the world even though God had cleansed it of those who were evil.

At the end of Noah's story, it was clear that the world was still in a bad position. If sin still existed, judgment could once again be executed. So God placed a rainbow in the sky, for the first time ever, to remind humankind that he would never again bring about a flood that would consume the entire world.[244] The rainbow symbolized grace. Even though God knew mankind was still inclined toward wickedness, he would be slow to anger.[245] The world was still in need of a savior, but God's covenant with Noah after the flood insured that he had something special in store for mankind.

Gilgamesh and Utnapishtim

The flood story of Gilgamesh is one of the most popular outside of the Biblical flood account. It is a legend about the Near Eastern king, Gilgamesh. Throughout this

---

243 Genesis 9:18-23.

244 Genesis 9:13.

245 Genesis 8:21.

epic, Gilgamesh seeks to obtain eternal life. Within this legend is a story of a flood that devastated the earth in the days of one of Gilgamesh's ancestors, Utnapishtim. Despite the fact that there are some significant differences between Noah's ark and Gilgamesh's flood, it is very important to notice the many similarities.

Gilgamesh encounters one of his most ancient ancestors and upon their encounter, Utnapishtim recounted a time when he had to construct a mighty sea vessel.[246] He recalled of the vessel, "The floor was 200 ft. square. . .the walls were 200 ft. high" and it was divided into six floors. He then explained that he had to load a sample of all living things onto his boat. After the boat was constructed a great storm hit and a flood covered the world. Everything caught up in the flood was killed and the ground was flattened.[247] The god Adad was the one responsible for the catastrophe. The people of the earth had created such a racket that Adad's rage prompted him to send a flood to wipe out the entire world's population. Utnapishtim caught wind of the god's plan to flood the world and loaded a sample of all living creatures onto his boat. As a result, life would be preserved and have a new beginning. In many ways Utnapishtim's story resembles that of the Genesis flood. The story of Gilgamesh contains some remarkable details that have convinced many to believe that there is more to this story than what meets the eye.

Certain experts have examined evidence in the region where Utnapishtim's story took place and have concluded that the flood in Gilgamesh's epic was local

[246] Werner Keller, *The Bible As History* (New York: Bantam Books, 1982), 33.

[247] Werner, 34-35.

to that region and not really global. Because of the great age of the Babylonian writings it has become popular to believe that it is the original flood story! If this claim is true, the Biblical account and other retellings would be forgeries of Utnapishtim's story. In his book *The Bible As History,* Werner Keller made the case that the Bible and the story of Gilgamesh described the same event and that the flood was indeed a local occurrence. However, the term "local" might be a little misleading. Keller believed that this was still an extraordinary event. He wrote, "According to Woolley the disaster engulfed an area north-west of the Persian Gulf amounting to 400 miles long and 100 miles wide. . .we should call it 'a local occurrence'-for the inhabitants of the river plains it was however in those days their whole world."[248] The flood Keller believes in was still enormous, but it was not a worldwide flood.

Keller mused at the incredible description of the Babylonian account: "Only someone who had himself seen the desolation caused by the catastrophe could have described it with such striking force."[249] To him, the ones who were described as "the gods" in Gilgamesh, the ones who escaped to the mountains, behaved too much like humans to be divine. Therefore, these gods were really humans that evacuated to the mountaintops in an attempt to escape the wrath of the flood.[250] The foundation for this theory involves geologic evidence that a tsunami covered a 400 mile span between 4000-

---

[248] Werner, 28.

[249] Werner, 35.

[250] Werner, 34.

2900 B.C. In 1929 A.D., an archaeological dig took place to investigate the mass tomb of Sumerian kings discovered at Tel al-Muqayyar. As they dug deeper and deeper they discovered an enormous clay deposit which they claimed could only be explained by a great flood. Because Utnapishtim's story was set in this region, it is only rational to conclude that his was the authentic and original flood account. Such evidence proves that the flood could not have been global, but a massive local flood.[251] But is there truly enough evidence to validate the claim that Gilgamesh contains the original flood story?

Anything is possible, but proponents of this view neglect geologic evidence that suggests that there was a worldwide flood. Fossils of ancient sea creatures across the world in areas that are no longer covered by water suggest that parts of the world used to be flooded. Of course, the possibility of a worldwide flood is never considered by scientists with old earth presuppositions. Considering global evidence of a flood, the geological date for a flood in that region between 4000-2900 B.C. could be erroneous. Not only do proponents of Gilgamesh's authenticity neglect global geologic data, they also neglect manuscripts that predate the writing of Gilgamesh's flood story.

It is doubtful that the flood account of Gilgamesh was original. The Sumerians and Amorites also had flood accounts. The Sumerians' account may date back to as early as 2000 B.C. and they may have had several versions of the flood story. The Amorites would have had closer connections to Abram, the Biblical patriarch, and their

[251] Werner, 23, 27-29.

account may predate Gilgamesh's record of the flood, as well. This would explain the similarities in the flood traditions and would cause serious problems for people that claim that the Gilgamesh epic's flood was the original.[252]

The detailed description of the devastation caused by the flood could be accounted for because there *were* eyewitnesses present to oversee the entire event. These people were Noah and his family. Noah and his family were recorded in the Bible as being the only surviving humans after the devastation of the flood. Naturally, they would have passed the flood tradition down to the next generation to commemorate God's great judgment on the world. The passing down of this tradition could have been done orally or by written record; it is evidenced that writing may have existed before the flood since detailed genealogies were kept. Either tradition, oral or written, would not be 100% necessary in light that the Bible is not just a compilation of written documents or recorded oral traditions, but is the inspired Word of God. Despite the age of any written document it must be assumed, if one takes the Bible seriously, that the Bible provides the only reliable account in regards to how the flood really happened.[253] If geologic evidence is considered to determine that there was a flood in Mesopotamia between 4000-2900 B.C., which correlates with the Gilgamesh epic, why is the global geologic evidence ignored regarding an even greater flood? The geologic column is a remarkable testimony to the catastrophic destruction caused by the great flood in the days of Noah. There would be several explanations to the clay deposits in Tel al-Muqayyar if this were considered.

---

[252] Morris and Whitcomb, 38.

[253] Morris and Whitcomb, 41.

One possibility is that an enormous flood, that was not global, occurred in Mesopotamia. In the Bible, God promised not to extinguish all of life by a flood again. Since that time there have still been floods. In New Orleans in 2005, hurricane Katrina caused massive devastation and flooding. In India, Haiti, and Japan tsunamis have more recently been recorded to claim hundreds of lives. This sort of occurrence happens on a fairly regular basis around the world. Floods and flood catastrophes are not rare occurrences, even in modern times. But, the flood account of legend has yet to be matched by those of our modern records.

It is also possible that Gilgamesh's flood relates to the Genesis flood account, geologically speaking. It may appear different in some regards, but the global flood was catastrophic and should not necessarily be expected to conform to any uniform process. Even though certain pieces of geologic data may suggest that there was a catastrophic local flood, it would still be possible that this flooding was part of the global flood recorded in Genesis. Aside from the evidence of whether or not Gilgamesh's flood was local or global, the Babylonian and Biblical stories contain a serious theological difference.

The God of the Bible and the gods of Gilgamesh's flood are distinctly different. The God of the Bible, for instance, chose to judge the world for different reasons than those of Adad.[254]

> Utnapishtim describes to him [Gilgamesh] how the gods were angry and they decided, for no moral reason that they would destroy mankind.

---

[254] Staats 2010, 13.

> Outside of his hut, Utnapishtim heard these words, "reed hut, reed hut, go build a boat." It appears that one of the gods had squealed and had brought that word to Utnapishtim, because the gods had decided, arbitrarily to destroy the whole human race. . .The gods had been terrified by the storm they had created because it developed beyond their control. They finally came down after the flood like hungry flies upon a sacrifice that was made because they were so hungry. In a week's time, they needed to be fed. . .
>
> . . .God did not decide to arbitrarily destroy the earth, but He, because of the violence that was going on, had to bring judgment. Yet, He would go to all the trouble to reveal to a righteous Noah and his family, the judgment coming because of His goodness and grace. He would do all of this for one man. This flood lasted, not for a week, but for a little over a year and when Noah came out, the Lord did not have to descend upon the sacrifice as a fly, but he accepted it as a beautiful act of worship to Him (Gen. 8:21-22). It is striking that when we compare the Ancient Near East with the Biblical account of the flood, that we see the mercy of God over against the arbitrariness of the gods.[255]

The gods of the Babylonian myth were devious. They attempted to keep the flood a secret so that no one would be spared. Utnapishtim stumbled across the news of the flood because of a leak in information from the gods.

---

[255] Staats 2010, 12-13.

The God of the Bible made it clear to Noah that God would bring about a great flood and even outlined the dimensions of the vessel that Noah was to build to save his family and the creatures of the earth. The God of the Bible was displayed as being a God of mercy and grace, even though his hand was forced to judge the entire world. The Babylonian gods begrudged mankind for petty reasons and brought about a global catastrophe that was intended to kill every living thing on earth.

It is quite likely that the flood described in Gilgamesh and the one described in Genesis are the same event. Nonetheless many scholars have, for whatever reason, decided to side with skeptics and concede that the Biblical account is not the original account of the flood. This is erroneous and foolish. If the Bible is the Word of God, it understands the events of the past better than secular scholars. If Gilgamesh is correct regarding the flood, should we also claim it has historic credibility regarding the gods? If one accepts an alternative account of the flood as truth, he or she might as well start worshiping the gods of that tradition.

Deucalion: Greek Flood Myth

There is a Greek flood myth that is certainly one that is noteworthy when reflecting upon the Biblical flood account. The remarkable similarities between the Greek flood and the Biblical flood are astonishing. The selected portion of this myth follows in sequence after Jove returned from among the mortals to tell the other gods of how wicked mankind had become.

> I had heard evil rumours of mankind and with the hope of proving them untrue I stepped down from Olympus incognito, no longer Jovian but extremely human, a traveler walking up and down the world. It takes too long to list the crimes I saw – rumours were less amazing than the truth. . .All men have joined in Hell's conspiracy since I have said it: all shall pay the toll of early death – and earth an early fall. . .[256]

No one resisted the temptation to accomplish evil, according to Jove's account. All humans set their hearts upon accomplishing evil and the god among them was disgusted by their lust for wickedness. Even though king Lycaon was the one who pushed Jove over the edge and convinced him of mankind's wickedness, sin was prevalent enough that the whole world could have been judged, aside from the lewd actions of Lycaon. This is consistent with what the Bible says concerning the pre-flood world in that it condemns the actions and intentions of mankind before the flood. Genesis 6:5 states, "The LORD saw how great man's wickedness on the earth had become, and that every inclination of the thoughts of his heart was only evil all the time." It brought God to the point where he finally said, "My Spirit will not contend with man forever, for he is mortal; his days will be a hundred and twenty years."[257] Ancient man was aware of the wickedness of the former world.

The only action that could correct these hopelessly corrupted people was judgment from a righteous God.

---

[256] Gregory, 36.

[257] Genesis 6:3.

Both accounts reveal that the minds of humans were set on evil. Their nature was transformed from that which was good into something that felt no inclination to do what was right. It was not just the fact that people were doing wicked things; mankind had no intention whatsoever of doing what was right in God's eyes. Nonetheless, a contingent of the Greeks showed reverence toward Jove upon his visitation. The goodwill of these people did not spare them from a wrath filled judgment.

> He planned a breed of men of heaven's make, different in spirit, better than the first. . .Then Jove raised thunderbolt against the earth – and checked the blow. . .Another doom for man came to his mind a death that stormed beneath the waves, and fell from air; and then dark rain began to fall. . .And as rain fell Iris, handmaid of Juno, In rainbow dress drew water from the earth's streams replenishing the clouds. Nor did rain cease. Nor was Jove's rage appeased by pouring heavens. Neptune arrived with armies of the waters, rivers assembled at his ocean's floor to hear his orders: "The hour is all short for long orations, open your locks and dykes, your streaming walls, and springs, unleash the horses riding in foam through waterfalls and waves." At his command the mouths of fountains opened racing their mountain waters to the sea. . .And almost every being that breathed on earth drowned as it met the flood; those who survived died of starvation on the shores of mountains. . .There in a little boat young Deucalion and his bride sailed to the

> mountaintop that now was island and stepped ashore. Their first thought was to pray. . .[258]

Defective people were exterminated to make way for a better breed of person. At the end of the flood a young man, named Deucalion, was noted to have survived along with his wife. It is difficult to determine whether or not he was supposed to be spared, because the story remains silent concerning his whereabouts, character, or favor from the gods. Jove clearly had a plan, but one cannot easily deduce the details of his plan. The gods did not appear to be mindful of any life forms throughout the horror of the catastrophe they wrought. Mercy was not at the forefront of the gods' minds after Jove had been offended by Lycaon and mankind.

Jove's decision to exterminate life was impulsive. The human race's judgment was sealed as a result of one man's horrific actions. Instead of looking over Lycaon's evil and recognizing the reverence of others, they had to get back at their offender. The lowlier people continued to worship Jove when he was on earth but their praise, at this point, meant nothing. The poor were nothing more than second class citizens. So even though the shepherds worshipped Jove, he did not spare them from the fate of the world. They were not worthy of his grace. This was a serious difference between Greek and Hebrew ideology.

The Bible never mentions Noah's status on earth and it does not mention anyone else's around this time, "But Noah found favor in the eyes of the LORD."[259] God

[258] Gregory, 37-39.

[259] Genesis 6:8.

clearly spelled out his plan to deliver his chosen person from catastrophe. A similar example of God's grace was displayed later in Genesis when God delivered Lot from the destruction of Sodom and Gomorrah. God's character is consistent throughout the entire Bible. He preserved those who honored him, despite the world's wickedness. Jove did not express this type of favor toward those who praised him on earth. For all the reader knows, Deucalion may have been an accident.

Deucalion was never mentioned as being an exception to the world's wickedness, nor did Jove state that "Deucalion has found favor in my sight" like God said of Noah. He was only accepted because of the sacrifice he made to the gods after the world had already been destroyed! It is possible that this story expresses that the gods do not always get their way. It is possible that Deucalion was a chosen vessel to accomplish the propagation of a new breed of man, but the story is not very clear regarding the true intention of the gods. The God of the Bible judged mankind because of the accumulation of sins over a span of time. Afterward, he promised Noah that he would never again flood the world. Deucalion's ability to elude the flood appeared to be more out of luck than of providence. In the case of Noah, God's hand guided and preserved him for the years to come.

Mercy was an afterthought to the Greek gods. They hated the wickedness of the human race enough to overlook any sort of goodwill toward Jove. The kind intentions of the weak and lowly were of no avail due to the wicked actions of their despicable king. One man and his wife happened to survive this catastrophe and appease the gods by remembering them through a sacrifice. The gods of the Greek myth operated on a system of instant gratification that was not much unlike the humans that they judged and destroyed.

Navajo Flood Myth

Dine Bahane is the Navajo creation myth. There are no people present in its flood story and God is not mentioned. The "Air-Spirit People" (the birds and insects) are the main focus of this flood myth. Yet it is very interesting that a flood story exists in the Western hemisphere. The flood stories of eastern cultures are theorized to have emerged from the Middle East and spread outward. *Dine Bahane* originated in a land that is an ocean away from the rest of the world. There are even certain elements of this story that resemble the other flood stories. For instance, the flood was a judgment sent as a result of the Air-Spirit-People's immorality.

> At To bil dahisk'id where the streams came together water flowed in all directions. One stream flowed to the east. One stream flowed to the south. One stream flowed to the west. One stream flowed to the north. . .Far to the east there was an ocean. Far to the south there was an ocean. Far to the west there was an ocean. And far to the north there was an ocean. . .It is also said that the Air-Spirit People fought among themselves. And this is how it happened. They committed adultery, one with another. Many of the men were to blame, but so many of the women.

> They tried to stop, but they could not help themselves.[260]

Original sin had corrupted the world and the Air-Spirit People were given over to depraved minds. They began to commit adultery and were unable to stop. The perversion of their nature led to worse sins that eventually offended the rulers of their land. They were powerless to resist the wickedness that dwelt in their hearts. Humans experienced a similar predicament in the book of Genesis.

Mankind's morality spiraled downward because of original sin. At first it was a failure to abstain from eating the fruit of one particular tree. Man disobeyed God and initiated the world's corruption. After the initial act of disobedience, the Bible specifically mentioned two prominent sins that preceded the flood: violence and adultery. Not long after the world's corruption, Cain murdered his brother Abel. Mankind's violent tendencies escalated from that point onward. Alongside murder, mankind engaged in sexual sins. Signs of sexual sin in Genesis are polygamy[261] and the interbreeding between angels and humans.[262] The sins of violence and adultery were also mentioned in *Dine Bahane*. The storyteller reveals the contrast between sacred order and unholy rebellion. The Air-Spirit People were meant to live at peace alongside their intended mate. Their blatant perversion of nature eventually caught the attention of their chiefs.

---

[260] Paul G. Zolbrod, *Dine Bahane* (Albuqurque: University of New Mexico, 1984), 35-37.

[261] Genesis 4:19.

[262] Genesis 6:9.

Teehoolsodii The One That Grabs Things In the Water, who was chief in the east, complained, saying this:

"They must not like it here," he said.

And Taltlaah aleeh the Blue Heron, who was chief in the south, also complained:

"What they do is wrong," he complained.

Ch'al the Frog, who was chief in the west, also complained. But he took his complaint directly to the Air-Spirit people, having this to say to them:

"You shall no longer be welcome here where I am chief," is what he said

"That is what I think of you."

And from his home in the north where he was chief, Ii;ni' jilgaii the Winter Thunder spoke to them also.

"Nor are you welcome here!" he, too, said to them.

"Go away from this land.

"Leave at once!"[263]

The chiefs became angry and bickered amongst themselves. Ch'al, the Frog, actually warned the Air-Spirit

---

[263] Zolbrod, 37.

People of his anger. He told them that he no longer wanted them in his land.

> But the people could not help it: one with another they continued to commit adultery. . .
>
> Four days and nights passed.
>
> Then the same thing happened. Those who lived in the south repeated their sins: the men with the women and the women with the men. . .
>
> That night the people held a council at Nahodoola in the south. . .At the end of the fourth night as they were at last about to end their meeting, they all noticed something white in the east. They also saw it in the south. It appeared in the west, too. And in the north it also appeared.
>
> It looked like an endless chain of white mountains. They saw it on all sides. It surrounded them, and they noticed that it was closing in on them rapidly. It was a high, insurmountable wall of water! And it was flowing in on them from all directions, so that they could escape neither to the east nor to the west; neither to the south nor to the north could they escape.
>
> So having nowhere else to go, they took flight. Into the air they went. Higher and higher they soared it is said.

> It is also said that they circled upward until they reached the smooth, hard shell of the sky overhead. When they could go no higher they looked down and saw that the water now covered everything. They had nowhere to land either above or below.[264]

There was nowhere on earth that was safe for the Air-Spirit People to land. The entire earth had become flooded by water. Gigantic tidal waves surrounded them and swept over the land. The floodwaters originated from the surrounding bodies of water. Many ancient cultures believed that much of the water in the flood came from tidal waves. Even in Genesis, credit is given to the "springs of the great deep."[265]

It is strange for *Dine Bahane* to neglect the rain waters that contributed to the flood. Most other flood accounts include some sort of massive rainfall. The Air-Spirit People were not completely helpless in evading the flood because they could fly. They did not need a boat or an ark to escape. They had nowhere to land once they took flight, but their ability to fly bought them time to assess the situation. The waters rose so high, though, that eventually they ran into the hard shell of the sky that enclosed the earth. The Air-Spirit People held out long enough that they found sanctuary in an opening in the waters. The world faced judgment but a remnant was able to evade the wrath of the flood. There was no divine providence or clear-cut plan of escape for the Air-Spirit People. Catastrophe struck and everybody did what

---

264 Zolbrod, 38, 39.

265 Genesis 7:11.

was necessary to survive. Despite some of the obvious differences, *Dine Bahane* definitely exhibits details that are pronounced throughout most other flood stories.

There are many common elements between this and the other flood stories. Everything starts with an authority of some sort becoming upset by the world. This authority decides that the only righteous action would be to judge all of the offenders throughout the earth. The form of the judgment is that of a catastrophic flood. The flood sweeps across the world with the intention of killing everything in its path, but something always comes along to provide salvation to a remnant of life. As unique as *Dine Bahane* might be, it follows this pattern. The different chiefs became upset with the Air-Spirit People. Ch'al the Frog and Ii;ni' jilgaii the Winter Thunder are the ones who caused the great flood. They intended to either drive out the Air-Spirit People or kill them off. The flood was catastrophic enough to destroy all life, but the Air-Spirit People were able to find an opening in the water where they could rest.

Dine Bahane preaches the sacred order of nature but disregards the significance of human guidance in the world. According to the Biblical creation account, mankind watched over the world to maintain its order. Not many creatures abstain from polygamy aside from humans, nor do many animals have the ability to abstain from violence. Animals act instinctually and are not judged for the deeds they commit. Mankind would have been the only creature capable of producing evil so awful that it deserved judgment! It is the only creature that has the ability to reason. This simple difference makes it absolutely necessary for humans to be judged for their transgressions. God himself is the one who designed the world to operate in such a manner.

The absence of God in *Dine Bahane* robs it of the One who is able to distinguish good from evil. Only he is capable of exacting righteous judgment. The Frog and the Winter Thunder acted in a manner consistent with the creation order, but they were not supreme authorities who truly had the right to call the Air-Spirit People to judgment. Why were the sins of the Air-Spirit-People wicked in the eyes of their chiefs? This story seems to acknowledge that certain deeds are good and others are wicked, but there is no explanation as to why.

However, as a Native American flood story, *Dine Bahane* creates an interesting predicament for modern theories concerning the origins of flood myths. Flood myths were not confined to the joined continents of Europe, Asia, and Africa, but also North America. According to those that believe in an old earth nomads that would have ventured into North America would have done so long before the invention of the flood stories of the Eastern hemisphere. The elements *Dine Bahane* shares with other flood legends should catch the attention of both seekers and skeptics alike. Stories of a worldwide flood did not just appear in the Americas by chance. The common elements of all of the flood stories cannot be explained through mere coincidence.

Consequently the missing elements, like God and man, are made up for by the actions of the Air-Spirit People, the chiefs that were present to judge the world, and the common knowledge concerning what was good and evil according to the created order. The people who invented the story of *Dine Bahane* were able to do so because they carried the story of the true global flood along with them as they migrated to North America. Certain elements were retained while many of the elements were altered. When one goes beneath the surface of this story, it is very clear that it preserves the ancient tradition of a catastrophic worldwide flood. This alone should catch the attention of anyone who is investigating this matter.

The Evolutionist Flood Myth

The scientific community teaches that the entire world was once submerged in water. Sure, it scoffs at any belief that there was a catastrophic global flood, or that a global flood was even possible. When their theory is properly examined, though, it is no more credible than a myth. When looked at critically, their mockery of this event is just plain foolish. According to the evolutionist, this submersion was not destructive or life threatening because it occurred during the earth's developmental stages. One might argue that had it not been for the global submersion, life would not have been able to develop! Their criticism of the notion of a global flood, in this regard, is not truly based on evidence, but faith.

The flood of scientific legend was part of a process that formed the earth. The earth was once a boiling mass of molten rock. The intense heat of the primordial earth caused water to evaporate from the molten mass. Once the vapor cooled in the blackness of space it rained back down as precipitation. The precipitation eventually flooded the world and cooled its molten mass. Most people that believe this theory also believe that life originated in the primordial ocean. There are many theories regarding how this may have occurred, but no single theory truly stands out. This theory of the earth's evolution greatly differs from the catastrophic legends of ancient times.

In chapter two, this immersion was likened to day two of Genesis, but because of the evolutionist's denial of a global flood, it must now be contrasted with the legends that claim that the world was once destroyed by water. All of the ancient flood stories were catastrophic, regardless of the religious tradition. The evolutionary flood was part of a process that was ultimately constructive. The ancient flood stories testify that life was extinguished as a result of the flood. The evolutionary theory professes that without the flood, life would never have emerged. The ancient flood stories claim that witnesses survived the flood who could transmit the story down to future generations. Not a single eyewitness was alive during the time of the evolutionary flood, but evolutionary scientists believe that their theory is superior to the testimony of the ancients! To modern ears the ancient stories might sound extraordinary, but the common elements of the different legends do not invite mockery. Evolutionists declare, "There was no worldwide flood!" They claim, "There is no such evidence to support these myths!" They taunt, "There is not enough water to cover the earth's entire surface!" But then, they blissfully teach, "In the earth's formational stages, it was once covered by water." Their testimonies are invalidated by their very own hypocritical statements! This makes the evolutionary flood the outsider.

The ancient world was in agreement. Genesis states that there was a worldwide flood. The epic of Gilgamesh, testified that there was a worldwide flood. Greek mythology reinforces the testimony of a worldwide flood. *Dine Bahane* preserved the story of the worldwide flood for a continent that was detached from the rest of the world! Their stories may not be identical, but one detail prevails: There was a worldwide flood!

Secular scientists think that they can speak out of both sides of their mouths. "The world could never be *flooded* in water, but it was indeed *covered* in water." They do not know what the primordial world was like. If there is evidence that the world was once entirely covered by water, it is only reasonable to concede that a worldwide flood, at one point in time, was possible. It does not conform to their presuppositions, but science is the pursuit of truth, not of presuppositions.

Chapter 22
Examining the Flood Stories

Based on these flood stories, it is easy to conclude that some sort of global or nearly global deluge took place. There are too many stories from different cultures to say that the worldwide flood was a myth. Some sort of great catastrophe happened on a scale that was noteworthy enough to be passed down from generation to generation. Some sort of great authority judged the world by flooding the earth. According to most flood stories, the authority was a god, gods, or God. According to *Dine Bahane*, the authorities were the chiefs of the land. Regardless, someone of holy status judged a world that betrayed its sacred order.

Except for *Dine Bahane*, the life forms responsible for the world's judgment were humans. Mankind had become utterly depraved and sought only to do evil. Their nature deteriorated so much that it angered their holy overseer and forced judgment to take place. Despite the judgment, there were survivors. These survivors witnessed the entire catastrophe. Some claim that only the noted survivors were witnesses to the flood, while others claim that there were undocumented survivors that catalogued the same event. There is no solid evidence that can prove one way or the other, but the legends testify that only the noted survivors were witnesses to the flood. The intent of the respective authority was to eliminate evil and propagate good.

Some stragglers may have remained on mountaintops outside of the view of the chosen survivors. Not every account of the flood says that the mountains were covered to their peaks. For instance, the Greek account does not teach that the mountains were fully covered and some of the finest Bible scholars would agree. Evolutionary scientists typically say that it would be impossible for the world, as it currently exists, to be fully immersed in water. Is it possible that the pagan myths are more credible in this area than the Bible?

In a word, the difference between the Biblical and pagan accounts is monotheism. The Biblical worldview is that there is only one God. The Greeks, and other pagan cultures, believed in a multitude of deities. It was thought that the gods dwelt upon mountaintops. For instance, in Utnapishtim's story, the gods that remained on earth fled to the tops of mountains to protect themselves from the flood waters. The Greek gods lived on Mount Olympus. The gods would not dare flood the mountains to their peaks because they would be destroying their home if they did such a thing. Yahweh did not need to run away from the flood. He is the God of heaven and earth. There were no other gods that he had to be concerned about. The Holy Spirit inspired the author of Genesis to note the great depths of the flood waters. Even the mountaintops would be covered. Everyone, then, would understand that there is only one God and he resides above his creation, not on top of mountains but in heaven. Regardless of the depth of flood waters, the legends agree that this was not a local occurrence. Unlike local floods, this flood would be remembered through the ages.

The likelihood of a massive local flood obtaining the label of a worldwide flood in the ancient world would have been instantly refuted. If a local flood decimated a region in the Fertile Crescent, other cultures would have been aware of the event. If someone survived the flood and informed the outside world of what had happened, they would not have bought in to a story that claimed that the event was a worldwide occurrence because clearly it was not! The most likely possibilities for such a false claim surviving would be if the story was formulated either long after it happened or if it did not happen at all. The testimony of ancient stories clearly states the worldwide nature of the flood. Given that reality, one must ask how the knowledge of a global flood could have spread.

A worldwide occurrence with chosen survivors would centralize the knowledge of the flood to one small group of people. This small group would propagate the memory of the flood by recounting it to their children. As the ensuing generations moved outward, the story would have travelled along with them and could have been edited as it travelled. It would not be likely for a local flood story to make this sort of journey because it would only have relevance to the locals who witnessed the event. It is logical enough to believe that the story of a massive flood started from a centralized location and blossomed outward to other tribes and nations but it would only have been taken seriously if it were relevant to the global community

The flood of the legends happened on a global scale. Each of the stories contains unique elements and common elements. Perhaps the most common element of the stories is the claim that it reshaped the entire world and was intended to extinguish all life. One can debate the supernatural implications of such a flood, but no one can deny that these stories date back several millennia and have been important parts of many cultures. If a massive local flood occurred in any region of the world, it did not relate to the ancient legends.

The Groundwork for Creationist Geology

There is no doubt that the story about the flood started with a small group of people and moved outward, but secular science has a hard time seeing evidence for a global flood. Their struggle is not that evidence is nonexistent; there is plenty of evidence for a global flood. The scientific community is simply scared to consider the possibility that the evidence from which they draw their conclusions has supernatural origins. The arguments for the age of the earth and the worldwide flood are rooted in geology. Geology is a field of study that is typically interpreted from a secular perspective and would never consider the idea that divine judgment is responsible for their body of evidence. It is for this reason that secular geology must be challenged.

Geology, the study of the earth through its rocks and fossils, is a field of science that has nearly been monopolized by those who believe in the Theory of Evolution. The Geologic Column is composed of the different layers of dirt dispersed through the earth, known as strata, and the different layers have been labeled in such a manner that they represent different eras in earth history. Because the general consensus of geologists is that the earth is billions of years old, the geologic column is interpreted as being the result of millions of years of death and the mass accumulation of dirt over time. In reality, this sort of logic is greatly irrational because the geologic column is not nearly as well organized as scientists pretend.

Nonetheless, certain conclusions can be deduced from observing the world buried beneath one's feet. For instance, through observing the abundance of fossilized creatures and plants, one might conclude that the earth was once swarming with life. In its infancy the earth was actually more habitable than what it is today! This could suggest that the world was created exactly as the Bible records. It might prove that the world was much better off before the advent of man. Alas, all that the fossils really tell anybody is that something, sometime in the past, was buried and its remains were preserved. Geologists typically side with the secular interpretation of natural data. Rarely does anybody in the scientific community bring up the problems of evolutionary geology even though there are many aspects of its paradigm that are worthy of scrutiny.

Every field of study has its problems and evolutionary geology is no different. There are many questions that have not received satisfactory answers from the evolutionary paradigm. Where did the dirt for each layer in the earth come from? How did mountains form? Why do trees protrude through multiple strata that represent millions of years? How did fossils form? Why are there massive fossil graveyards throughout the world? To answer these questions from an evolutionary perspective a person would have to assume one of two possibilities: 1) a whole lot of coincidence or 2) a miracle. It is possible that maybe the "prehistoric world" was a lot more unstable and a lot more random than the world we know today, but if that were true, why should anyone believe that evolution could have sustained life in such a chaotic and dangerous environment? Evolutionists do have theories concerning these abnormalities, but they require some serious mental gymnastics. Nobody truly knows how these phenomena occurred, from a geological perspective.

The presupposition that nothing supernatural or catastrophic could have influenced the creation of the geologic column is intentionally narrow-minded. One can concede that it is fair enough for an atheist to throw out the possibility of supernatural influence. But how can one throw out the possibility that a catastrophe was responsible for some of the world's geology? It becomes absurdly suspicious when reasonable enough possibilities are thrown out just for the sake that they might justify another person's religious beliefs. There are times in science when certain theories should be dismissed but that time should not be reserved merely to protect one's own biases against religion or catastrophism.

Aside from supernaturalism, the creationist's perspective is rooted in catastrophism. The concept of catastrophism merely implies that some sort of remarkable catastrophe changed the physical attributes and operations of the world at some point in time. For instance, young earth creationists believe that a world-wide catastrophe is responsible for the geologic column as it exists today. This does not necessarily presuppose a divine hand, but would be considered unlikely otherwise. This perspective states that the geologic column was not formed over millions or billions of years. It also does not state that it has to be an orderly column. Instead, it was created by the global flood that was documented in the book of Genesis. According to this perspective, there were no "geologic eras" because the strata would have been laid down in the time frame of a year.

In their book *The Genesis Flood,* John Whitcomb and Henry Morris went in depth in explaining creationist geology. They pointed out that some strata, according to the evolutionary model, are out of the scientifically accepted order. "It is not at all unusual for strata to be found completely out of the approved order, with 'old' strata resting comfortably on top of 'young' strata. And all of this. . .bears extremely hard on the theory of uniformity [evolution] and the geologic ages."[266] If each layer took millions of years to form, how can they possibly be out of order? If the layers were laid by a catastrophic flood, abnormalities would be expected. The creationist explanation is more satisfactory in this instance. This correlates with the geologic inconsistencies regarding the burial and preservation of different organisms.

Similar organisms could likely be found in similar strata, according to this premise, but it is not necessarily required. The order in which life forms were buried makes more sense from a creationist perspective because it allows for the inconsistencies that are observed. Marine creatures are most often acknowledged to be in the lowest strata of the geologic column. If a global flood

[266] Morris and Whitcomb, 272.

occurred this would make sense. These creatures were already below the land dwelling creatures. One would expect to find these creatures in the lower strata because of the stirring up of the ocean floor.[267]

In the higher layers, it would be expected that the creatures of greater mobility would be found. Once again, this is exactly what is observed. Birds are often found in higher layers of strata because they could take to the air while the world was being flooded. Other vertebrates (especially those of higher intelligence like humans) would have been able to escape to higher ground before finally being overtaken by the flood and would generally be expected to appear higher in the geologic column.[268] The evolutionary perspective believes that the different layers represent the gradual evolution of life over long spans of time.

There is no such thing as reconciling the two views of geology. It is unlikely for an atheist to adopt a theistic construct for geology, but many creationists have accepted a construct that is secular. It is not that one side or another has better evidence for their theory. It is more of a matter that both sides find their interpretation of the evidence to be more convincing than that of the other side. Even though there are many theists who adopt an evolutionary model of geology, it is not because they find the secular model more compelling. Rather, it is because most people are ignorant to the young earth model for geology. It should be easy for a creationist to observe that secular geology creates more mysteries than what it solves.

[267] Morris and Whitcomb, 273.

[268] Morris and Whitcomb, 275-276.

The Death of the Dinosaurs and the Flood

The secular misinterpretation of the geologic column is the culprit for one of the greatest mysteries of all time: What happened to all of the dinosaurs? How did such incredible creatures just all of a sudden go extinct when they were at the top of the food chain? When the geologic column is interpreted correctly, the mystery about what happened to the dinosaurs is quickly solved. Because of the general acceptance of the Theory of Evolution, there have been many theories regarding the extinction of the dinosaurs. All of these different theories are a hindrance to discovering the true reason for the disappearance of the dinosaurs.

No single theory, thus far, has been able to account for all of the geologic factors suspected in their demise. One theory says that all of the volcanoes erupted at once.[269] Another says that an asteroid struck the earth and wiped them out.[270] And yet another suggests that their own flatulence produced so much methane that they induced global warming and the climate change killed them![271] Most of the theories created by scientists involve some factor that radically changed the world's

---

[269] Live Science, "Volcanoes, not asteroid, may have killed off dinosaurs." http://www.foxnews.com/story/0,2933,310826,00.html (accessed May 18, 2012).

[270] Ken Ham, *The Great Dinosaur Mystery Solved!* (Green Forest, Arkansas: Master Books, 2009), 12.

[271] NewsCore, "Dinosaurs 'gassed' themselves into extinction, British scientists say" http://www.foxnews.com/scitech/2012/05/07/dinosaurs-farted-their-way-to-extinction-british-scientists-say/?intcmp=features (accessed May 18, 2012).

climate because the "prehistoric world" appeared to be much warmer than the ages that followed. Many factors must be considered when analyzing the geologic column and the death of the dinosaurs.

Secular scientists might be on to something with the different conclusions they have made. There is evidence that there was amazing seismic activity in the past. There is evidence that an asteroid struck the earth. Most scientists are convinced that the climate of the old world was much different from the world today. Secular theories attempt to make sense of each individual factor, but they typically view each one as being a part of its own event. The Biblical flood account could explain all of these geologic phenomena and combine them into one enormous catastrophe.

Seismic activity is the key to solving the mystery of the dinosaurs. The global flood described in the Bible would have required high seismic activity. The Bible recalls that the "springs of the great deep burst forth."[272] This simple phrase would include such processes as volcanic eruptions, water geysers, earthquakes, and tsunamis.[273] Such chaotic activity would have swept up plants and animals in tremendous mudslides, which would have given birth to fossil graveyards. An asteroid striking the earth would have shaken the foundations of the world. But the flood did not eliminate the dinosaurs, although it probably contributed to their ultimate demise. If the flood in Noah's day happened as it was described in the Bible, a sample of every kind of animal was preserved.

---

[272] Genesis 7:11

[273] Cadwallader, 37.

Two popular theories contend that the dinosaurs were not killed off by one swift catastrophe but that they phased out over time. The secular theory that advocates this is that dinosaurs evolved into birds. Most people are familiar with this theory. The other theory, the one espoused by creationists, is that dinosaurs continued to live after the flood but gradually died off due to a dramatic post-flood climate change, limited food, and extermination brought upon by humans. History testifies to the creationist's theory that dinosaurs and humans lived together.

Historically speaking, one must understand that the word "dinosaur" was not introduced until 1841. If humans ever encountered dinosaurs before 1841, they would not have called them "dinosaurs." Was there any creature recorded in history that bore the description of a dinosaur? From a linguistic perspective the answer is "yes." The word dinosaur literally means "terrible lizard." There are many legends about "terrible lizards" that caused trouble for peasants and kingdoms. Accounts of these beasts have been recorded throughout history but have been dismissed in modern times as being mythological. Before the modern era, they were called "dragons."[274]

With all of the factors considered, it is not far-fetched to say that dinosaurs and humans once lived together. The mystery of the dinosaurs' disappearance only exists because the popular Theory of Evolution supposes that dinosaurs died off sixty five million years ago, long before any human would have been able to experience

[274] Cadwallader, 33.

one. Geologic evidence, when viewed from the proper perspective, can be interpreted in such a way that proves that the worldwide flood was a reality. Legends of dragons are scattered throughout the world and many of these dragons fit the descriptions of recognizable species of creatures that we would call dinosaurs. The secularist theories of dinosaur extinction and the evolution of reptiles into birds create more problems than what they solve. After all, what is easier to believe: that the myth of dinosaurs evolved from dragons, or that birds exist because of dinosaurs?

Chapter 23
A Hero of Old

I sit upon a mountaintop, watching the waves rise higher and higher. Time moves slowly as I count down the moments leading up to my untimely death. You will never hear any stories about me, but in my day people sang songs of my greatness. I am one of those that you would call the Nephilim. . .a giant!

I can tell you stories about many terrible things. I could tell you the story of how violence entered the world. I could tell you stories about mighty beasts that breathed fire and trampled the likes of men as though they were nothing but grass. The world I was born into was dangerous. That was why I was raised to be a warrior. My mother and my companions always warned me to never become weak. If I could become strong, the world would not overtake me.

I descend from a line of humans that has only known war since the time of the great departure. Cain, our patriarch, killed his brother Abel in the first act of violence. He ran away for fear of his life and told all of his brothers and sisters that if they harmed him, God would exact vengeance on them. The mark placed on his head verified his claim. Like a beast of the field, his brand warned away those who sought easy prey. They knew that God would avenge his death if anyone harmed him.

Yet, this justification was used by many people long after Cain. Lamech was a murderer in the line of his father Cain. He was the second man to claim that he would be avenged by God if anyone would harm him. This started feuds between clans. Eventually, these feuds escalated into war. God's entire creation descended into chaos and unruliness.

My birth was not intentional. I came into the world through an unnatural event that was not blessed by God. I am what you might call an abomination! One of the angels from heaven came down to earth and birthed me through a human mother. I do not know my father. I only know that natural man is powerless against my strength.

You will hear stories that attribute my abilities to other people. You will hear of men that stood taller than the largest horses. You will listen to tales of warriors that could hurl boulders as though they were toys. This is a memory of a time when violence gripped the world and war raged from all corners of the earth. I honed my skills to be the greatest of them all. Ironically, my strength does not pose a threat to the enemy that is scaling this mountain upon which I sit. I have ignored the warnings from God's servant and this is my reward.

I had once encountered a man of peace, a man of God, named Noah. He warned us about a great catastrophe that would destroy the world. We were warned that God was going to release the waters from heaven and cover the earth with the waters below. The name of the catastrophe was a "flood." Noah was building an enormous vessel that he claimed would protect anyone who took refuge inside. He called it an "ark."

Many people participated in building this ark, but not I. There was not enough to be gained for me, or so I thought. None of the workers, outside of Noah's family, believed the claim about the impending flood. They continued their lives and I continued mine.

Over a hundred years had passed and the ark Noah was building had reached completion. The animals boarded the vessel from all over the world. The very sight should have aroused suspicion in the minds of the skeptics. It seemed as though he had every sort of animal you could possibly imagine. Still, we did not heed his warnings.

Finally, Noah's predictions came true. It started with a massive shaking of the ground. Everyone alive trembled in fear because no one had ever experienced anything like this. The heavens suddenly collapsed from above! Water fell from the sky like the great falls of the earth. A dark shadow mounted over us. I looked up to see what appeared to be an enormous, white, rolling mountain. It rapidly approached and spelled out certain death for anyone caught in its wake. I was miles away, but I knew that this was what Noah warned us about.

Nobody believed that it was coming, so no one was prepared. Newlyweds perished beneath the bombardment of waves. Merchants and their businesses were destroyed by the horrendous currents. Fire sprung forth from the ground and consumed anyone who was trapped in its fury. Without warning and in a matter of moments, most of the world's life was exterminated. I hurried to the nearest mountain and thought to myself, "Maybe if I can find Noah, I can escape this disaster with my life."

There was no time to seek out Noah. I had become stranded on the edge of the mountain and the flood waters were rapidly rising. I climbed to the top, hoping that I could escape this fate. Once I reached the top, I discovered that nothing was going to stop these flood waters from reaching me. It was only a matter of time before I would join all of the others who had perished at the hand of God.

In the distance, I saw a massive object. It appeared to be Noah's ark. I signaled it in hopes that he could rescue me. It was of no use. The ark that he constructed was not a boat. He could not steer it upon his own will. The ark was at the mercy of the waves. Clearly, it was meant only to preserve the life of those inside.

This was one mistake I could never make right. Even if I could go back and get into the ark, could God have ever forgiven me for the wicked life I lived? I was responsible for much bloodshed in which I took pride. Now, I am facing the wrath of God. There is no escape. This is my appointment with the Creator.

Section 5
Babel and Conclusions

Introduction

The last stop on this tour through the first eleven chapters of Genesis is the Tower of Babel. The Tower of Babel is a structure shrouded in mystery. Some people claim to know what it was, while others believe that the Tower has forever been lost. The account of Babel shows how all of mankind gathered into one location and defied God.

> Now the whole world had one language and a common speech. As people moved eastward, they found a plain in Shinar and settled there. They said to each other, "Come, let's make bricks and bake them thoroughly." They used brick instead of stone, and tar for mortar. Then they said, "Come, let us build ourselves a city, with a tower that reaches to the heavens, so that we may make a name for ourselves; otherwise we will be scattered over the face of the whole earth." But the LORD came down to see the city and the tower the people were building. The LORD said, "If as one people speaking the same language they have begun

> to do this, then nothing they plan to do will be impossible for them. Come, let us go down and confuse their language so they will not understand each other." So the LORD scattered them from there over all the earth, and they stopped building the city. That is why it was called Babel – because there the LORD confused the language of the whole world. From there the LORD scattered them over the face of the whole earth.[275]

At first, it is difficult to understand why God scattered the people from Babel. Was it because he did not want them to make progress? Could it be that God wanted to suppress knowledge? Was God afraid that they would overthrow him? The people of the earth wanted to better themselves and to show off their incredible ingenuity. Pride, the gateway to nearly every sin, was why God disrupted their progress. Their efforts sought to undermine God and exalt human accomplishment. In a sense, they were the first humanists.

The building of the city of Babel took root in man's selfish desire to be independent from God's rule. They erected the infamous Tower of Babel to declare their intentions: they would stay put in Shinar. The tower's name declared its ability to reach heaven. God saw what they were doing and knew that it was wicked. He despised their efforts and decided to halt their building project, scramble their languages, and scatter humanity throughout the earth.

Many have speculated that the gathering of all people at Babel was against God's will. God commanded

[275] Genesis 11:1-9.

mankind in Genesis 1:28 to "fill the earth, and subdue it." People were not created to overpopulate one area, but to scatter and populate the entire world. Mankind refused to obey God's simple commandment. John Sailhammer comments, "The focus of the author since the beginning chapters of the Book of Genesis has been both on God's plan to bless mankind by providing him with that which is 'good' and on man's failure to trust God and enjoy the 'good' God had provided."[276] The God of the Bible is good and he seeks the best for those he created. Human effort to be as great as God has been its undoing. Original sin was committed in the hope that eating from the Tree of the Knowledge of Good and Evil would put humans on an equal plain with God. God's command to avoid the tree was simple, just as his command to populate the entire earth was, but people do not trust God enough to take him at his word.

Ever since creation, mankind has struggled to obey God. They initially defied him in Eden, continued to defy him throughout the world, and returned to defy him once again after the flood. The construction of Babel was in blatant defiance to worshipping the one true God. It appeared that humanity would never learn its lesson and submit to God's rule. Only by disrupting the evil that unfolded at Shinar could God provide mankind with an opportunity to repent from its evil ways.

[276] Gaebelein Vol. 2, 105.

Chapter 24
The Tower of Babel

The Tower of Babel was the pinnacle of mankind's disobedience. The people of the world built the city of Babel with the sole intention of receiving glory. The intention for the city of Babel, also known as Babylon, could be deduced from its very name. The name Babel means "the gate of God."[277] The Babylonians wanted to bridge the gap between God and man. They wanted to make it possible for mankind to touch the divine on its own will and obtain immortality by its own efforts. By nature, these efforts were evil.

It was in vain that Babylon and its tower were constructed. Everything about the construction of Babel was to declare man's independence from God. First of all, they wanted their building materials to be a result of their own ingenuity. They constructed everything out of brick instead stone. God created stone; man created brick. God's created material was a much more reliable substance than mankind's manufactured product.[278] Second,

---

277 Lasor, Hubbard, and Bush, 20.

278 Ronald F. Youngblood, *Nelson's New Illustrated Bible Dictionary* (Nashville: Thomas Nelson Publishers, 1995), 147.

the people who built the city proclaimed that they wanted to make themselves a name. To accomplish this, they devised a plan that would prevent them from being scattered throughout the earth. The city was built around a great tower that served as a beacon for mankind.[279] The beacon sent out a signal to other people that proclaimed freedom from God.[280] Third and finally, the people set out on a journey that was in the direction of their wicked ancestors. All of the transgressors of Genesis inevitably moved eastward from Eden. In its early chapters, it seems as though east was the direction of the rebellious heart.[281] The Tree of Life was placed at the east end of Eden.[282] After murdering his brother, Cain moved east of Eden.[283] After the flood, mankind gradually travelled east into the plain of Shinar, where they founded Babel.[284] Whether it was conscious or subconscious, the people of Babel travelled eastward, following after their uncle, Cain, and mimicking his way of life. Previously, God demolished mankind for its disobedience and despicable nature. The flood should have created fear in the human heart toward its righteous God. At Babel, mankind made it clear that they would continue to sin fearlessly despite their knowledge of God's wrath.

---

[279] Genesis 11:4.

[280] Youngblood, 147.

[281] Gaebelein 1990, 105. This was also symbolic when Adam and Eve moved eastward away from Eden and when Cain moved eastward after killing Abel.

[282] Genesis 1:24.

[283] Genesis 4:16.

[284] Genesis 11:2.

One might think that after a global flood, humans would lose their will to sin. It was only because of his faith that God preserved Noah, who was noted as being an upright man.[285] This example should have been enough to set mankind's heart straight. What is often forgotten, though, is that Noah indulged in wine and became drunk not long after stepping off of the ark.[286] Noah, too, was a sinner who sinned against God after the catastrophic flood. Sin still existed and it continued to corrupt the hearts of people. After several generations of offspring, mankind was becoming as sinful as ever and had to be divided.

No doubt, the story of Babel is bizarre. Generations after a worldwide flood all of the people of the world gathered into one region and built a city with a tower that reached all the way up to heaven. It sounds like a myth. Myths often attempt to explain the unexplainable, and one might make the case that Babel was an attempt to explain the origins of the various languages. Today, most people do not believe that all languages came about at once. Instead, the majority of people believe that languages slowly evolved over time. Was Babel just a myth? Did ancient man really build a tower that stretched upward toward heaven?

Most evidence in relation to the first eleven chapters of Genesis is speculative and Babel is no different. To the best of mankind's understanding, the Tower of Babel has not been identified beyond the shadow of a doubt. But there are many clues that may reveal the identity and

---

[285] Genesis 6:9.

[286] Genesis 9:21.

location of the Tower of Babel. A highly popular theory is that the Tower of Babel was a ziggurat. Many ziggurats have been discovered in Mesopotamia and they were constructed with bricks as described in Genesis.

> The location of two dozen ancient temple-towers of Mesopotamia, called ziggurats and possibly illustrative of the Tower of Babel, are now known. These towers were gigantic artificial mountains of sun-dried bricks. The oldest one recovered is that of Uruk (biblical Erech, Gen. 10:10), from the fourth millennium B. C. Other famous ziggurat ruins remain at Ur, Borsippa and Babylon.[287]

Archaeological evidence that links the Bible to history is compelling.

Nonetheless, none of the archaeological discoveries to date have positively identified the structure or location of the Tower of Babel. The inability to uncover the Tower of Babel could be attributed to one of several possibilities: 1) the Tower of Babel was nothing more than a myth, 2) it has been buried deep underneath the surface of the ground, 3) it was destroyed by man, 4) it was destroyed by God, or 5) it is merely unrecognizable. Given these possibilities, one might conclude that it is impossible to prove the existence of the Tower of Babel.

Fortunately, Babylonian mythology testifies to the historicity of the Tower of Babel. *Enuma Elish*, a source that has commonly been used throughout this project, details the building of a great city that housed cultic

---

[287] Unger, 19-20.

monuments that were dedicated to the gods. After the god Marduk defeated Tiamat, the other gods became jubilant. Their rejoicing resulted in an enormous building project that would commemorate Marduk's accomplishment:

> Marduk made his voice heard and spoke, addressed his words to the gods his fathers, "Over the Apsu, the sea-green dwelling, In front. . .Esharra, which I created for you, (Where) I strengthened the ground beneath it for a shrine, I shall make a house to be a luxurious dwelling for myself And shall found his cult centre within it, And I shall establish my private quarters, and confirm my kingship. Whenever you come up from the Apsu for an assembly, Your night's resting place shall be in it, receiving you all. Whenever you come down from the sky for an assembly, Your night's resting place shall be in it, receiving you all. I hereby name it Babylon, home of the great gods. We shall make it the centre of religion." The gods his fathers listened to this command of his. . .[288]

> The Annunnaki made their voices heard and addressed Marduk their lord, "Now, O Lord, that you have set us free, what are our favours from you? We would like our night's resting place to be in your private quarters, and to rest there. Let us found a shrine, a sanctuary there. Whenever we arrive, let us rest within it." When Marduk heard this, His face lit up greatly, like daylight. "Create Babylon, whose construction you requested! Let its mud bricks be

[288] Stephanie Dalley, *Myths of Mesopotamia* (Great Britain: Oxford University Press, 2000), 259.

> moulded, and build high the shrine!" The Anunnaki began shoveling. For a whole year they made bricks for it. When the second year arrived, They had raised the top of Esagila[289] in front of. . .the Apsu; They had build a high ziggurrat for the Apsu. They founded a dwelling for Anu, Ellil, and Ea likewise. In ascendancy he settled himself in front of them, And his "horns" look down at the base of Esharra.[290]

The construction of this great city was a monumental achievement. It was supposed to be the center of religious practice and was marked out with many religious structures to commemorate the gods. It was believed that the gods would come down from heaven and camp out in the towers that were built. The gods were not shy about having shelters built to commemorate their greatness. One must ask, though, did gods really construct Babylon?

It is believed that ziggurats were built by kings with the intent to carry out religious acts. Some would even go as far to say that kings built them with the intention to show that their office was higher than the priesthood, as a ziggurat was built higher than a temple.[291] In ancient times, temples were constructed on platforms so that they would rest on a level higher than the commoner's house. This would show that the status of the gods was higher than that of man. It also acknowledged that the dwelling

---

[289] *Esagila is the Temple of Marduk; Esharra is the name of several temples, including one of Anu in Uruk and one of Assur in Assur city

[290] Dalley, 262, 321.

[291] John Lendering, "Zigguraat," Livius.org, http://www.livius.org/za-zn/ziggurat/ziggurat.html (accessed June 13, 2011).

place of the gods was in the heavens. A structure that was elevated higher than the commoner was necessary in order to draw the attention of the gods. Priests dwelt in temples, but kings dwelt in ziggurats. Ziggurats were much more awe inspiring than the temples. In essence, a ziggurat was built to declare that the kings were closer to the gods than even the priests. These colossal structures normally included a shrine at the top so that it was visible and that it would not be overlooked by the patron god of the city.[292] In light of this information, Genesis shines some beautiful light on the account of *Enuma Elish*.

The Biblical account of the construction of Babel echoes Marduk's command for the construction of a city. The purpose for this city's construction is revealed in *Enuma Elish*. It required the building of religious structures that would be dedicated to Marduk and the other gods. The Temple of Marduk was to be the center of religion. Such a designation would make this city the center of the world. In Genesis, it is inferred that the construction of Babel was a sign of mankind's desire to become religiously independent from God through its own religious practices. It appears that people felt that they owed it to themselves to immortalize their own names. The establishment of Babylon created a central place of worship. It would have been the capital of the world. According to the Bible, everyone traveled to the land of Shinar to establish this great city.[293] Not only did the people discover a great city to live in, they also discovered their gods: the deified kings and queens. All

[292] The British Museum, http://www.mesopotamia. co.uk/ziggurats/story/stoset.html (accessed June 13, 2011).

[293] Lendering, (accessed June 13, 2011).

these rulers needed to establish their authority was a symbol, a gateway to God.

A great structure is eventually revealed in the Babylonian writings: Etemenanki. Etemenanki was a massive ziggurat. Many experts believe that Etemenanki was the historic identity of the long lost Tower of Babel. Many artists, however, do not picture a ziggurat when they hear the term "tower" used in reference to the Tower of Babel. Is it possible that the Tower of Babel was a ziggurat and not really a tower as most people perceive? *Enuma Elish* was originally written in Akkadian, and the Akkadian word for "ziggurat" is "zaqaru." Zaqaru means to rise high.[294] So a ziggurat is a structure that is tall. According to the legend, Etemenanki was supposedly three hundred feet tall![295] This was not the biggest ziggurat ever constructed, but it would have been colossal for this time in history. The name Etemenanki actually means "House Platform of Heaven and Earth."[296] The Akkadian word for Babel means "Gateway to God."[297] It is easy to see the connection, now, between the Tower of Babel and Etemenanki.

The names Etemenanki and Babel convey a very similar message. They both declare that they are the way to God. Ironically, the Bible points out that the name "Babel," in Hebrew, translates as "confusion." The

---

[294] Lendering, (accessed June 13, 2011).

[295] David Noel Freedman, *Eerdmans Dictionary of the Bible* (Grand Rapids, Michigan: William B. Eerdmans Publishing Company, 2000), 138.

[296] The British Museum (accessed June 13, 2011).

[297] Youngblood, 147.

languages were confused at Babel. Mankind departed from Babel in utter disillusionment because they had abandoned the one true God to pursue idols of their own creation.[298] As a result, many people believe that God either destroyed the Tower of Babel or prevented its completion before he sent mankind away.

Historically, Etemenanki was destroyed multiple times and had to be rebuilt. Supposedly the Hittites had destroyed it after the death of Hammurabi, and Nebuchadnezzar rebuilt it during his reign.[299] Etemenanki's destruction and reconstruction might cause some to question whether Etemenanki was the Tower of Babel described in the Bible. In Genesis 11:8, God came down to halt the building of the mighty structure and the city of Babylon. What happened to the tower after its construction was halted? Did God destroy the tower?

Historically there is no mention of strange events, natural or supernatural, that would have implied divine judgment of this sort. Upon closer reading, the Bible does not indicate that God destroyed the tower but only halted its construction. It is never mentioned that God permanently halted its construction or directly brought about its destruction. It is possible, and likely, that someone else took up the reigns to the project and followed it through to completion. It is also possible that it was destroyed by another nation sometime later in history.

It is speculated that the Hittites were the first to destroy Etemenanki. This would not necessarily imply that God's hand was absent from the act, because God

[298] Genesis 11:8-9.

[299] Keller, 318.

often used armies to accomplish his will and he may have used the Hittites to decimate the Tower of Babel. This would not have occurred immediately after God halted the construction of Babel, but sometime afterwards. The Hittites would have traveled from a foreign land to accomplish this, and the Bible says that all of the people of the world were gathered at Babel. Their journey alone proves that the Bible is not referring to a foreign power's interference with Babel's progress.

According to the Bible, it appears that only the city remained incomplete. The Tower may have reached completion before the city's people dispersed. Some translators claim that there was no tower; rather, they believe that the original language implies that the city itself reached toward the heavens. This suggests that the account details the construction of a "towering city" with no mention of an actual tower. Such a stance ignores the political ramifications of a tower. Even today, nations construct massive buildings and towers to declare their superiority to the rest of the world. It is more likely that the original language is referring to a city with a tower as a political and religious center. A ziggurat would serve such a purpose. One would be built to bring the king nearer to the gods and set him above his subjects. This tower declared to God that the people of Babel were liberated from him.

Ultimately, the monuments of Babel were a sign that the world was in a state of rebellion. The city itself was a home to rebellious people, so God's concern was not so much that the people were erecting a tower but that they were refusing to obey his command to spread across the earth. After confusing their language, God forced them to move. The city was probably left in an incomplete state. People could no longer settle in Babylon because they could not communicate with one another. Before people permanently settled, its construction halted. The mass confusion of language would have prevented people from settling in Babylon.

There is harmony between the Bible and the Babylonian myth. The city of Babylon, or Babel, was constructed with religious intent. It was a testimony that mankind did not need God to establish order in their civilization. The building of this city was revolutionary! The Babylonian description deifies the founders of Babylon. *Enuma Elish* praises Marduk for the construction of the Temple, the ziggurats, and other religious structures that existed in Babylon. Perhaps the people who built Babylon intended for themselves to become the ancestral gods of their people.

The author of the Babylonian story viewed the construction of Babylon as a marvelous occurrence. Marduk dreamt of the idea after defeating Tiamat. The other gods were grateful to build Babylon for him. It was supposed to be the world's center for religious practice. It established an order that mankind's purpose on earth was to appease the gods through worship and sacrifice. Since Babylon was supposed to be the world's center for religion, it was meant to be the most important city on earth.

The Bible states that people were constructing this city, with its tower, to declare their own splendor. According to the Bible, God did not appreciate the building of Babel. It does not give the exact reason as to why God disrupted its building but the implication was that the people who were constructing it would pride themselves in its completion. "So the Lord scattered them from there over all the earth, and they stopped building the city."[300] There is disagreement concerning the fate of Babylon's construction. *Enuma Elish* does not describe the disruption of its construction. This brings into question whether or not God really did stop it from being completed. On the other hand, the Bible says that Babel was not constructed by gods but by people. This casts a shadow of doubt upon *Enuma Elish's* account. Many rulers of ancient civilizations have claimed that they descended from the gods. This direct descent from divine beings was how rulers established their authority. Authoritative rulers always enslave mankind to do their bidding. Because of man's deification of royalty, the Biblical account's assertion that mortals were responsible for the construction Babel is more likely.

Furthermore, the Bible accurately predicted the ultimate fate of Babylon through its prophets. The writers of *Enuma Elish* marveled at the work of their hands as they constructed Babylon. The Bible conveys the message that Babylon was a city doomed to fail. Etemenanki was actually destroyed on multiple occasions. Isaiah prophesied the eradication of Babylon:

> Babylon, the jewel of kingdoms, the pride and glory of the Babylonians, will be overthrown by God like Sodom and Gomorrah. She will never be inhabited or lived in through all generations; there no nomads will pitch their tents, there no shepherds will rest their flocks. But desert creatures will lie there, jackals will

---

[300] Genesis 11:8.

> fill her houses; there the owls will dwell, and there the wild goats will leap about. Hyenas will inhabit her strongholds, jackals her luxurious palaces. Her time is at hand, and her days will not be prolonged.[301]

German archaeologists "had to clear away a million cubic feet of rubble before they had exposed part of the temple of Marduk on the Euphrates."[302] A city that blasphemes God Most High deserves such an end. Surely enough, the once great city of Babylon met its fate as the Bible predicted. The Bible accurately predicted the fall of Babylon. Its description of its construction should be equally trusted.

Evidence that a city with a magnificent tower once existed is overwhelming. There is no doubt that Babylon was once the center for cult activity in the world. Its idolatrous and egotistic polytheism was a precursor to the city's confusion. The confusing of the languages at Babel put mankind in its rightful place and prevented it from alienating itself from the one true God.

---

[301] Isaiah 13:19-22.

[302] Keller 315, 317.

Chapter 25
The Confusing of Tongues

Deconstructing the common language mankind spoke would have been horrifyingly divisive. One moment they could communicate clearly through one language; the next moment they could not communicate at all. God scrambled the language of mankind so that people would have to migrate and settle in other regions throughout the earth. After mankind lost its ability to communicate with one another, the world became a place unlike anything that had been experienced up to that point in history.

The confusing of the languages at Babel is one of the most fascinating and observable repercussions of the first eleven chapters of Genesis. Scientists today still struggle to unravel the origins of the different languages, despite the revelation given through this account. There certainly is an evolutionary explanation for the development of the multitude of languages, but a great mystery has emerged through the study of a person's lifespan of developmental acquisition of language. This mystery is that it appears as though the acquisition of language is programmed into the human genome.

Kathleen Berger wrote in her textbook *The Developing Person: Through the Life Span*,

> Language with thousands of basic vocabulary words, hundreds of idiomatic phrases, dozens of grammar rules, and many exceptions to those rules, is the most impressive intellectual achievement of the young child. In fact, language is the most impressive accomplishment of all humans: It differentiates our species from all others and is probably the reason human brains are more complex than those of any other animal. . .a 2-year-old human has three times as much brainpower as a full-grown gorilla.
>
> Infants are equipped to learn language even before birth, partly due to brain readiness and partly due to their auditory experiences during the final prenatal months.[303]

Most people have heard the old saying, "It is what separates us from the animals." Verbal language truly does separate us from the animals. Kathleen Stassen Berger believes that language in humans is something innate. Spoken language, for humans, is simply "meant to be." If language is preprogrammed into humans, God must have designed this ability with special intentions in mind.

The sudden change from one language into many had serious repercussions. Cooperation among large numbers of people would be nearly impossible. The traditions that they once held dear, such as the stories about

[303] Berger et al., 158-159.

Creation, the Fall, and the Flood, would soon be altered. Their worship of God would be misdirected. One might argue that God hindered the human race from worshipping him, but such an accusation neglects the fact that mankind already chose to worship false gods before God confused their language. The people "exchanged the glory of the immortal God for images made to look like a mortal human being and birds and animals and reptiles."[304] The stories about the Creator God had been altered to boast the glory of man. Some men were even deified and given the glory that God truly deserved. Confusing the languages would create a problem that mankind would not soon resolve.

Today, many languages still exist. In fact, new ones continue to evolve. What was once called English a few hundred years ago is now called "Old English." Mankind has attempted to overcome language barriers through translators and education in foreign languages. In countries where people are exposed to multiple languages, they acquire a second, third, and sometimes even more languages. In such cases, the human ability to acquire language from an early age comes in very handy. Communication has leapt many obstacles and has even begun to overcome distance through the advances of modern technology. Despite such advances, communication through spoken language is becoming a lost art. Is it possible that mankind's advancements in communication could lead to another Babel scenario?

Language is an essential component of the human being. God designed mankind with the ability to acquire

---

[304] Romans 1:23.

and speak language. Confusing the languages divided the people of the world and warped the common traditions that they all held dear at one point in history. Despite feeble efforts to reconcile a divided world to itself, humanity remains in a state of confusion. Only God can bring reconciliation to a world that has been divided by language.

Chapter 26
The World That Now Is

Language: the greatest human achievement. The world does not lack the ability to communicate through various spoken languages. Communication has evolved much since the first words uttered by a human being. Written language was developed to communicate to mass numbers of people. Written language was transcribed onto walls, tablets, and other mediums to communicate messages to people who may never meet the one who wrote them. Letters would be transmitted through couriers that would travel great distances in short amounts of time to deliver important messages to loved ones, business partners, and kings. Words then transcended the mediums of physical transcription and took to the airwaves. They would be translated through dots and dashes, radio signals, satellites, and so forth to connect people on one side of the world with the other. Such an advantage in communication would appear to be a great advantage for mankind, but what has it produced?

People are more confused today than they have ever been. The various outlets for communication have allowed for everyone to post their thoughts, beliefs, and retelling of events that impact the lives of others across the globe. Media outlets contradict other media outlets, while one person contradicts another. One says that war is brewing and another says that all is well. Who can you believe? Who can you trust? Their words are scrambled, garbled, and confused. It has led to a culture where only one thing matters to each and every individual: self.

Walk down a street in a big city. People drive cars through heavy traffic. Men and women in business suits walk intently toward their next destination hoping for their next big break. The homeless beg on street corners, hoping someone will notice them. Lights, signs, and newspaper stands warn people of traffic, great deals, and economic woes. From the ground up, there is an aura that breaks the mood and that is when everything sinks in. It is all meaningless. Despite all of the methods and modes of communication, it all means nothing.

Each and every person lives a life without meaning and completely in vain. There is nothing different between the beggar and the wealthy person. They both anticipate their next big break and a gateway to their heart's desire. One day, they will both be dead and have nothing to show for their efforts. This problem is not new.

The city of Babel was an exercise in human futility. The people that built the city of Babel and its tower were desperately trying to make a mark on the world. Their names would be etched in stone and the memory of them would span through eternity. Both the city and the Tower of Babel have been destroyed. Nobody cares about its former grandeur. Nobody cares about the civilization that once thrived in Babylon. The people responsible for its construction are only remembered in stories that nobody can recall. It is all gone and it is all forgotten.

But, the Babel mentality has been resurrected. The new atheism has ushered in the next era of human vanity. Cosmetics, music, art, and entertainment are driven with three factors in mind: me, myself, and money. Modern buildings dwarf the Tower of Babel and are even called "skyscrapers" because they "scrape" the high heavens. Since there is no God, life must be lived for something: "I live for me!" Such an attitude can only spawn evil.

Why is there so much hate in the world? Atheists wish to blame religion for all acts of hate, but the true culprit for hatred is selfishness. The Apostle James puts it this way: "What causes fights and quarrels among you? Don't they come from your desires that battle within you? You want something but don't get it. You kill and covet, but you cannot have what you want."[305] Schools teach kids to love themselves and to only seek after their own interests. A display in the Answers in Genesis Creation Museum states, "Once people abandon the authority of God's Word, there's no sure foundation for morality and justice in the world. Human reason can be used to justify evil of every sort."[306] In most modern countries, God's Word has been abandoned in formal education and has been replaced by humanism. Not only is this indoctrination unrestrained, it is greatly promoted.

The result is hopelessness. An entire culture has been developed based on evolutionary presuppositions. There is no right, there is no wrong. There is no good and there is no evil. The entire evolutionary purpose can be summed up in three words: "You are here." Other than that, there

[305] James 4:12.

[306] Creation Museum, *Who's Your Brother?* (St. Petersburg, Kentucky, 2011).

is no certainty. The foundation of the Theory of Evolution is the premise that there is no God. If God does not exist, there is nothing more to life than one's own existence.

Life is an accident. It is here today and gone tomorrow. Life's sole purpose is to die. There may be a couple of joys along the journey from birth to death, but it all fades away in an instant.

Children grow up worshiping death. They dress in black, wear images of skulls, and mar their bodies as though they were nothing special. The meaning of life is no longer a mystery to them. There is no meaning.

The dark times in which we live still have hope, for the Apostle John tells us that the darkness cannot overcome the light.[307] Hope can be found in the light bearer, Jesus. He is the Way, the Truth, and the Life.[308] In him, life can be experienced to the fullest.[309] All things make sense in light of our Risen Savior.

The world is confused, and I am here to bear witness of that truth. Just like everyone else, I use a cell phone, computer, and all of the devices and gizmos that make our modern lives go 'round. I have been down the streets of the big city and have seen the futility of it all. But there is one thing that I have experienced that has brought joy to man and woman, rich and poor, black and white: Jesus. He is the answer because he is the Savior who is true to the world. Accept him into your life and you will never be the same.

---

[307] John 1:5.

[308] John 14:6.

[309] John 10:10.

Chapter 27
Jesus and the Beginning

The premise of this book has been that a reliable testimony is only transmitted through a reliable witness. Outside of a witness's testimony, one can only ponder over evidence and deduce fanciful speculations. A person born after 1969 A.D. would not know about the moon landing outside of the testimony of a reliable witness. In the grand scheme of things, no one can know anything outside of his or her own experience. Is there anyone that mankind can turn to and receive nothing but the truth?

Many scientists will continue to claim that all things came into existence through a natural method. They will further claim that all of the evidence supports an evolutionary theory. Popular media and secularists have a stranglehold on the "acceptable interpretation" of evidence. Yet, their evidence remains silent. The stars do not speak, no record of the earth's formation is etched in stone, and fossils lack a meticulously drawn family tree. There is only one Being that bears witness to the events of the past, and he will live forever.

In the book of Job, the title character, Job, goes through many hardships that nearly wreck his relationship with God. But God revealed himself through a whirlwind and asked him questions to test his understanding of the circumstances he was going through. God's first question was, "Where were you when I laid the earth's foundations? Tell me, if you understand."[310] God knew where Job was at the world's foundation; he was nothing more than a thought in his mind. Do you question God's authority?

God asks, "Where were you when I laid the earth's foundations?" Not a single human witnessed this event, whether he or she believes God was involved or not. God was the only One present before time existed. God knew every individual person before he or she was born: "Before I formed you in the womb I knew you, before you were born I set you apart."[311] God is the only faithful witness concerning the creation of all things.

Humans can devise imaginative theories and fanciful fairy tales concerning the universe's existence, but not a single person has the authority to declare one "true" and the other "false." At the conclusion of C. S. Lewis's book, *Till We Have Faces*, the main character of the book, Orual, was on her deathbed and was reflecting upon a complaint she had against God. She felt that nothing God had done in her life made sense. But according to God, everything worked out according to plan. She wrote, "I know now, Lord, why you utter no answer. You are yourself the answer. Before your face questions die away. What other would suffice? Only words, words; to be led out to battle against other words."[312] That is really

---

[310] Job 38:4.

[311] Jeremiah 1:5.

[312] C. S. Lewis, *Till We Have Faces* (San Francisco: HarperCollins HarperSanFrancisco, 1956), 308.

what all arguments come down to in regards to origins: words "led out to battle against other words." One's determination of truth is a matter of faith.

This book opened up with an argument between Richard Dawkins and Michael Behe. Dawkins and Behe could argue until the sun melts away, and one would never concede to the other. Neither accepts the authority behind the other's words. Dawkins argues according to his knowledge and understanding, while Behe argues according to his knowledge and understanding. No one, except for God, can make an argument backed by authority.

The Bible claims that Jesus is the Son of God and that he came down to the earth to make God known. The Apostle John wrote about Jesus at the opening of his Gospel: "In the beginning was the Word, and the Word was with God, and the Word was God. He was with God in the beginning. Through him all things were made; without him nothing was made that has been made. In him was life; and that life was the light of men."[313] Later on in his Gospel, John recorded a prayer that was spoken by Jesus: "I have brought you glory on earth by completing the work you gave me to do. And now, Father, glorify me in your presence with the glory I had with you before the world began."[314] John believed that Jesus existed outside of time before the creation of the world, and he had forever co-existed with the Father God in eternity.

The co-existence between Jesus and the Father infers one profound truth: Jesus is the eternal God. Another Scripture from John states, "Your father Abraham

---

[313] John 1:1-4.

[314] John 17:4-5.

rejoiced at the thought of seeing my day; and he saw it, and was glad. . .I tell you the truth. . .before Abraham was born, I am."[315] The divine claim made by Jesus was clearly understood by his Jewish listeners. In the Old Testament, God identified himself to Moses as "I AM." In John's gospel, Jesus applied this title to himself. The title "I AM" is a description of God's eternal presence, that he "is," "was," and forever will "be."[316] He directly connected himself to the God of the Old Testament in this statement and the ancient patriarchs who followed him.

The four topics discussed in this book (creation, the Fall, the flood, and the scattering of the nations from Babel) were all foundational to God's calling of the ancient patriarchs Abraham, Isaac, Jacob, and their descendants. Their stories proceeded only after the world became such a mess that God had to make provisions just to allow it to exist. Their lives were shadows of the coming Christ, a living prophecy comprised of imperfect humans guided by an all-powerful God. Christians must assume that the patriarchs were real, for without the patriarchs salvation did not truly descend from the Jews.[317] The authenticity of the early characters of the Bible validates the truth of Jesus' claims. Any Joe could make false assertions like "the world is flat," "we never landed on the moon," or that "life was seeded on earth by Martians." Authority is established on a truthful declaration of reality. The only one that could give a 100% accurate testimony concerning reality is the very

[315] John 8:56, 58.

[316] Revelation 1:8.

[317] John 4:22.

God who brought all things into being. Only he knows all things. Humans are limited to the amount of knowledge they can acquire. Michael Behe asserts that there are only two ways that a person can know anything: the first is through personal experience and the second is by authority.[318] The problem is that many people rely on authorities that exaggerate their understanding of reality. Doing this leaves one's knowledge at the whim of another person's opinion or interpretation of the truth.

All knowledge is dependent on faith. Personal experience can be misinterpreted by a person, and many of the worldly authorities are corrupt, deceptive, and downright evil. Authorities can range from the "laws of nature" to the doctor who tells you that "if you eat three double quarter pounders a day, you may become fat." Not all authorities are reliable and not all of them are relevant. Satan was an authority to Eve in the Garden of Eden, and he deceived her. He misled Eve so that she would place her faith in him. Because of such deception, faith can be a dangerous thing.

Even atheists like Richard Dawkins have faith. He has faith that God does not exist. He has faith in his own intellect and his ability to discern truth from lies. He has faith that all things evolved from inanimate material through natural processes that were unrestricted by a divine hand. Dawkins must have great faith to espouse this sort of worldview because if he were wrong, he would be at enmity with the Creator of the universe! On the other hand, if he is correct, he would be better off believing in something else.

---

[318] Behe, 184.

Jesus is an authority in whom people can place their faith. From a worldly perspective, he was peaceful, assertive, intelligent, and willing to die for his beliefs. Who in all of history has been remembered because of his or her empty tomb? Who else, after only three active years in service, could create a worldwide movement that would last two thousand years? Jesus claimed to be God. This was the claim for which he was condemned and there is no way around that, lest we disregard the writings of the New Testament.

If Jesus is God, that means he has always existed. So if Jesus always existed, he existed before Abraham as well, which means that he would have been a witness to all of the events that preceded Abraham. He would be the only one to know, beyond a shadow of a doubt, the history of the universe from beginning to end. There is no shame in going all in with the Bible because it is an all or nothing wager. The Bible is reliable and it is validated because of Jesus' divine origin. Viewing Jesus in this way gives him supreme authority.

Not everyone considers the Bible to be completely true, even inside of the realm of Christianity. In fact, most Christians will accept what Jesus has to say in the New Testament but disregard everything that was said in the Old Testament. They will often claim that the Genesis creation account was not meant to be literal, Adam and Eve never existed, Noah and the flood were not real, and that Babel never happened. But if a Christian is one who follows the teachings of Jesus, what does Jesus say about the world that then was?

Jesus addressed the events that happened at the dawn of creation. At times he even quoted Genesis to provide a foundation for certain doctrinal issues. In Mark's gospel he answered the Pharisees concerning the legality of divorce according to the Law of Moses. Jesus told them, "At the beginning of creation God 'made them male and female.' 'For this reason a man will leave his father and mother and be united to his wife, and the two will become one flesh.' So they are no longer two, but one."[319] Jesus testified that God created man and woman together at the beginning of creation. In this particular passage, Jesus quoted the very words of Genesis regarding their creation! Man and woman were created together at the beginning of time and they were specially created in the image of God.[320]

In the Gospel of Matthew, Jesus expressed the unique sort of love that God has for mankind above all of creation:

> Look at the birds of the air; they do not sow or reap or store away in barns, and yet your heavenly Father feeds them. Are you not much more valuable than they?. . . And why do you worry about clothes? See how the flowers of the field grow. They do not labor or spin.. . . If that is how God clothes the grass of the field, which is here today and tomorrow is thrown into the fire, will he not much more clothe you—you of little faith?[321]

God is the caretaker of the natural world. He cares deeply about the birds, flowers, and other works of creation. His

---

[319] Mark 10:6-8.

[320] Genesis 1:27.

[321] Matthew 6:26, 28, 30.

punch line was, "Are you not much more valuable than they?" Genesis makes it clear that mankind is of higher value than animals or plants, and Jesus reinforced the truth of Genesis. Jesus believed in the authenticity and authority of the first book of the Bible.

Jesus believed the Old Testament in its entirety. He once rebuked the Pharisees with the words, "And so upon you will come all the righteous blood that has been shed on earth, from the blood of righteous Abel to the blood of Zachariah son of Berekiah."[322] If Jesus was the Son of God, he would be unable to lie. According to Jesus' testimony, Abel was a real person. If Abel was a real person, Adam and Eve, who were his parents, must also have been real! Jesus believed that the story about Cain and Abel was not a fable, but an actual event in history. If this was an actual event in history, Jesus must also have spoken the truth concerning the existence of Satan.

Satan is real and he was involved in man's fall from the Garden of Eden. The devil is not a figment of someone's imagination, he is a real entity. As mentioned earlier, Jesus saw Satan fall from heaven. During his earthly ministry, Jesus rebuked Satan on multiple occasions. Satan, even at the world's beginning, was a real and active force that sought to destroy mankind and prevent its redemption. If Jesus acknowledged the truth of the existence of the devil, his testimony concerning Noah would be of no surprise.

Jesus taught about the Day of the Son of Man and warned that "Just as it was in the days of Noah, so also will it be in the days of the Son of Man. People were

---

[322] Matthew 23:35.

eating, drinking, marrying and being given in marriage up to the day Noah entered the ark. Then the flood came and destroyed them all."[323] This testimony confirms that Jesus believed Noah was real, the ark was real, and that the flood destroyed everyone who was not on the ark was real. Not long after the landing of the ark on dry land, the world was gathered into one place and built the city of Babel. Jesus never addressed Babel directly, but he did prophesy about a future event that would echo Babel's splendor and futility.

In the book of Revelation, Jesus described a Babel-like situation. The Apostle John recorded these words although Jesus himself provided the revelation:

> The sixth angel poured out his bowl on the great river Euphrates, and its water was dried up to prepare the way for the kings from the East. Then I saw three impure spirits that looked like frogs; they came out of the mouth of the dragon, out of the mouth of the beast and out of the mouth of the false prophet. They are demonic spirits that perform signs, and they go out to the kings of the whole world, to gather them for the battle on the great day of God Almighty. "Look, I come like a thief! Blessed is the one who stays awake and remains clothed, so as not to go naked and be shamefully exposed." Then they gathered the kings together to the place that in Hebrew is called Armageddon.[324]

All of the kings gathered into one land and intended to oppose God. They will gather with the purpose of

---

[323] Luke 17:26-27.

[324] Revelation 16:12-16.

being present on the great day of battle with God. A division took place as a result: "The great city split into three parts, and the cities of the nations collapsed. God remembered Babylon the Great and gave her the cup filled with the wine of the fury of his wrath."[325] The name of this doomed city was Babylon, which is synonymous with Babel. At Babel, God judged the people, divided them, and halted the building of their city. According to the prophecy, God would split the city of Babylon, cause them to collapse, and give her the cup of his wrath. In both instances the city experienced divine judgment. This serves as a warning to those who think that they can gather and oppose the Living God.

Jesus' authority supports each one of the events within the first eleven chapters of Genesis. Do you accept the authority of Jesus? Do you believe his words? It is easy for us to complain two thousand years later that, "If God is real, why does he not reveal himself?" He has revealed himself to us! He stepped down from his throne and became a man. He atoned for all of the wickedness that mankind did, is doing, and will do in the future. Everyone is welcome to receive the truth of God!

There is no way to prove that the records in the Bible are true. One can cite archaeology, uncover lost scrolls, and even walk down the streets that Jesus traveled. One must make a leap of faith in order to believe. There is nothing foolish about faith; everyone employs faith. It even takes faith to accept the Theory of Evolution. The difference is the source of testimony. There are people who speak truth and there are people who only seek to

[325] Revelation 16:19.

win the favor of others. The Apostle Paul wrote, "the time will come when men will not put up with sound doctrine. Instead, to suit their own desires, they will gather around them a great number of teachers to say what their itching ears want to hear. They will turn their ears away from the truth and turn aside to myths."[326] Who is it that speaks truth and who is it that tickles the ears of his or her listeners? Those who testify concerning Jesus are priests, pastors, and other Christians. The teachers of evolution are professors, scientists, and atheists. Nobody's thoughts are truly original, so do not be fooled into thinking that the acceptance of the one and the rejection of the other make a particular person cleverer than those with whom he or she disagrees. It is a matter of faith.

Faith in any belief creates yet another danger. "If I believe in the wrong God, what will my punishment be?" "If I do not believe in God and there is a God, what consequences will I face?" "What if there is no God and I currently believe in God?" We all have faith in something. Yet, faith is only blind for those whose eyes are not set upon Jesus.

Just as there is no other name that can save mankind, neither can anyone else's words bring life aside from Christ. His testimony is trustworthy because he was there in the beginning. He testifies to the events detailed throughout this book: God, Creation, the Fall, the Flood, and Babel. One can either accept or reject the words of Jesus, but no one can merely ignore them. Where do you place your faith?

---

[326] 2 Timothy 4:3-4

Chapter 28
A New Beginning

You have read selections from many ancient stories and it is my hope that you can fully realize the truth of the Bible. My highest priority, even if you already accept the notion of a literal seven day creation six thousand years ago, is that you may come to know the Lord and Savior Jesus Christ. The Tower of Babel was not the final judgment of God. If you were to continue reading in Genesis, you would see that God reached out to a man named Abram. Abram was born to a pagan family in the land of Canaan.

God made a promise with Abram: "I will make you into a great nation, and I will bless you; I will make your name great, and you will be a blessing. I will bless those who bless you, and whoever curses you I will curse; and all peoples on earth will be blessed through you."[327] Because of his devout love, God never gave up on mankind. He even promised that he would bless the world through his chosen people. Abraham was the beginning of that sacred promise, but the promise would experience some difficult times because of mankind's inability to fulfill their end of the promise.

---

[327] Genesis 12:2-3.

Throughout the entire Old Testament, man was proven to be spiritually wicked. God had to step into his creation and intercede on mankind's behalf. This was accomplished through the man, Jesus Christ. After Jesus' death, resurrection, and ascension, something phenomenal occurred on the day we call Pentecost.

> When the day of Pentecost came, they were all together in one place. Suddenly a sound like the blowing of a violent wind came from heaven and filled the whole house where they were sitting. They saw what seemed to be tongues of fire that separated and came to rest on each of them. All of them were filled with the Holy Spirit and began to speak in other tongues as the Spirit enabled them. Now there were staying in Jerusalem God-fearing Jews from every nation under heaven. When they heard this sound, a crowd came together in bewilderment, because each one heard them speaking in his own language. Utterly amazed, they asked: "Are not all these men who are speaking Galileans? Then how is it that each of us hears them in his own native language?[328]

Outside of the context of Babel, it is easy to miss the contrast between Pentecost and mankind's former corruption. Babel was the removal of a common language. Pentecost was the restoring of a common language. It allowed people to taste the glory of God's kingdom so that Jesus' disciples could spread the news of God's good will.

---

[328] Acts 2:1-8.

The Prophet Joel referred to the pouring out of the Holy Spirit as the "last days."[329] Despite the course of history as it was set forth in Genesis, Jesus Christ became the turning point of history. Mankind was once on an unstoppable downward skid toward destruction, but through Jesus, hope was restored so that people could be reconciled to God. The world was once void of hope. Now, despite the world's darkest hours, the world is full of hope. We live in a new world. We expectantly wait for God's final judgment so that we may be reunited with our Savior in heaven. There is no way to know when Jesus will return, but he has warned that there will be signs that lead up to the world's conclusion. The Apostle Peter wrote:

> Knowing this first, that there shall come in the last days scoffers, walking after their own lusts, and saying, Where is the promise of his coming? For since the fathers fell asleep, all things continue as they were from the beginning of creation. For this they willingly are ignorant of, that by the word of God the heavens were of old, and the earth standing out of the water and in the water: Whereby the world that then was, being overflowed with water, perished: But the heavens and the earth, which are now, by the same word are kept in store, reserved unto fire against the day of judgment and perdition of ungodly men.
>
> But beloved, be not ignorant of this one thing, that one day is with the Lord as a thousand years, and a

[329] Joel 2:28.

> thousand years as one day. The Lord is not slack concerning his promise, as some men count slackness; but is longsuffering to us-ward, not willing that any should perish, but that all should come to repentance. But the day of the Lord will come as a thief in the night; in the which the heavens shall pass away with a great noise, and the elements shall melt with fervent heat, the earth also and the works that are therein shall be burned up. Seeing then that all these shall be dissolved, what manner of persons ought ye to be in all holy conversation and godliness, Looking for and hasting unto the coming of the day of God, wherein the heavens being on fire shall be dissolved, and the elements shall melt with fervent heat? Nevertheless we, according to his promise, look for new heavens and a new earth, wherein dwelleth righteousness.[330]

The journey is not over. God's plan for redemption continues and mankind must continue to strive against the evil of the world.

My prayer for the reader is that he or she will not just read with fascination, considering the marvelous similarities between the stories of different cultures throughout the world. I want each person to consider the unique and common details of each story. Is it possible that all of the myths of creation evolved from one false story? Or did they evolve from one true creation account? Consider if you will, that there is such thing as absolute truth. Every religion challenges the perception of absolute truth. Inherently, every ideology promotes a

[330] KJV 2 Peter 3:3-13.

unique worldview, complete with its own presuppositions. One must step out in faith if he or she wishes to believe in anything. One who refuses such advice will never be able to make sense of the world that currently exists. If you are a Christian, I pray that this book has strengthened your faith in the Holy Scriptures. If you are not, I pray that you may come to a saving faith. I pray that the Holy Spirit worked upon your heart as you read this book. I also pray that you will be compelled to examine the Bible by reading it from cover to cover. Jesus once rebuked the Sadducees, who would be like today's liberal Bible scholars, with the words, "You are in error because you do not know the Scriptures or the power of God."[331] Do not make the same mistakes as the Sadducees. Those who read the Holy Bible with an open heart, seeking after the truth, will not be let down with what it has to offer.

May the God of Creation, Judgment, and Redemption be with you now and forevermore. May the light of his Son Jesus illuminate your darkest road to give you guidance and may the riches of his love lead you to His Kingdom which is to come. Amen.

---

[331] Matthew 22:29.

References

AOL. "Earliest Human Footprints Discovered." 2009. http://news.aol.com/article/earliest-human-footprints-found-in/360312 [Last accessed on February 26, 2009 (no longer available)]. Related Article: BBC News. "Earliest 'human footprints' found." 2009. BBCNews.com. http://news.bbc.co.uk/2/hi/7913375.stm [accessed July 4, 2011].

BBC News. "Earliest 'human footprints' found." 2009. BBCNews.com. http://news.bbc.co.uk/2/hi/7913375.stm [accessed July 4, 2011].

Behe, Michael J. 2006. *Darwin's Black Box: The biochemical challenge to evolution*. New York, New York: Free Press.

Berger, Kathleen Stassen. 2005. *The Developing Person: Through the life span*. New York: Worth Publishers.-Aslin, Richard N., Jusczyk, Peter W., & Pisoni, David B. 1998.Speech and auditory processing during infancy: Constraints on and precursors to language. In William Damon (Series Ed.), Deanna Kuhn and Robert Siegler (Vol. Eds.), *Handbook of child psychology: Vol. 2. Cognition, perception, and language* (5th ed., pp. 147 – 198). New York: Wiley.

Brown,A. Philip II, and Bryan W. Smith. 2008. *A Reader's Hebrew Bible,* from A. Phillip Brown II and Bryan W. Smith (Hebrew Old Testament), and Richard J. Goodrich and Albert L. Lukaszewski (Greek New Testament). 2008. *A Reader's Hebrew and Greek Bible.*Grand Rapids, Michigan. Zondervan .

Bruchac, Joseph. 1992. *Native American Animal Stories.* Golden, Colorado: Fulcrum Publishing.

Cadwallader, Mark W. 2007. *CREATION: Spelled out for us all.* Conroe Texas: CTS Publications.

Comfort, Ray. 2001. *Hidden Wealth Series: Scientific facts in the Bible.* Gainesville, Florida: Bridges – Logos Publishers.

Cooper, Bill. 1995. *After the Flood.* Norfolk, England: New Wine Press.

Creation Museum. 2011. *Who's Your Brother?* St. Petersburg, Kentucky.

Dalley, Stephanie. 2000. *Myths of Mesopotamia: Creation, the flood, Gilgamesh, and others.* Great Britain: Oxford University Press.

Darwin, Charles. 2004. *The Origin of Species.* New York: Barnes and Noble Classics.

Dawkins, Richard. 2008. *The God Delusion*. New York, New York: Mariner Books.

Deyoung, Don. 2006. *Thousands. . .Not Billions*. Portland, Oregon: Master Books.

Extreme Science. "A Geologic History of Earth." 2010. http://www.extremescience.com/zoom/index.php/geolo.gic-earth-history [accessed July 17, 2010].

Freedman, David Noel. 2000. *Eerdmans Dictionary of the Bible*. Grand Rapids, Michigan: William B. Eerdmans Publishing Company.

George B. Johnson, Jonathan B. Losos, Peter H. Raven, and Susan R. Singer 2005. *Biology, 7th ed*. Madison, Wisconsin: McGraw Hill Higher Education.

Ghandi, M. K. 1949. *Non-Violence in Peace and War, vol. 2*. Ahmedabab-14. 160, as cited in Peter J. Hadreas. 2007. *A Phenomonology of Love and Hate*. Burlington, Vermont: Ashgate Publishing Company.

Giancoli, Douglas C. 2005. *Physiscs: Principles with applications, 6th ed.* Upper Saddle River, New Jersey: Pearson Prentice Hall.

Gregory, Horace. 2001. *The Metamorphoses: Ovid*. New York: Signet Classic.

Grogan, Geoffrey W. and Frank E. Gaebelein, ed. 1990. *The Expositor's Bible Commentary, vol. 6*. Grand Rapids, Michigan: Zondervan.

Ham, Ken. 2009. *The Great Dinosaur Mystery Solved!* Green Forest, Arkansas.

Hamilton, Edith. 1999. *Mythology: Timeless tales of gods and heroes*. New York: Warner Books.

Hawking, Stephen "Life in the Universe." 1996. http://hawking.org.uk/index.php?option=com_content&view=article&id=65 [accessed July 16, 2011]

Hawking, Stephen "Life in the Universe." http://www.rationalvedanta.net/node/131 [accessed July 16, 2011].

Heaney, Seamus. 1987. *Beowulf: A new verse translation*. New York: W. W. Norton & Company.

Heliopolis (literally translated by Wallace Budge). 1969. *The Gods of the Egyptians*. Vol. 1. Dover, New York, 308-313, paraphrased in Cooper, Bill. 1995. *After the Flood*. Norfolk, England: New Wine Press.

Holy Bible: Containing the Old and New Testaments in the King James Version. 1984. Nashville: Thomas Nelson Inc.

Holt, Jim. *Wall Street Journal* science writer, as quoted in, Comfort, Ray. 2001. *Hidden Wealth Series:*

Scientific facts in the Bible. Gainesville, Florida: Bridges – Logos Publishers.

Kazan, Casey. "Stephen Hawking: 'humans have entered a new stage of evolution.'" 2009. The Daily Galaxy. http://www.dailygalaxy.com/my_weblog/2009/07/stephen-hawking-the-planet-has-entered-a-new-phase-of-evolution.html [accessed July 16, 2011]).

Keller, Werner. 1982. *The Bible as History*. New York: Bantam Books.

Lao-tzu. 1991. *Tao-te-ching*. Tr. Leon Wieger. English version by Derek Bryce. Lampeter: Llanerch Publishers, p.13, as quoted in Cooper, Bill. 1995. *After the Flood*. Norfolk, England: New Wine Press.

Lasor, William Sanford, David Allan Hubbard and Frederic Wm. Bush. 1996. *Old Testament Survey*. Grand Rapids, Michigan: William B. Eerdmans Publishing Company.

Lendering, Jona. "Ziggurat, revised April 1, 2006." http://www.livius.org/za-zn/ziggurat/ziggurat.html [accessed June 13, 2011].

Lewis, C. S. 1980. *Mere Christianity*. San Francisco, California: HarperCollins, HarperSanFrancisco.

Lewis, C. S. 1956. *Till We Have Faces*. San Francisco: HarperCollins HarperSanFrancisco.

Live Science. "Volcanoes, not asteroid, may have killed off dinosaurs." 2008. http://www.foxnews.com/story/0,2933,467764,00.html [accessed May 18, 2012]

Lombardo, Stanley. 2000. *The Essential Homer*. Indianapolis, Indiana: Hackett Publishing Company Inc.

Lubenow, Marvin L. 1992. *Bones of Contention: A creationist assessment of human fossils*. Grand Rapids, Michigan: Baker Books.

Lubenow, Marvin. "The human fossils still speak!" 1993. http://www.answersingenesis.org/creation/v15/i2/fossils.asp [accessed July 4, 2011]. First printed in *Creation, vol.15, 10-13*. 1993.

Luther, Martin. 1986. *What Martin Luther Says: A practical in-home anthology for the active*. St. Louis Missouri: Concordia Publishing House. Quoted in Ken Ham. 2006. *Answers. . .With Ken Ham: Did God create in 6 literal days?* Produced by Mark Looy and Jim Kragel. Recorded at Cedarville University, Ohio: Answers in Genesis in Association with Cedarville University.

McDowell, Josh. 2006. *The Last Christian Generation*. Holiday, Florida: Green Key Books.

Martin Palmer with Elizabeth Breuilly. 1996. *The Book of Chuang Tzu*. New York: Penguin Arkana.

Morris, Henry M. and John C. Whitcomb. 1961. *The Genesis Flood: The Biblical record and its scientific implications*. Phillipsburg, New Jersey: Presbyterian and Reformed Publishing.

Murray, John Courtney. 1964. *The Problem of God*. London: Yale University Press.

Neil A. Cambell, Jane B. Reece, Lisa A. Urry, Michael L. Cain, Steven A Wasserman Peter V. Minorsky, and Robert B. Jackson. 2008. *Biology, 8th ed*. New York: Pearson Benjamin Cummings.

NewsCore. "Dinosaurs 'gassed' themselves into extinction, British scientists say." 2012. http://www.foxnews.com/scitech/2012/05/07/dinosaurs-farted-their-way-to-extinction-british-scientists-say/?intcmp=features [accessed May 18, 2012].

Nordenskiold, Erik. 1935. *The History of Biology*. New York: Tudor Publishing Co.

Palmer, Martin and Elizabeth Breuilly. 1996. *The Book of Chuang Tzu*. New York: Penguin Arkana.

Sailhamer, John H. and Frank E. Gaebelein, ed. 1990. *The Expositor's Bible Commentary, vol. 2*. Grand Rapids, Michigan: Zondervan.

Snelling Andrew. "Radioisotopes and the Age of the Earth." 2007. http://www.answersingenesis.org/

articles/aid/v2/n1/ radioisotopes-earth [accessed July 17, 2010].

Staats, Gary. 2001. *Christological Hebrew Grammar: A study of creation: Genesis 1:1-2:3*. Austin, Texas: WORDsearch.

Staats, Gary. 2010. *Short Meditative Thoughts on the Bible and Life*. Findlay, Ohio: Dr. Gary Staats.

Staats, Gary. "OT 501 Pentateuch" (lecture, Winebrenner Theological Seminary, Findlay, OH, June, 8 2010).

Strobel, Lee. 2004. *The Case for a Creator.* Grand Rapids, Michigan: Zondervan.

Strong, James. 1990. *The New Strong's Exhaustive Concordance of the Bible*. Nashville: Thomas Nelson Publishers.

The British Museum. "Ziggurats." http://www.mesopotamia.co.uk/ziggurats/story/sto_set. Html [accessed June 13, 2011]

The Holy Qur'an: With English translation and commentary, vol.1, Surah Al-Fatihah – Surah Al-Baqara. 1988. Great Britain: Islam International Publications Limited. Hazrat Tahir Ahmad.

The Holy Qur'an: With English translation and commentary, vol.2, Surah Al-Imran – Surah Al- Tauba.

1988. Great Britain: Islam International Publications Limited. Hazrat Tahir Ahmad.

Unger, Merrill F. 1980 *Unger's Bible Handbook: An essential guide to understanding the Bible*. Chicago, Illinois: Moody Press.

Wallace, Bruce. 1968. *Topics in Population Genetics*. New York: W. W. Norton Company Inc.

Webster's Dictionary. 2003. New York: Harper Collins.

West, M.L. 1999. *Hesiod Theogony Works and Days*. NewYork: Oxford University Press

Wikiquote. (http://en.wikiquote.org/wiki/Bill_Maher). Quoted from an interview on The O'Reilly Factor, September 26, 2006, Fox News [accessed September 27, 2011].

Youngblood, Ronald F. 1995. *Nelson's New Illustrated Bible Dictionary*. Nashville: Thomas Nelson Publishers.

Zolbrod, Paul G. 1984. *Dine bahane: The Navajo Creation Story*. Albuquerque: University of New Mexico Press.

CPSIA information can be obtained at www.ICGtesting.com
Printed in the USA
BVOW03s0427060813

327757BV00001B/3/P

9 781626 977259